AF791756

DTP

(Desktop Publishing)

Training Guide

by

Satish Jain

B.Sc., B.E. (II Sc), M.E. (II Sc), M.Tech. (IIT Kanpur),
Wing Commander (Retd.)
Ex Professor of Information Technology,
Institute of Information Technology & Management,
GGS Indraprastha University, Delhi.

and

M. Geetha

B.Com., Diploma (IT)

BPB PUBLICATIONS

B-14, CONNAUGHT PLACE, NEW DELHI-1

FIRST EDITION 2015

REPRINT 2023

ISBN : 978-81-8333-552-2

LIMITS OF LIABILITY AND DISCLAIMER OF WARRANTY

The information contained in this book is true and correct and the best of Author's & Publisher's knowledge. We are committed to serve students with best of our knowledge and resources. We have taken utmost care and attention while editing and printing of this book but Author and Publisher should not be held responsible for errors, omissions and any other unintentional mistake that might have crept in. However, errors brought to our notice shall be gratefully acknowledged and attended to.

All trademarks referred to in the book are acknowledged as properties of their respective owners. This book is written solely for the benefit and guidance of the students.

Distributors:

COMPUTER BOOK CENTRE
12, Shrungar Shopping Centre, M.G.Road
BENGALURU-560001
Ph: 25587923, 25584641

MICRO BOOKS
Shanti Niketan Building, 8,Camac Street,
KOLKATA-700017 Ph: 22826518, 22826519

MICRO MEDIA
Shop No. 5, Mahendra Chambers,150 DN Rd.
Next to Capital Cinema, V.T. (C.S.T.) Station,
MUMBAI-400 001, Ph: 22078296, 22078297

DECCAN AGENCIES
4-3-329, Bank Street,
HYDERABAD-500195
Ph: 24756967, 24756400

BPB PUBLICATIONS
B-14,Connaught Place,
NEW DELHI-110001
23325760, 43526249

BPB BOOK CENTRE
376 Old Lajpat Rai Market,
DELHI-110 006, Ph: 23861747

INFOTECH
G-2, Sidhartha Building,
96 Nehru Place,
NEW DELHI-110 019
Ph: 26438245

BPB PUBLICATIONS
20, Ansari Road, NEW DELHI-110002
Ph: 23254990/91

Published by Manish Jain for BPB Publications, B-14, Connaught Place, New Delhi – 110001 and Printed at Manipal Technologies Limited, Manipal

Dedicated to

Mata Raj Rajeshwari and Sri Sai Baba

whose blessings overcome all hurdles in life

BOOKS *by Prof. Satish Jain*

According to CBSE New Syllabus of year 2010–11 (for Class IX to Class XII)

- **Foundation of Information Technology for Class IX (code 165)**
- **Foundation of Information Technology for Class X (code 165)**
- **Computer Science with C++ Language** ***made comprehensive*** **for Class XI (code 083)**
- **Computer Science with C++ Language** *made comprehensive* **for Class XII (code 083)**
- **Informatics Practices** ***made comprehensive*** **for Class XI (code 065)**
- **Informatics Practices** ***made comprehensive*** **for Class XII (code 065)**

'O' Level made simple Books (According to NIELIT (DOEACC) Syllabus effective from July, 2010 Examination)

- **IT Tools and Business Systems** *(covering M1-R4, A1-R4 and B1.1-R4 papers)* **(*Also available in Hindi*)**
- **Internet Technology and Web Design** *(covering M2-R4, A2-R4 and B1.2-R4 papers)* **(*Also available in Hindi*)**
- **Programming and Problem Solving through `C' language** *(covering M3-R4, A3-R4 and B1.3-R4 papers)* **(*Also available in Hindi*)**
- **Application of .Net Technology** *(covering M4.1-R4 paper)*
- **Introduction to Multimedia** *(covering M4.2-R4 paper)*
- **Introduction to ICT Resources** *(covering M4.3-R4 paper)*
- **BPB 'O' Level *Course*** *(Covering: IT Tools and Business Systems, Internet Technology & Web Design and Programming and Problem Solving through 'C' Language) (Also covering A1-R4, A2-R4, A3-R4 as well as B1.1-R4, B1.2-R4 and B1.3-R4 papers)*

'A' Level made simple Books (According to NIELIT (DOEACC) Syllabus effective from July, 2010 Examination)

- **Computer System Architecture** *(covering A4-R4 and B1.4-R4 papers)*
- **Structured System Analysis & Design** *(covering A5-R4 and B1.5-R4 papers)* **(*Also available in Hindi*)**
- **Data Structure Through C++** *(covering A6-R4 and B2.1-R4 papers)* **(*Also available in Hindi*)**
- **Introduction to Database Management Systems** *(covering A7-R4 and B2.2-R4 papers)*
- **Basics of OS, Unix and Shell Programming** *(covering A8-R4 and B2.3-R4 papers)*
- **Data Communication and Network Technologies** *(covering A9-R4 and B2.4-R4 papers)*
- **Introduction to Object Oriented Programming through Java** *(covering A10.1-R4 and B2.5.1-R4 papers)*
- **Software Testing and Quality Management** *(covering A10.2-R4 and B2.5.2-R4 papers)*

BOOKS by Prof. Satish Jain *(Contd...)*

'O' & 'A' Level BPB's Golden Solutions for NIELIT (DOEACC) Examination Question Papers

- `O' Level—**IT Tools and Business Systems** (*Also covering A1-R4 and B1.1-R4 papers*)
- `O' Level—**Internet Technology & Web Design** (*Also covering A2-R4 and B1.2-R4 Papers*)
- 'O' Level—**Programming & Problem Solving through `C' language** (*Also covering A3-R4 and B1.3-R4 Papers*)
- `O' Level—**ICT Resources** (*covering M4.3-R4 paper*)
- `O' Level—**Introduction to Multimedia** (*covering M4.2-R4 paper*)
- `A' Level—**Data Communication and Network Technologies** (*Also covering A9-R4 and B2.4-R4 papers*)

'O' Level CHM (Computer Hardware Maintenance) Made Simple (According to NIELIT (DOEACC) Syllabus)

- **Electronics Components and PC Hardware** (*covering CHM–O1 paper*)
- **PC Architecture** (*covering CHM–O2 paper*)
- **Computer Peripherals and Networking** *(covering CHM O3 paper)*
- **System Software, Dignostics and Debugging Tools** (covering CHM O4 paper)
- **Course on Computer Concepts (CCC)** *made simple* (According to NIELIT (DOEACC) Revised Syllabus of year 2011 Examination) (***Also available in Hindi***)
- **Basic Computer Course (BCC)** *made simple* (According to NIELIT (DOEACC) Syllabus of year 2011 Examination)

Training Guides for Application Packages

- **CorelDRAW Graphics Suit X3** (Version 13) ***Training Guide***
- **Photoshop CS3 and CS5/CS6** ***Training Guide***
- **PageMaker-6.5 and 7.0** ***Training Guide***
- **MS Office 2007 and 2010** ***Training Guide***
- **MS Word 2007 and 2010 Training Guide**
- **MS Excel 2007 and 2010** ***Training Guide***
- **MS PowerPoint 2007 and 2010** ***Training Guide***
- **Internet** ***Training Guide***
- **Windows 7/8** ***Training Guide***
- **Dreamweaver CS5** ***Training Guide***
- **Flash Professional CS5/CS6** ***Training Guide***
- **Illustrator CS5** ***Training Guide***

Preface

The objective of this book is to meet the growing need of PC users to learn and become proficient in using software packages namely Photoshop CS6, CorelDRAW X5, and PageMaker 7. In addition, the basic of Desktop Publishing is also discussed in simple English. This guide is based on step-by-step learning methodology.

Unit 1 introduces you, Fundamentals of DTP. The first Chapter discusses the basics role of DTP in creating various media Publication.

Unit 2 introduces you with Adobe Photoshop CS6. This package is very powerful image editing software. This package is used for Web and Multimedia designers, digital photographers and videographers to work with graphics.

Unit 3 introduces you popular graphics package namely, CorelDRAW Graphics Suite X5. This package has been explained with several examples, so that novice can easily comprehend it.

Unit 4 deals with the page layout package namely PageMaker 7. Set of illustrations are given to enable first time users to be comfortable with this package.

An Appendix is added that contains `Questions based on the Software Packages' discussed in the book.

We shall feel obliged to the readers if they send us their critical opinion of the presentation, readability and coverage in this book and send us suggestions in improving the subject matter. They may e-mail to us on *bpb@vsnl.com*.

Authors

14th August, 2015

Contents

CHAPTER 1

Fundamentals of DTP

Introduction

Desktop publishing is the use of the computer and software to create visual displays of ideas and information. Desktop publishing documents may be for desktop or commercial printing or electronic distribution including PDF (Portable Document Format), slide shows, e-mail newsletters, e-pub, and the Web.

This Chapter explains the various features of DTP (Desktop Publishing) and provides you enough knowledge and skills to know the powerful concepts of DTP.

What Is Desktop Publishing?

Desktop publishing (DTP) is generally regarded to have three types. These are image editing, illustration and page layout. Desktop publishing is the process of using certain types of software and the computer to combine text and graphics to create a well laid out documents, such as brochures, newsletters, books, etc. Desktop publishing is also known as DTP. Using a page layout software, desktop publishing helps documents for printing on a computer which are for either large or small scale publishing.

Hardware costs made desktop publishing systems impractical for most users in the past. But as the prices of personal computers and printers have fallen, desktop publishing systems have become increasingly popular for producing newsletters, brochures, books and other documents that formerly required a typesetter machine.

Once you have produced a document with a desktop publishing system, you can output it directly to a printer. Offset printing produces higher-quality documents, especially if color is used, but is generally more expensive than laser printing.

Word Processing vs Desktop Publishing

In the '80s, when desktop publishing had just made an entrance, DTP programs were not very user-friendly and required prior experience in the field. Similarly, the first word processing programs were exactly that - programs for dealing with text and text only. At that time, desktop publishing and word processing were two different procedures.

Today, desktop publishing programs are so user-friendly that they can be used almost without prior training. This is helped by the fact that many of the word processing features have been incorporated into them. Word processing programs have also evolved greatly and can now handle non-text elements like images, illustrations and tables. Today, the line between word processing and desktop publishing has become blurry.

What is WYSIWYG?

A particularly important feature of desktop publishing systems is that they enable you to see on the display screen exactly how the document will appear when printed. Systems that support this feature are called WYSIWYGs (What You See Is What You Get).

Hardware Requirements for DTP

A Personal Computer (PC), a scanner and a printer are the minimum requirements for bringing out publications using DTP. The RAM (Random Access Memory) requirement is 128-256 MBs and the hard disk capacity is 20–40 GBs. A 17″ color monitor with higher resolution is required. Zip drive or a CD (compact Disk) writer is required for data transfer and storage, and also a video card is required to process images so they can be displayed on monitor. The video card is a device, which enhances the picture quality of colored images in the monitor. Most of the PCs have built-in video cards.

Desktop Publishing Software

Graphic designers and non-designers use DTP software alike. Different software programs provide different skill levels and used in home, offices, and professional enterprises. Top high-end DTP programs include QuarkXPress, Adobe Illustrator, Photoshop, PageMaker and CorelDRAW and Scanning software.

Text and Graphics used by DTP

The various types of software generally used by DTP operations are listed below:

(a) Text editors

(b) Word processors

(c) Page layout applications

(d) Vector and raster graphics

Let us discuss them one-by-one:

Text Editors

A text editor is a type of program used for editing plain text files. In a plain text file, one byte of data (8 bits) represents a character of text. The most common computer alphabet is the American Standard Code for Information Interchange (ASCII). Text editors are often provided with operating systems or software development packages, and can be used to change configuration files and programming language source code. Microsoft (MS) Windows comes with a very simple Notepad, text editor.

Word Processors

A word processor (more formally known as document preparation system) is a computer application used for the production (including composition, editing, formatting, and printing) of any sort of printable material.

Word processors are descended from early text formatting tools (sometimes called text justification tools, from their only real capability). Word processing was one of the earliest applications for the personal computer in office productivity. Although early word processors used tag-based markup for document formatting, most modern word processors take advantage of a graphical user interface. Most are powerful systems consisting of one or more programs that can produce any arbitrary combination of images, graphics and text, the latter handled with type-setting capability. Microsoft Word is widely used computer word processing system.

Page Layout Application

Page layout is the process of placing and arranging text and graphics on the page to produce documents, such as newsletters, brochures, books, etc. Page layout refers to the actual document page and its composition. The primary software programs for desktop publishing are called page layout applications. PageMaker was the first desktop publishing or page layout program that made it easy to arrange and rearrange text and graphics.

The best known professional page layout software programs are: InDesign, FrameMaker, QuarkXPress, and Corel Ventura. Mid-level page layout programs include MS Publisher. Desktop publishing dramatically brought down the cost of page layout, causing many projects to be taken in house.

Vector and Raster Graphics

Vector Graphics

Vector graphics is the creation of digital images through a sequence of commands or mathematical statements that place lines and shapes in a given two-dimensional or three-dimensional space. In physics, a vector is a representation of both a quantity and a direction at the same time. In vector graphics, the file that results from a graphic artist's work is created and saved as a sequence of vector statements. For example, instead of containing a bit in the file for each bit of a line drawing, a vector graphic file describes a series of points to be connected. This results in a much smaller file size.

At some point, a vector image is converted into a raster graphics image, which maps bits directly to display space (and is sometimes called a bitmap). The vector image can be converted to a raster image file prior to its display so that it can be ported between systems.

A vector file is sometimes called a geometric file. Most images created with tools, such as Adobe Illustrator and CorelDRAW are in the form of vector image files. Vector image files are easier to modify than raster image files (which can, however, be reconverted to vector files for further refinement).

Bitmap image

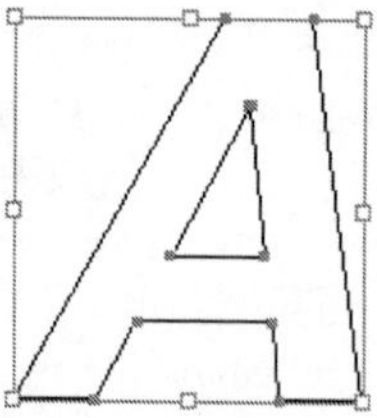
Vector Graphic

Animation images are also created as vector files. For example, Shockwave's Flash lets you create 2-D (Two Dimensional) and 3-D (Three Dimensional) animations that are sent to a requestor as a vector file. Software used to create vector graphics is also referred to as object-based editing software.

The image to the left below is representative of a bitmap and the image to the right is representative of a vector graphic. They are shown at four times actual size to exaggerate the fact that the edges of a bitmap become jagged as it is scaled up.

The jagged appearance of bitmap images can be partially overcome with the use of "anti-aliasing". Anti-aliasing is the application of subtle transitions in the pixels along the edges of images to minimize the jagged effect (below left). A scalable vector image will always appear smooth (below right)

Anti-Aliased Bitmap Image

Smooth Vector Image

Bitmap images require higher resolution and anti-aliasing for a smooth appearance. Vector-based graphics on the other hand are mathematically described and appear smooth at any size or resolution. Bitmaps are best used for photographs and images with subtle shading. Graphics best suited for the vector format are page layout, type, line art or illustrations.

Raster Graphics

Raster graphics is that style of graphics in which the image is broken up into a matrix of picture elements (pixels). The matrix will have a certain number of rows, each containing a certain number of pixels. Each pixel can be assigned any number of colors. The number of colors depending upon the "depth" of the image, often expressed as the number of bits needed to encode all the colors. Typical bit depths used today are: 1 (two colors, usually black and white), 2 (four colors, usually shades of gray), 4 (16 colors), 8 (256 colors), 16 (65,536 colors), etc.

The number of rows and columns gives you the resolution. If there are c columns and r rows, the image is referred to as r x c image. If the image is to have a certain physical size, this size combined with the number of pixels give you the number of (dpi) dots per inch of the image, which is a measure of its resolution. The higher the dpi, the smaller the dots, and the harder it is to see them as individuals.

A raster image editor works by manipulating each individual pixel. Most pixel-based image editors work using RGB (Red, Green, Blue) color model, but some also allow the use of other color models, such as CMYK (Cyan, Magenta, Yellow, key (black)) color model.

Printing and Finishing Phase of Desktop Publishing

After a document is designed and the file prepared for printing, the last step in desktop publishing is the actual printing, along with any finishing touches required. The final document may be printed to a desktop printer or it may be sent out for printing.

There are many ways to get it printed and ideally you will have to decide on a printing method prior to starting the design project, such as the range of printing methods and when to use which type of printing process. Printing techniques, offer different ways in which printing may be accomplished, such as lithography, letterpress, gravure, and laser printing. Printing techniques use simple mechanisms for rapidly applying colors to substrates, such as paper or plastic to form multiple reproductions of original images for mass distribution.

Digital/Desktop Printing

Desktop printing is important to desktop publishing. It was primarily the introduction of the Apple LaserWriter, a PostScript desktop printer, and PageMaker for the Mac that kicked off the desktop publishing revolution. Inkjet and laser printers are the most common type of desktop printers and are generally used for personal small volume printing and proofing.

Offset Lithography Printing

Lithography is mainly used by commercial printers, printing companies that will print thousands of copies of the same item, in one production run. Lithography machines can print on both sides of paper/card and they rely on four basic colors; yellow, cyan (type of blue), magenta (type of red) and black. This is also known as the CYMK process. Offset printing is generally used to undertake litho printing. Figure 1.1 shows the structure of an offset lithography printing machines.

1. The printing plate has the image to be printed. The image stands out slightly from the printing plate surface.
2. The printing plate is kept dampened. Ink is applied to the plate but it is repelled from the dampened surfaces which are the non-image areas.

3. As the printing cylinder rotates the ink is transferred to the rubber blanket cylinder.
4. The ink, now on the rubber blanket cylinder, is pressed onto the paper or card as it is pulled through the machine. (The paper is trapped between the blanket cylinder and the impression cylinder - these pull the paper through the machine).

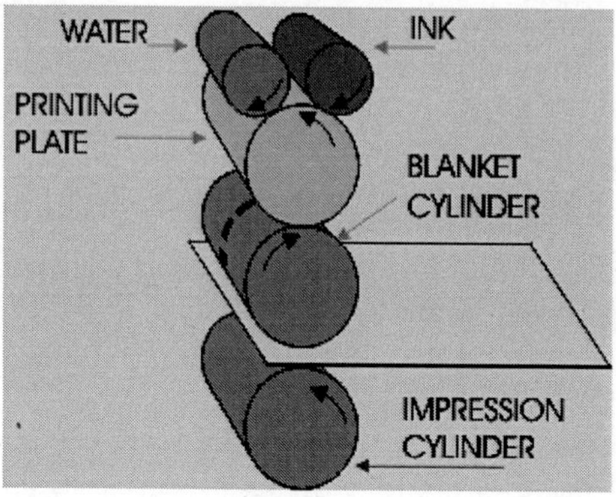

Figure 1.1 Offset lithography printing machine

With some modern lithography printing machines the image is put onto the printing plate by shining ultraviolet light through a negative (similar to a photograph negative). The plate is coated with a chemical which allows the ink (made from oil) to attach to the image area. If different colors are needed for the final print - the same card/paper will be sent through the machine and each time different negatives and colors will be applied. This is done until the print, which may be a poster, is completed.

Laser printing

A laser printer is a common type of computer printer that rapidly produces high quality text and graphics on plain paper. A laser printer is a popular type of personal computer printer that uses a non-impact photocopier technology.

Laser printers have many significant advantages over other types of printers. Unlike impact printer, laser printer speed can vary widely, and depends on many factors, including the graphic intensity of the job being processed. The fastest models can print over 200 monochrome pages per minute (12,000 pages per hour). The fastest color laser printers can print over 100 pages per minute (6000 pages per hour).

The standard resolution in laser printers today is 600 dots-per-inch (dpi). This resolution is sufficient for normal everyday printing including small desktop publishing jobs. A high-end production printer might have a resolution of 2400 dpi.

CHAPTER 2

Basics of Photoshop CS6

Introduction

The latest edition, Photoshop CS6 is a new release with an updated interface, several new features and several improvements that will allow you to work faster and more efficiently. It is a graphic design and image enhancement program that runs on both Windows and Macintosh platforms. Photoshop comes in two editions: Photoshop CS6 and Photoshop CS6 Extended. Photoshop CS6 Extended edition has the same features included in the Standard edition.

Photoshop's ability to manipulate digital images, restore old photographs, as well as create digital artwork from scratch. The images created with any digital camera or photographic film images converted to digital format through the use of a scanner. Once an image is opened in Photoshop, the designer can manipulate the image in different ways, such as correcting color, reducing dust and scratches in an old image.

Photoshop CS6 / Photoshop Extended CS6 System Requirements

Photoshop CS6 runs 64-bit on Mac OS X, Windows Vista, and Windows 7. It can also run in 32-bit mode on Windows XP (although Photoshop Extended's 3D (Three Dimensional) features and some (Graphics Processing Unit) GPU-accelerated functions are not available on XP).

- Intel Pentium 4 or AMD (Advanced Micro Devices) Athlon 64 processor.
- Microsoft Windows XP with Service Pack 3 or Microsoft Windows 7 with Service Pack 1.
- 1 GB of RAM (Random Access Memory).
- 1 GB of available hard disk space for installation.
- 1024 x 768 display (1280 x 800 recommended) with 16-bit color and 512 MB (1 GB recommended) of VRAM or Virtual RAM.
- OpenGL 2.0–capable system
- DVD-ROM (Digital Versatile/Video Disk-Read Only Memory) drive
- Broadband Internet Connection

Starting Photoshop CS6

To start Photoshop CS6, do this:

1. Click **Start** menu, highlight **Programs**, and choose **Adobe Photoshop CS6**.
2. The Photoshop CS6 opens and the window appears as shown in Figure 2.1.

Exploring the New Photoshop Interface

The default Photoshop interface includes the Menu bar, Tools panel, Options bar,

Figure 2.1 Photoshop window Elements

canvas area, and several panels, such as Color, Adjustments, and Layers. All these panels are present in groups. You can collapse or expand a panel as per your requirement. You can also make a panel as a floating panel or collapse it into an icon to increase the canvas area.

Now let us discuss the Photoshop CS6 interface elements beginning with the Menu bar.

Menu bar

Each Menu in the Menu Bar represents a group of commands that can enable you to make transformations to all or part of an image and to manipulate files. The Menu Bar replaces the Application bar in Photoshop CS6. At the right-most corner of the Menu bar it displays three button; Minimize, Restore, and Close. In addition, the Mini Bridge button is now available as a tab below the canvas area.

Options Bar

The Options bar or Control Panel is situated below the Menu bar in the Photoshop screen as shown in Figure 1.1. The **Options** bar displays options specific to the tool we have selected from the Tools palette. For example, if we select Brush Tool, it will display options specific to the Brush Tool, such as the Brush Preset Picker, Toggle the Brush Panel, Painting Mode, Opacity for Brush Stroke.

Document Window

When we open a Photoshop file, it appears with screen components. The name of the file appears in the Title bar of the Document window. You can move a window by clicking in the document window's Title bar and dragging it to a new location in the workarea. At the bottom of the document window shows information about the open file.

The Photoshop program window contains the following components:

Image Window—The Image window contains the image to be edited. This is the area where we work and only this part of the screen gets printed.

Image Title bar—Title bar appears on the top of image document tabs as shown in Figure 2.2. The Title bar of the image displays vital information about the image opened. For example, Flower3 is the name of file, .jpg is file format of the image, 100% resembles the zoom size at which the image is appearing in the window, RGB indicates the color mode of the image, and 8 represents its bit size.

Figure 2.2 Document window

Document Info—At the bottom of every document window and displays information, such as the current magnification and file size of the active image.

Panels

Panels are small adjustable windows that provide the access to common commands and options. By default, these panels are combined into groups known as panel groups and appear to the right side of the Photoshop window. For instance, by default, the Color panel is grouped with the Swatches panel. You can click the name of the tab in which you want to work with, to activate it. Panels in a panel group can be collapsed into tabs or icons, where in the tabs form displays the icons and names, and the icons form displays only the icons.

You can customize the panel arrangements in the following ways:

- Press the **Shift+Tab** keys together for hiding/showing all panels exclude the Tools panel.
- Drag the Panel tab to a desired location to unlock and make the panels as floating panels. By default, panels are docked into the right side of the Photoshop window.

- Click the icon of the respective panel for display the expanded panel view with commands and options.
- Click the panel icon again or click the double arrows in the title bar for closing the panel.
- Click the panel menu icon at the upper right corner of a panel to open a panel menu.

Tools Panel

The toolbox holds tools for creating and editing images. The first time you start the application, the toolbox appears on the left side of the screen. The toolbox is a collection of drawing tools (See Figure 2.3). When you want to use a particular tool, just click on that tool. The mouse pointer will change its shape according to the tool selected. Then you can click the tool pointer on your canvas and start your work. The following are the tools in Photoshop's toolbox:

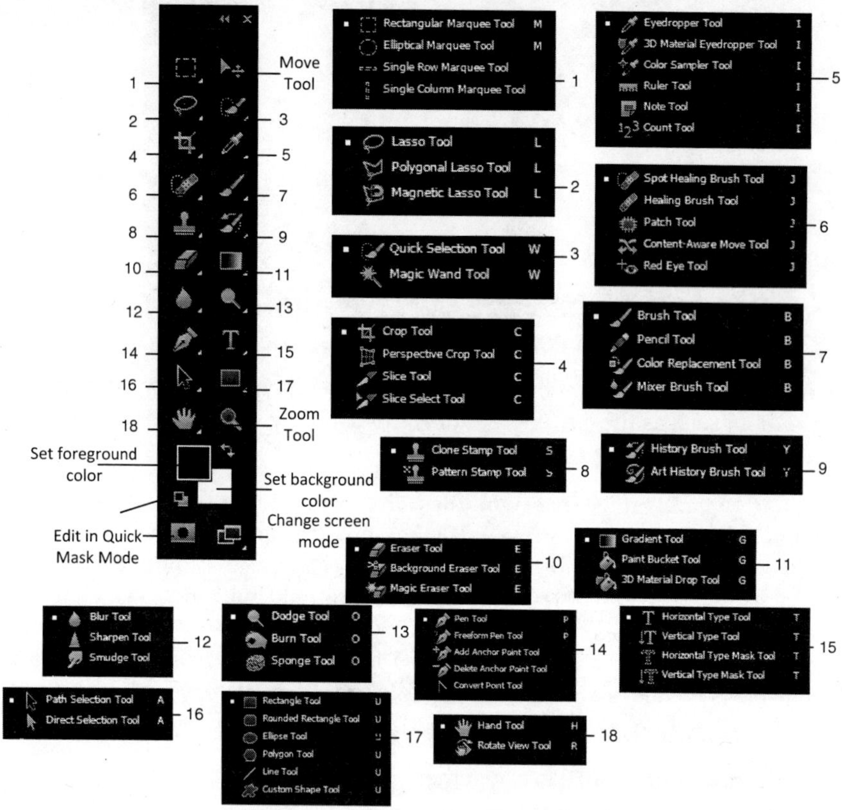

Figure 2.3 Toolbar with Flyouts

To use the Tools panel efficiently while working in Photoshop.

- Press the V key on the keyboard at any point to activate Move Tool. The name and the shortcut key appear in the tooltip when you place your cursor over any tool. For instance when you place the cursor over Move Tool, the tooltip appears as Move Tool (V) where V is the shortcut key for the Move Tool.
- Click the hold the mouse button to open a flyout to access the additional tools. A small triangle on a tool means that some additional tools are present and hidden under the main tool.
- Click the double arrows in the title bar of the Tools panel to bring the Tools panel into the two-column and vice-versa. The Tools panel is in the one-column view by default.
- Click the Title bar at the top of the Tools panel to create a floating Tools panel.
- Press the Tab key to hide/show all the panels, including the Tools panel.
- Press the Caps Lock key on the keyboard to change the shape of the pointer for the painting tools to crosshair. To return to the standard cursor, press the Caps Lock key again.

Using Rulers

Rulers help you position the images. When you need to position selections based on measurements, turn on the rulers. When you no need them turn them off.

To show and then hide rulers, do this:

1. Click the **View** menu choose **Rulers**. The rulers will appear on the image. A check mark indicates that the rulers are shown on the image.
2. Again click the **View** menu. Choose **Rulers**. The rulers will disappear from the image.
3. *Alternatively,* press **Ctrl+R** to toggle between showing and hiding rulers.

Position with Guides and the Grid

Guides and the grid help you position the images. Guides appear as non-printing lines that float over the image. You can move and remove guides. You can also lock them so that you do not move them by accident. The Lock Guides option under the View menu lets you lock the guides; you cannot move the guides when they are locked.

Guides and grids behave in similar ways:

- Selections, selection borders and tools snap to a guide or the grid when dragged within pixels. Guides also snap to the grid when moved. You can turn this feature on and off.
- Guide spacing, along with the guide and grid visibility and snapping, is specific to an image.

- Grid spacing, along with the guide and gird color and style is the same for all images.

You can use Smart Guides to help align shapes, slices and selections. They appear automatically when you draw a shape, or create a selection or slide.

To place a Guide, do this:

1. Click the **View** menu choose **New Guide...** . The **New Guide** dialog box appears as shown in Figure 2.4.
2. In the **New Guide** dialog box, choose the **Horizontal** or **Vertical** orientation and enter **Position:** list box. Click OK button.

   The horizontal guide appears at the 0 position as shown in Figure 2.4.

To select a Grid, do this:

1. Click the **View** menu choose **Show**. A sub menu appears, select **Grid** from the sub menu. Or **Ctrl + '** keys together.

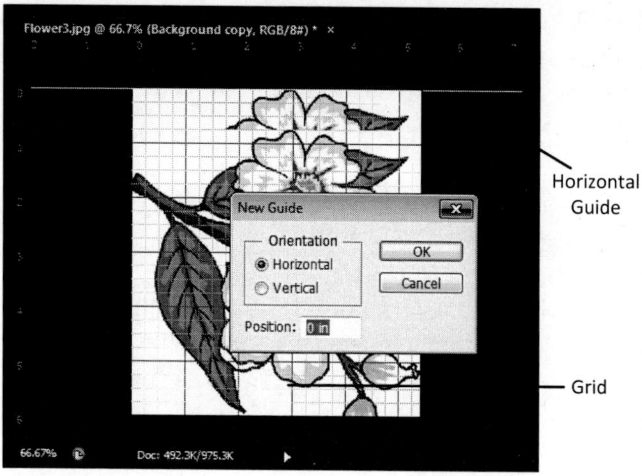

Figure 2.4 New Guide dialog box

Hold down Alt key, and drag from the vertical ruler to create a horizontal guide. Alternatively, drag from the horizontal ruler to create a vertical guide.

To Move a Guide, do this:

1. Select the move tool.
2. Position the pointer over the guide. The pointer turns into a double-headed arrow.
3. Drag the guide to move it.

To Remove a Guide, do this:

1. To remove a single guide, drag the guide outside the image window.
2. To remove all guides, choose **View** menu and select **Clear Guides**.

Opening an Existing File

There are many ways to open an existing file in the workarea. You can Open Recent command from the File menu. A list of previously opened files will appear in the menu list. Choose a file to open it.

To open an existing file, do this:

1. Click the **File** menu and choose **Open Recent**. A list of **Open Recent File** list appears, select the desired file you want to open. Or
2. Click the **File** menu and choose **Open**. *Alternatively,* press **Ctrl + O** keys together. The **Open** dialog box appears as shown in Figure 2.5.
3. If you want to open a file with a format of your choice, click the down arrow of the **Files of type:** drop-down list and select a format of the file, which you want. For example, if you want to open a JPEG (Joint Photographic Experts Group) file, then select Photoshop JPEG (*. Jpg, *jpeg, *jpe) from the drop-down list.
4. Navigate to the file location.

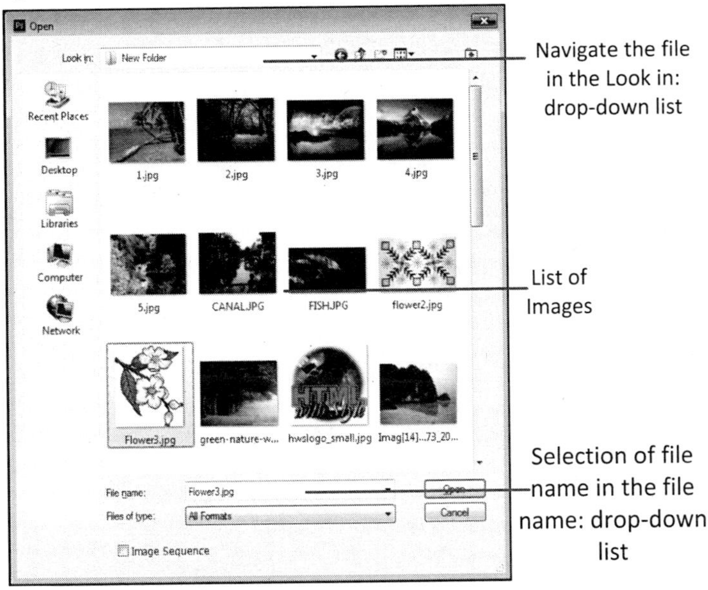

Figure 2.5 Open dialog box

Creating a New Document

You can use Photoshop CS6 to either edit an existing document or create a new document from scratch. Photoshop gives you a variety ways to create a new document.

To open a new file, do this:

1. Click the **File** menu and choose **New...** . *Alternatively,* press **Ctrl+N** keys together. The **New** dialog box appears as shown in Figure 2.6.

2. In the **Name:** text box type the name of your file. This name will be used whenever you want to open your file again after saving it.
3. Click the **Preset:** drop-down list to select the document size. Preset list consists some already defined size. Select any one of them.

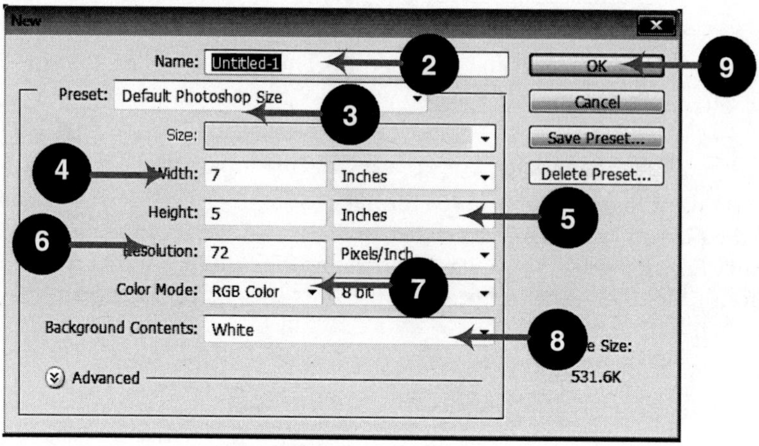

Figure 2.6 New dialog box

4. Click the **Width:** text box to change the width of the image. If you want to change the unit, click on the down arrow to see the unit list. Then select any unit of measurement of your choice.
5. Click the **Height:** text box to change the height of the image. If you want to change the unit, click on the down arrow to see the unit list. Then select any unit of measurement of your choice.
6. Click the **Resolution:** text box to change the resolution of the image. If you want to change the resolution unit, click on the down arrow to see the resolution unit list. Then select any resolution unit of your choice. Resolution change will enable you to sharpen the image.
7. Click the down arrow in the **Color Mode:** drop-down list to see the Color Mode list. The various mode options are Bitmap, Grayscale, REG Color, CMYK Color, Lab Color. Then select a desired mode.
8. The **Background Contents:** In drop-down list; choose the desired option to change the background of an image. If you select White, the image will have a White Background. If you select Background Color, the canvas will be filled with the background color. If you select Transparent, option opens a checkboard pattern for the new image. This indicates that the image lacks a Background layer.
9. After you have set the desired settings, click OK button to save the settings.

The new document (Untitled-1) appears in the middle of the canvas areas as shown in Figure 2.7.

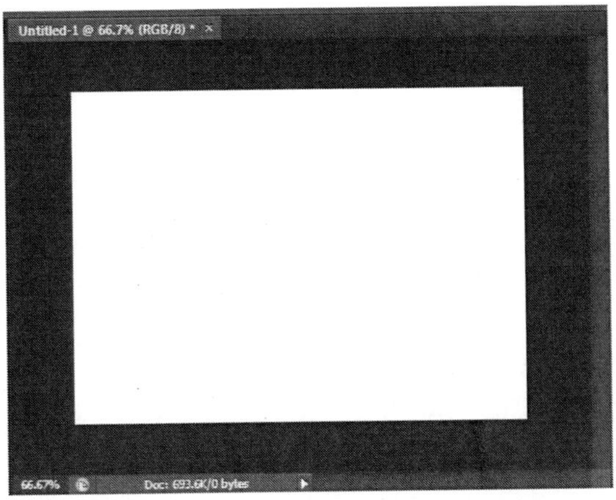

Figure 2.7 New document window

Saving a Document

After you have created a file or made changes to an existing file, you need to save the file. You can save a file with its current filename, location, and format or with a different filename, location, format and options. You can also save a copy of a file while leaving the current file open on your desktop.

To save current file, do this:

1. Click the **File** menu and choose **Save...** . *Alternatively,* press **Ctrl+S** keys together.
2. Photoshop saves your file and leaves it open for use.

To save a file with a different name and location, do this:

1. Click the **File** menu and choose **Save As...** . *Alternatively,* press **Alt + F + A** keys together. The **Save As** dialog box appears as shown in Figure 2.8.

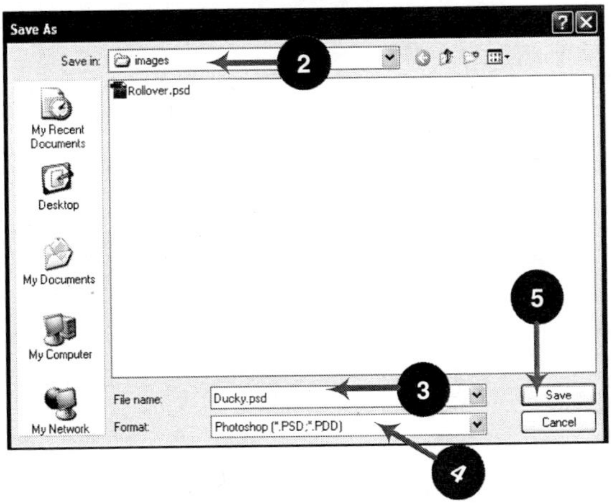

Figure 2.8 Save As dialog box

2. Navigate the location where you want to save the file in the **Save in:** drop-down list.
3. Click the **File name:** text box, then type a new name for your file.
4. Select a format in the **Format:** drop-down list to save your document. In our case, we have selected **Photoshop (*.PSD, *.PDD)** format. Here, PSD stands for Photoshop Document.
5. Click the **Save** button to save the document with the specified settings. The **Save As** dialog box will close. Photoshop saves the file and leaves it open for use.

Working with Photoshop Views

The Zoom tool is located towards the bottom of Photoshop's toolbox, and resembles a magnifying glass. The maximum magnification of a Photoshop document is 3200%, and the minimum size is 1 pixel.

Using Zoom Tool

Photoshop gives you a variety of ways to view your images. One way to zoom is to use Zoom Tool, which appears similar to a magnifying glass. You can click its icon in the Tools panel or simply press Z key on the keyboard. *Alternatively,* you can click on the image with Zoom Tool to zoom in, and press the Alt key while clicking (Alt-click) the image to zoom out. You can also press the Ctrl and plus (+) keys simultaneously to zoom in; and Ctrl and minus (–) keys together to zoom out.

Increase or Decrease the Zoom Magnification of an Image, do this:

1. Select the **Zoom tool** on the toolbox.
2. Select the options which are available in the **Options** bar (See Figure 2.9).

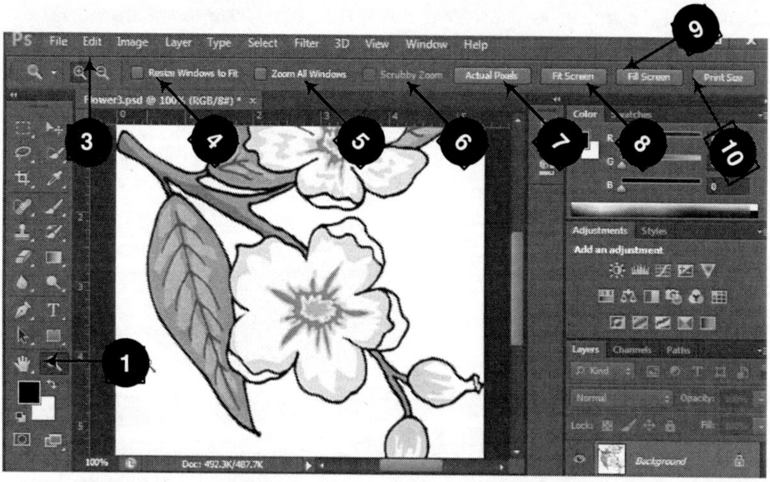

Figure 2.9 Selecting zoom tool with zoom options bar

3. Click the **Zoom In** or **Zoom Out** button on the Options bar, and then click in the document window to increase or decrease the zoom.
4. Select the **Resize Windows to Fit** check box on the Options bar to resize the active document to fit the current window.
5. Select the **Zoom All Windows** check box on the Options bar to zoom all open document windows to the same magnification.
6. Select the **Scrubby Zoom** check box to zoom continuously. You can drag left to zoom out or right to zoom in.
7. Select the **Actual Pixels** option on the Options bar to view your image at 100 percent magnification. You can also press Ctrl+1 keys together, or double-click Zoom Tool in the Tools panel to display image at 100 percent.
8. Select the **Fit Screen** option to resize the active image window to fit the available space on your screen in the Document window.
9. Select the **Fill Screen** option to fill the workarea within the monitor screen.
10. Select the **Print Size** option to display and adjust the size of image to be printed.

Using Hand Tool to Navigate the Image Area

Hand Tool is used to navigate from one part of the image to another. Usually, when you zoom in, it hides some portion in the Document window is unable to display all images. In such cases, you can use Hand Tool to drag the hidden portion to the visible area of the Document window.

When Hand Tool is active, following options are available in the Options bar:

- **Scroll All Windows:** It allows scrolling all open windows simultaneously.
- **Actual Pixels:** It displays your image at 100 percent magnification.
- **Fit Screen:** It allows resize the active image window to fit the image inside the Document window.
- **Print Size:** It displays the size of image which is to be printed.

Exiting Photoshop CS6

After finishing you work with Photoshop, you can close the document and exit from the application. You can close open documents one at a time (choose Close from the File menu or click the Close button on the Document tab). If you have not saved the document you are currently working on, Photoshop offers you to save your document or discard the changes. If you save the changes, the content of the document remains unchanged until you open it again and make changes to it.

To close the document and exit Photoshop, do this:

1. Select **File** menu and choose **Close** from the **Menu** bar to close the active document.
2. You can notice the active document window is closed.
3. Select **File** menu and choose **Exit** from the **Menu** bar to exit Photoshop.

CHAPTER 3

Working with Images and Selections

Introduction

In this Chapter, we will learn about the methods available in Photoshop CS6 for working with images, the difference between Bitmap and Vector images. In addition, we will also learn how to select any part or full image and apply changes on them according to the requirements. For selecting any image or part of an image, we have to simply drag around the area, which we want to select using a Selection Tool.

Compare between Vector and Bitmap Images

When we talk about graphics, we can differentiate among the graphics into two classes. One is bitmap (or raster graphics) and other is Vectors. Bitmap graphics are created by a rectangular grid of picture elements (pixels) to represent image. Bitmap images are resolution-dependent, that is, they contain a fixed number of pixels. Enlarging a bitmap graphic re-distributes the pixels in the grid, often making the edges of the image to appear jagged.

Vector images are made up of objects like lines, curves, and shapes, placed on top of each other to create an image. A vector image can be described using mathematical definition. Vector graphics are resolution independent, that is, they can be displayed on output devices of varying resolutions without losing quality. Thus, moving, resizing or reshaping a vector graphic will not distort the image quality and user can easily modify these attributes.

Understanding Image Resolution

The term `resolution' refers to the number of small squares, known as pixels, which describe an image and establish its detail. Resolution is determined by pixel dimensions, or the number of pixels along the width and height of an image.

The number of pixels per unit of length in an image is called the image resolution, usually measured in pixels per inch (ppi). An image with a high resolution has more pixels (and therefore a larger file size) than an image of the same dimensions with a low resolution. Images in Photoshop can vary from high resolution (300 ppi or higher) to low resolution (72 ppi or 96 ppi).

The number of pixels per unit of length on a monitor is the monitor resolution, and usually measured in pixels per inch (ppi). Image pixels are translated directly into monitor pixels. In Photoshop, if the image resolution is higher than the monitor resolution, the image appears larger onscreen than its specified print dimensions. For example, when you display a 1×1-inch, 144-ppi image on a 72-ppi monitor, the image fills a 2×2-inch area of the screen.

As you know, the resolution of an image is pixel-dependent. You can understand this better after you become familiar with the term pixel, discussed in the next Section.

Understanding Pixel

To understand the concept of pixel logic, open an image in the Photoshop Document window and view the image at two different resolutions. In our case, an image is shown in two different resolutions, i.e., 18 (pixels per inch) ppi and 72 ppi as shown in Figure 3.1. As you notice in Figure 3.1, the lower resolution of the image appears pixelated or blurred as compared to the higher resolution version.

Figure 3.1 Two different types of resolution of an image

Changing the Resolution of an Image

It is easy to change the size of an image. You can either resize the image or resize the canvas. Resizing image means making image to specify image size in terms of printed dimensions and image resolution. Changing pixel dimensions affects not only size of an image on-screen but also its image quality and its printed characteristics.

To change the resolution of an image, do this:

1. Open an image in Photoshop.
2. Click **Image** menu and choose **Image Size...** . *Alternatively,* press **Alt+Ctrl+I** keys together as shown in Figure 3.2. The **Image Size** dialog box appears.
3. Type a value in the **Resolution:** text box in the **Document Size:** section. In our case, we have typed **150**, as shown in Figure 3.3.
4. Click the **OK** button in the **Image Size** dialog box.

Note that the values in the **Width:** and **Height:** text boxes in the **Pixel Dimensions:** section change when you change the resolution value. Moreover, note that with the increase in pixel resolution, document size also changes. The resolution of the image changes, as shown in Figure 3.4.

Figure 3.2 Selecting Image Size... option from the Image menu

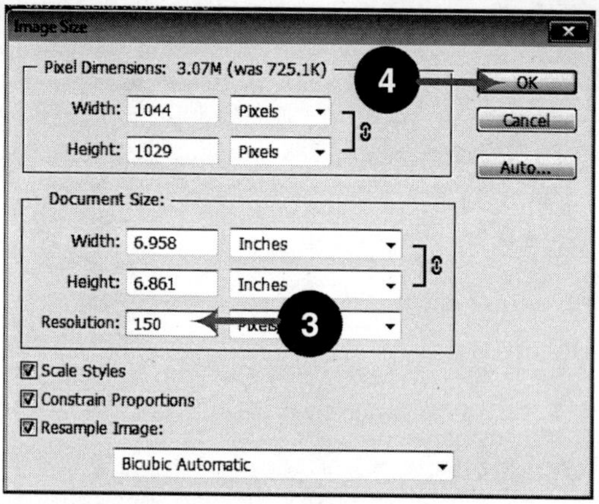

Figure 3.3 Image Size dialog box

Figure 3.4 The resolution of the image get changed

Change the Size of a Document

Document size is defined as the height and width of an image. The height and width can be increased or decreased in a constrained proportion, that is, if you increase the width of the file, the height increases automatically in the same proportion. This can be done by selecting the **Constrain Proportions** check box in the **Image Size** dialog box.

To change the document size of an image, do this:

1. Open an image in Photoshop.
2. Click **Image** menu and choose **Image Size...** . *Alternatively,* press **Alt+Ctrl+I** keys together as shown in Figure 3.5.
3. Type a value in the **Width:** text box in the **Document Size:** section. In our case, we have typed **15**, as shown in Figure 3.5.
4. If the **Constrain Proportions** check box is selected in the **Image Size** dialog box, the value in the **Height:** text box changes automatically. In addition, the values in the **Width:** and **Height:** text boxes under the **Pixel Dimensions:** are also changed.
5. Click the **OK** button as shown in Figure 3.5.
6. The size of an image changes according to the width and height, specified by you in the **Image Size** dialog box as shown in Figure 3.6.

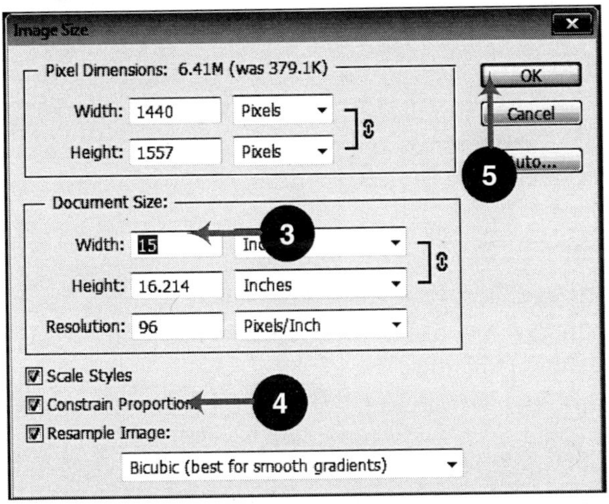

Figure 3.5 Image Size dialog box

Resample an image

Changing the pixel dimensions of an image is called *resampling*. Resampling affects not only the size of an image onscreen, but also its image quality and its printed output—either its printed dimensions or its image resolution. When you change the resolution and document size of an image, the Resample Image check box appears as selected by default.

Figure 3.6 Changing the document in the image dialog box

Editing Images

In Photoshop CS6, image editing is one of the familiar common commands, such as rotating, cropping, etc. We will learn to make changes to the image. In addition, you will also learn how to adjust the size of the canvas and create a duplicate of the image.

Rotate an Image

The Rotate canvas commands let you rotate or flip the image vertically or horizontally. The commands do not work on individual layers or parts of layers, paths, or selection borders. You can rotate an image at a predefine angle or at an angle of your choice.

To rotate an image, do this:

1. Open the image that is to be rotated in Photoshop.
2. Click the **Image** menu highlight **Image Rotation**. A sub menu option appears as shown in Figure 3.7.
3. Choose **Flip Canvas Horizontal** or **Vertical** options. You can check that the image is rotated at 90° CW as shown in Figure 3.8. In our case, we have chosen **Flip Canvas Horizontal**.

To rotate specific rotation through dialog box, do this:

1. Click the **Image** menu highlight **Image Rotation** and choose **Arbitrary...** . The **Rotate Canvas** dialog box appears as shown in Figure 3.9.
2. In the **Rotate Canvas** dialog box, choose the radio button beside the **Angle:** option **°CW** or **°CCW**. (In Photoshop **CW** and **CCW** mean to rotate clockwise or counterclockwise, respectively). The default value 0 gets highlighted. Type the value; say 45 degree in the **Angle:** text box.

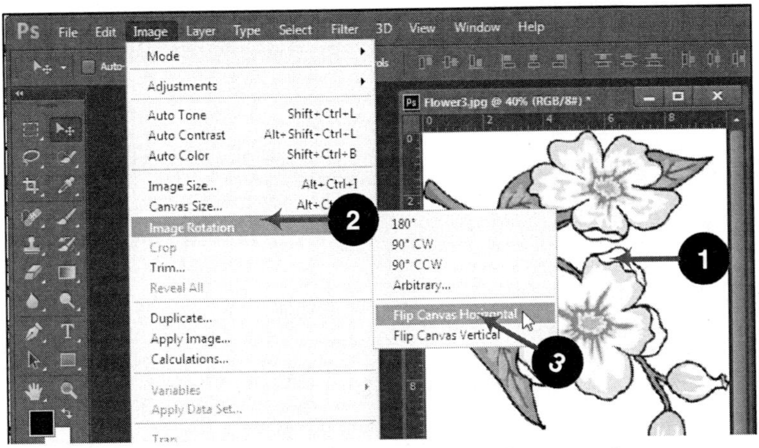

Figure 3.7 Selecting Image Rotation showing sub menu

Figure 3.8 The image has rotated to Flip Canvas Horizontal

3. Click the **°CW** radio button to rotate clockwise.
4. Click the **OK** button.
5. The image rotates at an angle of 45 degree as shown in Figure 3.9.

Cropping an Image

Cropping is the process of removing portions of an image. It also reduces the size of the document. There are several ways to crop images in Photoshop CS6. You can crop an image using the Crop Tool and Cropping with the Marquee Tool. Each of these cropping methods works in different ways.

To crop an image using the Crop Tool, do this:

1. Open the image to be cropped.

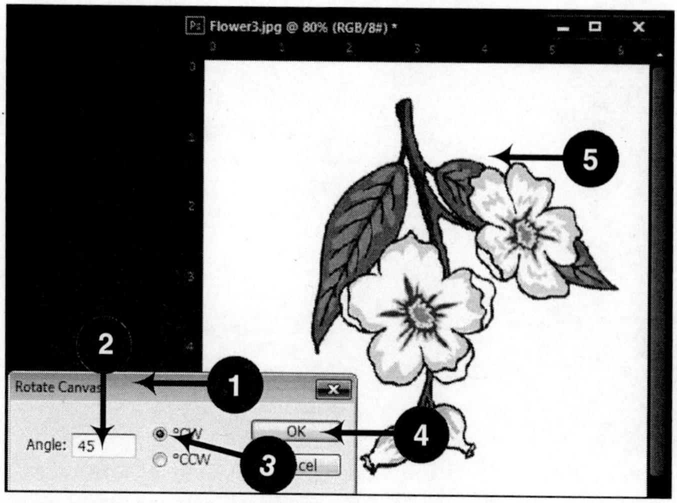

Figure 3.9 The image gets rotated at an angle of 45 degree

2. Select the **Crop** tool in the **Tools** panel or press the **C** key on the keyboard to select it as shown in Figure 3.10.

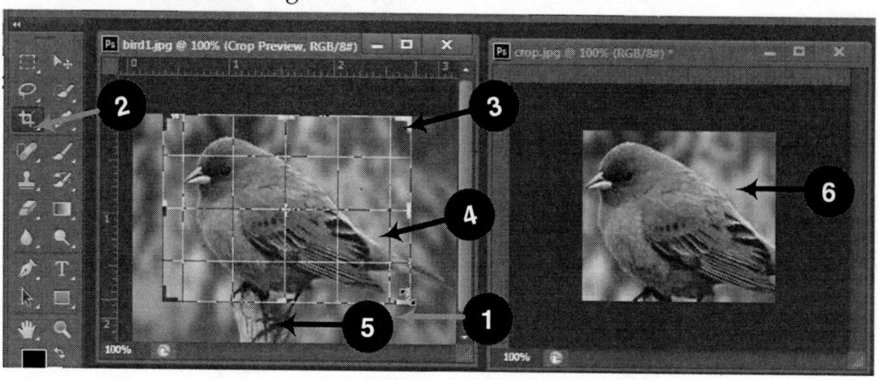

Figure 3.10 The selected part of the image get cropped

3. The crop box has multiple handles that you can use to resize and rotate it.
4. Drag the mouse-pointer over the image to create a rectangular selection over the part of an image that you want to keep and then release the mouse button (See Figure 3.10).
5. Instantly, a marquee with handles at the corners and sides of the image. Note that the remaining portion of the image is covered with a black shield as shown in Figure 3.10.
6. Press the **Enter** key to crop the portion of the image and deselect the crop tool. The image is cropped, as shown in Figure 3.10.

Change the Canvas Size

The canvas size is full editable area of an image. The canvas size command lets you increase or decrease an image's canvas size. Increasing the canvas size adds space around an existing image, while decreasing the canvas size crops the image. When you increase canvas size, it fills the extra area with the current background fill color.

To change the size of the canvas, do this:

1. Open the document whose canvas size you want to change.
2. Click **Image** menu and choose **Canvas Size...** . *Alternatively,* press **Alt + Ctrl + C** keys together.
3. The **Canvas** dialog box appears as shown in Figure 3.11. It displays the current canvas dimensions and file size in the **Current Size:** section.

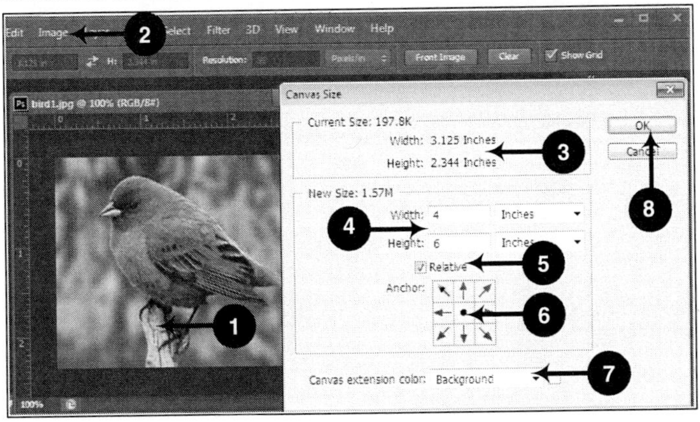

Figure 3.11 Canvas Size dialog

4. In **New Size:** section, enter values in **Width:** and **Height:** text boxes to specify width and height of canvas. You can also specify the unit of measurement in drop-down list next to text boxes.
5. Select **Relative,** and enter the amount you want to add or subtract from the image's current canvas size. Enter a positive number to add to the canvas, and enter a negative number to subtract from the canvas.
6. For **Anchor:**, click a square to indicate where to position the existing image on the new canvas.
7. In the **Canvas extension color:** drop-down list, choose one of the following options:

- Foreground to fill the new canvas with the current foreground color.
- Background to fill the new canvas with the current background color.
- White, Black or Gray to fill the new canvas with that color.
- Other to select a new canvas color using the Color picker.

8. Click the OK button to apply the new canvas size settings and close the dialog box. The image with extended canvas (white area) appears.

Making Color Adjustments

All Photoshop Color Adjustment tools work essentially an existing range of pixel values to a new range of values. The difference between the tools is the amount of control they provide. Color Adjustment tools and their option settings are accessed in the Adjustments panel.

The process of color corrections using the tools and methods are known as color adjustments. Photoshop introduced the Adjustments panel to access all the commands and dialog boxes related to color corrections from a single window.

The Adjustment panel is active by default, when you start Photoshop the Adjustment panel is not displayed in the Photoshop window, click **Windows** menu and choose **Adjustments** from the Menu bar to access it.

When adjusting your image, you can use various commands in the Properties panel. Presets are available, such as Auto Contrast and Color, Curves, Color Balance, Brightness/Contrast, and Selective Color Adjustment layers.

Levels Adjustment

Photoshop CS6 uses Levels adjustment to correct the tonal range (i.e., the light and dark pixels) and color balance of an image by adjusting intensity levels of image shadows, midtones and highlights. The Levels adjustment in the Adjustments panel appears with two different levels: Input Levels and Output Levels, along with a histogram. It shows the amount of pure black, pure white and between black and white. Input levels allow you to change the specific values for highlights, shadows and midtones in an image.

The several elements and options in the Levels adjustment are as follows:

- Move the Black slider for the Input Levels to the left or right direction to decrease or increase the level of shadow in an image.
- Use the Gray and White sliders to increase or decrease the levels of midtones and highlights in the image respectively. The Input slider at the middle is used to adjust the gamma value in the image.
- Use the Black and White sliders of the Output levels to limit the darkest and lightest pixels of the image. The default Output sliders are at level 0 and 255, where the pixels are black and white respectively.

There are several elements and options in the Levels adjustment as shown in Figure 3.12.

After exploring several elements of the Levels adjustment in the Adjustments panel, let us now use the level adjustments to correct the tonal range and the color balance of an image.

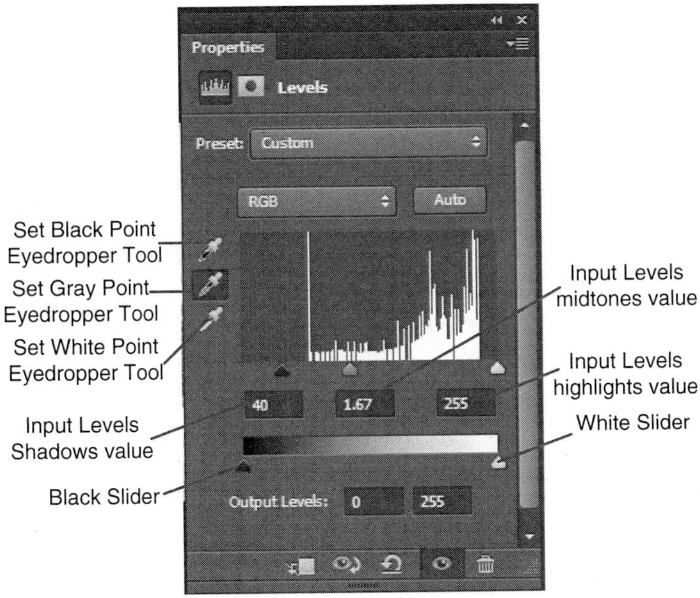

Figure 3.12 Level adjustment options

To correct the tonal range of an image, do this:

1. Open the image for tonal correction using Levels adjustments.
2. Click the **Create a new Levels adjustment layer** icon in the Adjustments panel to create a Levels adjustment layer and open in the Properties panel with all the settings, as shown in Figure 3.13.

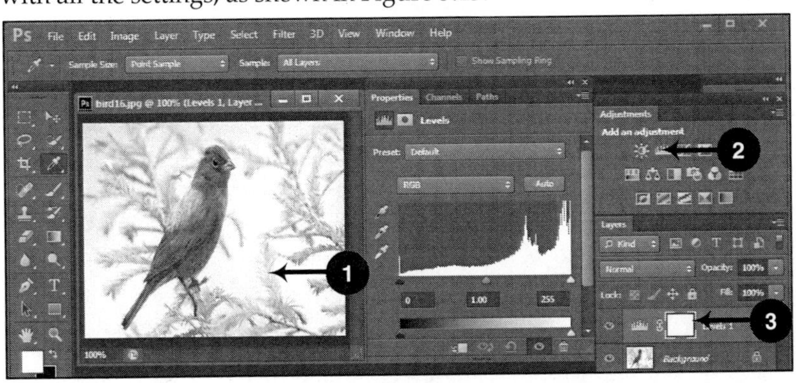

Figure 3.13 Selecting create a new levels adjustment layer in the Adjustment panel

3. The above image has higher level of shadows and lower level of highlight as depicted by the histogram. You can also see an adjustment layer named Level 1 is created in the Layers panel.

4. Type a value in the **Adjust shadow Input level** text box to increase the shadows in the image. In our case, we have typed 19.
5. Type a value in the **Adjust highlight Input level** text box to decrease the highlights. In our case, we have typed 145 as shown in Figure 3.14.

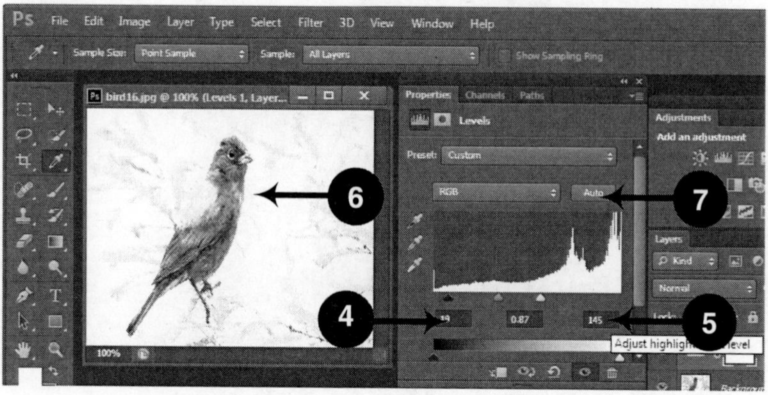

Figure 3.14 The image gets lighter shadow

6. The color corrected image appears as shown in Figure 3.14.
7. Click **Auto** button to adjust levels automatically.

Brightness/Contrast Adjustment

The Brightness/Contrast adjustment lets you make simple adjustments to the tonal range of an image. When you click the Create a New Brightness/Contrast Adjustment Layer icon, the settings appear in the Properties panel. Moving the brightness slider to the right increases tonal values and expands image highlights, to the left decreases values and expands shadows. The contrast slider expands or shrinks the overall range of tonal values in the image. When you click the Brightness/Contrast icon in the Adjustments panel, both the Brightness and Contrast sliders appear with the default value 0 in the Properties panel.

When Use Legacy is selected, Brightness/Contrast simply shifts all pixel values higher or lower when adjusting brightness. Figure 3.15 (right side) shows an original image and Figure 3.15 (left side) shows the same image after its brightness and contrast levels have been increased.

Working with Selections Tools

Selection means to select any part or full image and apply changes on them according to the requirements. For selecting any image or part of an image, we have to simply drag around the area, which we want to select using a Selection Tool.

Making a selection is a two-step process. First, you select one of the Selection Tools in the Tools panel. Second, you drag or click on the image to select specific portion of the image.

There are different types of tools in Photoshop CS6 for selection, such as Marquee Tool, Lasso Tool and Magic Wand Tool. All these tools are explained in the following sections.

Figure 3.15 The left side Brightness/Contrast applied in the image

Using Marquee Tools

Marquee Tool is placed in upper left corner of the Photoshop toolbox. Marquee Selection Tools helps us to select areas of an image in geometrical patterns. We can select areas of an image in rectangular, square, elliptical or circular shapes by using various Marquee Tools. If we enable one of these tools and select an area of an image by dragging the mouse, the selected area of the image will get surrounded by a dashed border. To make changes to the selected portion of the image, click on the small black arrow on the Marquee Tool in the Toolbox. The Marquee Selection fly-out is activated as shown in Figure 3.16.

The tools contained in the Marquee Selection fly-out are as follows:

- **Rectangle Marquee (M)**—This Tool allows us to select portions of an image in the shape of rectangle, or to make a square, press Shift key.
- **Elliptical Marquee (M)**—This Tool allows us to select portions of an image in elliptical shape, or to make a circle press Shift key.
- **Single Row Marquee**—This Tool allows us to select a single row of pixels of an image.
- **Single Column Marquee**—This Tool allows us to select a single column of pixels of an image.

Selecting a Rectangle

To make a Rectangular selection, do this:

1. Open an image.
2. Click on the small black arrow on the bottom right side of the Marquee Tool. The **Marquee fly-out** appears as shown in Figure 3.16.
3. Click the **Rectangular Marquee Tool**. The shape of the mouse pointer changes to + (Plus Sign).

4. Place the mouse pointer over the image and drag around the area you want to select. A dashed border surrounds the area you have selected as shown in Figure 3.16.

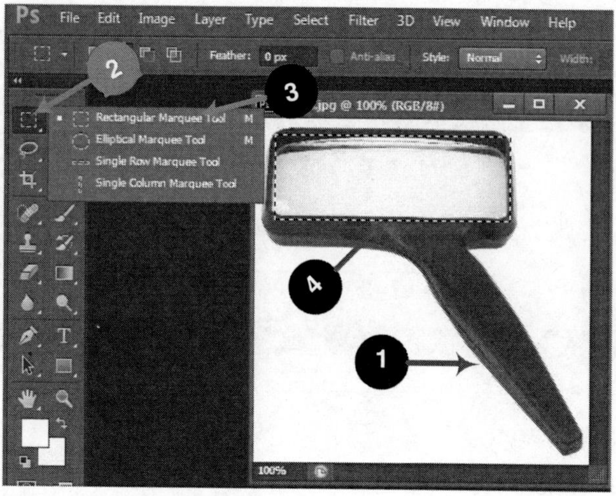

Figure 3.16 Selecting Rectangular Marquee Tool on the image

5. The **Marquee Tool Options bar** will appear on the top (See Figure 3.17).

   New selection – Clicking this option allows us to make a new selection.

   Add to selection – Clicking this option allows us to add some area of the image to the existing selection. For example, if you miss a part of image to select, clicking the new selection will be added to the previous selection and both the selections will be treated as one selection.

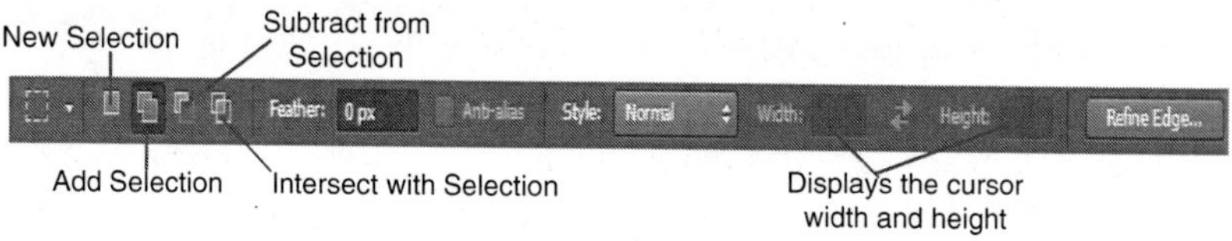

Figure 3.17 Marquee Tool Options bar

   Subtract from selection – Clicking on this button allows us to subtract some of the portion of the image from the selection. For example, if we make a new selection, then new selection will be subtracted from the previous selection.

   Intersect with selection – Clicking on this button allows us to select only the intersected part of two selections.

   Feather: – This option is used to create soft edges around the selection. Enter a numerical value (0 to 1000) to create a feathered selection edge.

   Anti-alias: – Creates a blurred, softer-edged selection. This option is enabled only when Elliptical Marquee Tool is active.

Style:—In the Style: option, Photoshop provides us with a number of styles with which we can make a selection.

- **Normal**—It creates default normal selection.
- **Fixed Aspect ratio**—It creates proportional selection where height and width are in proportion. Enter the Fixed Ratio values in the Width: and Height: boxes.
- **Fixed Size**—Creates selections of specific dimensions. This option enables the Width: and Height: options in the Options bar. You have to specify the height and width value for a selection area in the Height: and Width: text boxes, respectively.

6. Drag the selection area; the cursor displays width and height in the **Width:** and **Height:** text boxes.
7. **Refine Edge...:** When you click this button on the Options bar, the Refine Edge dialog box appears which is used to view the current selection against different backgrounds for easy editing. By default, the Refine Edge... button is enabled only when there is a selection.

Using Lasso Tool

Another way to make a selection in an image is to use the Lasso Tool. The Lasso Tool lets you draw straight edges and freehand around an object and thus create a selection. Click on the small black arrow on the Lasso Tool in the Toolbox. Hold down the **Alt** key, and then drag to draw straight-line segments. Releasing the mouse instructs the Lasso Tool to close the selection shape. The Lasso Tool fly-out is activated as shown in Figure 3.18.

The Lasso Tool fly-out contains the following tools:

Lasso Tool (L)—The Lasso Tool is useful for drawing freeform segments of a selection. To make a selection, click and drag around the area you want to select.

Polygonal Lasso Tool (L)—The Polygonal Lasso Tool is useful for drawing straight-edged selections in an image. This Tool is ideal to select objects with straight edges, such as buildings.

Magnetic Lasso Tool (L)—In Magnetic Lasso Tool, we can quickly select objects with complex edges.

To make a selection using Lasso Tool, do this:

1. Open an image.
2. Click the small black arrow on the bottom right side of the Lasso Tool. The **Lasso fly-out** appears as shown in Figure 3.18.
3. Click the **Lasso Tool**. Place the mouse pointer over the image and drag it around the image. A dashed border surrounds the area from the image as shown in Figure 3.18.
4. The **Lasso Tool** options bar will appear below the menu bar (See Figure 3.18).

5. The four rectangular buttons on the options bar allow you to make a **New selection**, **Add to the selection**, **Subtract from a selection** or **Intersect with a selection**. Click on any one of them, which is required.
6. Enter in the **Feather:** text box (from 0 to 1000) to get the soften edges effect. It smoothens edge transition. Click **Anti-alias** check box.

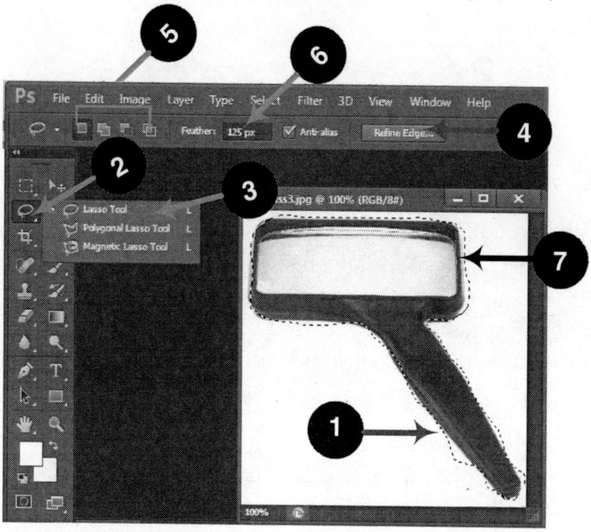

Figure 3.18 Selecting image with Lasso tool

7. After applying the above options, the picture looks soften and with smooth edges.

Using Polygonal Lasso Tool

Polygonal Lasso Tool draws straight segments. To make a selection, click multiple times surrounding the area you want to select. This tool is ideal to select objects with straight edges, such as buildings.

To make a selection using Polygonal Lasso Tool, do this:

1. Click the image.
2. Click the small black arrow on the bottom right side of the Lasso Tool.
3. Click the **Polygonal Lasso Tool** to make it to activate.
4. Do one of the following depending on the image you select:
   - To draw a straight segment, position the pointer where you want the first straight segment to end, and click. Continue clicking to set endpoints for subsequent segments.
   - To draw a straight line at a multiple of 45°, hold down **Shift** key as you move to click the next segment.

- To draw a freehand segment, hold down **Alt** key and drag. When you finish, release **Alt** key and the mouse button.
- To erase recently drawn straight segments, press the **Delete** key.

5. Click the image to set the starting point to complete the selection.

   The **Options** bar now displays the options available for the Polygonal Lasso Tool (See Figure 3.19).

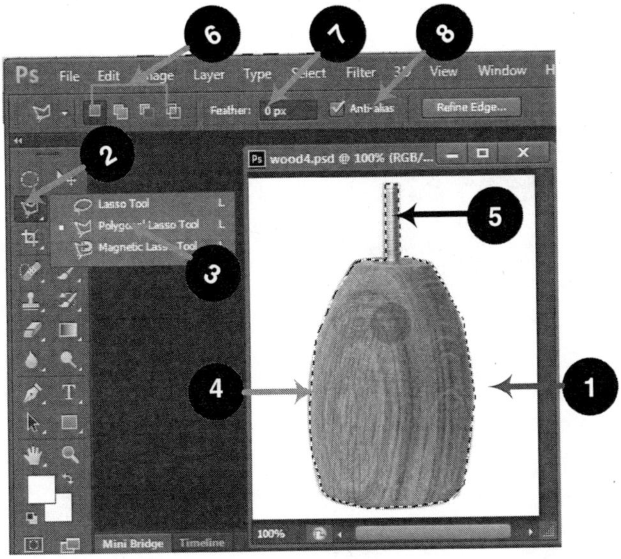

Figure 3.19 Selecting Polygonal Lasso Tool

6. The rectangular buttons in the options bar allow you to make a **New selection, Add to the selection, Subtract from a selection** or **Intersect with a selection**. Click on any one of them, which is required.
7. Enter in the **Feather:** text box (from 0 to 1000) to get the soften edges effect.
8. To smoothen edge transition, click **Anti-alias** check box.

   Figure 3.19 shows a selection made using the **Polygonal Lasso tool**.

Using Magnetic Lasso Tool

The **Magnetic Lasso Tool** will follow the visible edge of the object, occasionally adding anchor points to the line as you move. Clicking the starting point or double-clicking the mouse not at the starting point instructs the Magnetic Lasso Tool to close the selection shape.

To make a selection using Magnetic Lasso Tool, do this:

1. Open the image.
2. Click the **Magnetic Lasso Tool** and make it to activate.
3. Click on an edge of the object to set the first anchor point.

4. Move the mouse-pointer along the edge of the object to draw a freehand segment.
5. To close the selection border, place the pointer on the start point and click. In Figure 3.20, we have made a selection using the **Magnetic Lasso Tool**.

Figure 3.20 Selecting the edge using the Magnetic Lasso Tool

6. The **Options bar** now displays the options available for the **Magnetic Lasso Tool** (See Figure 3.21).

Figure 3.21 Magnetic Lasso Tool Options bar

7. The four rectangular buttons in the options bar allow you to make a **New selection, Add to the selection, Subtract from a selection** or **Intersect with a selection**. Click on any one of them, which is required.
8. Make an entry in the **Feather:** text box (from 0 to 1000) to get the soften edges of a selection. In our case, we have typed 25 px.

Feathering effects become apparent only after you move, cut, copy, or fill the selection.

---

9. Click **Anti-alias** check box to get the jagged edges smooth for a selection, and softening the color transition between edge pixels and background pixels.
10. In the **Width:** list box, enter the value of the pixels. The Magnetic Lasso Tool detects edges within the specified distance from the pointer. The default width is 10 pixels.

11. In the **Contrast:** list box, enter the value between 1 to 100%. The default edge contrast is 10 percent. A higher value detects the edges contrast sharply with their surroundings and a lower value detects lower-contrast edges.
12. In the **Frequency:** list box, enter the value from 0 to 100. The default value for frequency is 77. Specify the rate at which the Lasso Tool sets fastening points.
13. If **Use table pressure to change pen width:** option is selected, then you can increase the width of pen by increasing the pressure.

Using Magic Wand Tool

The Magic Wand Tool is used to select adjacent areas of color in an image. The Magic Wand tool creates a selection based on the shift in brightness ranges within an image. If there is a definable shift in the brightness of the pixels, it can be a very powerful tool for the selection of odd-shaped areas. The selection depends upon a value referred to as the Tolerance setting. The higher the Tolerance setting value, the wider the range of selected pixels.

To make a selection using Magic Wand Tool, do this:

1. Select the **Magic Wand** Tool in the Toolbox.
2. Click the image. The **Magic Wand** tool lets you select an area of consistent color without having to trace its outline.
3. Note that the **Options** bar changes to the **Magic Wand Options** bar (See Figure 3.22).

Figure 3.22 Magic Wand Tool Options bar

4. The rectangular buttons on the options bar allow you to make a **New selection**, **Add to selection**, **Subtract from selection** or **Intersect with selection**. The Magic Wand tool's pointer changes depending on which option has been selected.
5. Click the **Sample Size:** drop-down arrow, and then select the number of pixels to sample size.
6. **Tolerance:** sets the tolerance level of the selection. The default value is 32 (See Figure 3.23). Lower levels create more tolerance, so small areas of color are selected. Higher numbers create less tolerance, so large areas of color are chosen.

   For example, Enter 50 in the box beside the Tolerance option. Click on only part of the image. All the adjacent pixels with the same color within the Tolerance range are selected as shown in Figure 3.23.
7. **Anti-alias** check box is used to create smooth edge in your selection. This allows you to soften the edges of a selection. In general, you must keep this option turned ON at all times when making selections with any tool.

8. **Contiguous** check box is used to select colors in the Tolerance level that are adjacent to each other. Uncheck it to select all pixels in the entire image using the same colors.
9. **Sample All Layers** check box is used to select colors in all of the layers that match the desired color. Uncheck it only to the active layer.

Figure 3.23 Set tolerance range using Magic Wand Tool

Adjust Selections Manually

You can use the selection tools to add or subtract from existing pixel selections. Before manually adding to or subtracting from a selection, you may want to set the feather and anti-aliasing values in the options bar to the same settings used in the original selection.

Adding to an Existing Selection

You can use the selection tools to add or subtract from existing pixel selections.

To add an existing selection, do this:

1. Open an image.
2. Make a selection using any of the selection tools, say **Elliptical Marquee** Tool as shown in Figure 3.24.
3. Hold down **Shift** key, and drag over the area you want to add in the selection. A plus sign appears next to the pointer where you are adding to a selection (See Figure 3.24).

Another way to add a selection by using the Expand commands. The Expand command is used to expand the area of an existing selection. You can also use the Contract command to reduce the area of an existing selection by a specific value.

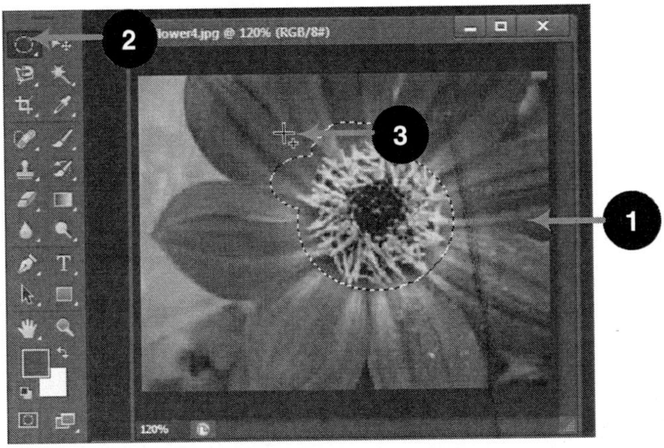

Figure 3.24 Adding an existing selection by pressing Shift key

1. Make a selection that you want to expand to a specific value.
2. Click the **Select** menu highlight **Modify**. A sub-menu appears. Select **Expand...** option as shown in Figure 3.25.

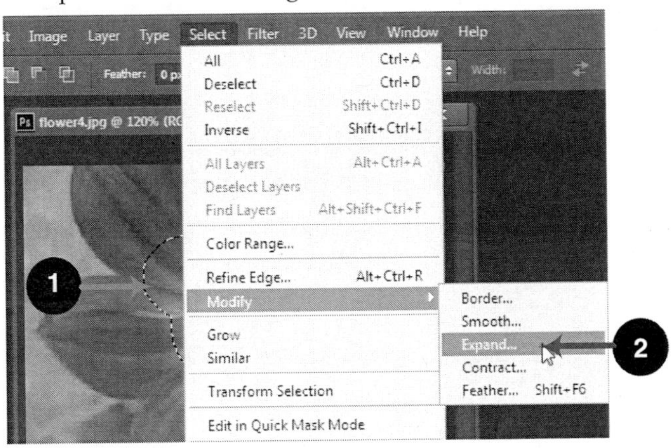

Figure 3.25 Selecting Expand command in the Select menu

3. The **Expand Selection** dialog box appears as shown in Figure 3.26.
4. Type the desired value in the **Expand By:** text box. In our case, we have typed 30 pixels.
5. Click the **OK** button.
6. The selection in the image expands by 30 pixels, as shown in Figure 3.26.

Subtracting from a Selection

Likewise, if you want to subtract or remove an area from the original selection, press and hold the **Alt** key. With the selection tool to reselect the area you want to remove from the selection.

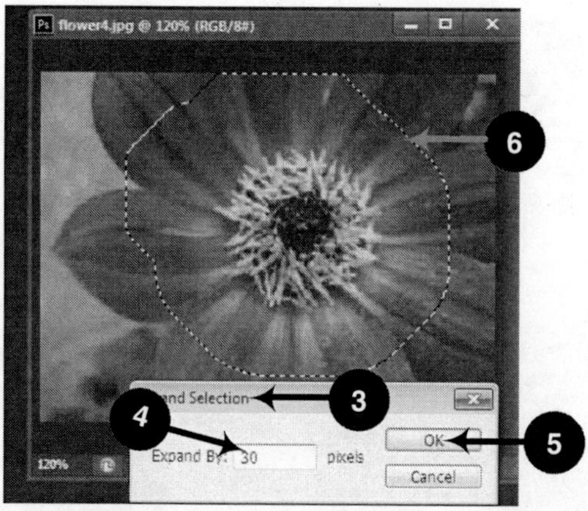

Figure 3.26 Using Expand Selection dialog to expand the selection

1. Open the image.
2. Make a selection using any of the selection tools, say **Elliptical Marquee** Tool as shown in Figure 3.27.
3. Hold down **Alt** key, and drag to subtract the selection. A minus sign appears next to the pointer when you are subtracting from a selection (See Figure 3.27).

Figure 3.27 Subtracting an existing selection by pressing Alt key

Similarly, you can use the Contract command to control or reduce the selection by the specified value.

Move a Selection

You can use the Move Tool to copy selections as you drag them within the images.

To move an image within the selection, do this:

1. Open an image.

2. Make a selection using the **Marquee Tool**.
3. Click the Move Tool on the toolbox or press key **V** from the keyboard. The **Move Tool** will become active with black arrow.

   Place the mouse-pointer inside the selection border.
4. Hold down and drag the mouse-pointer to move the selection as shown in Figure 3.28.

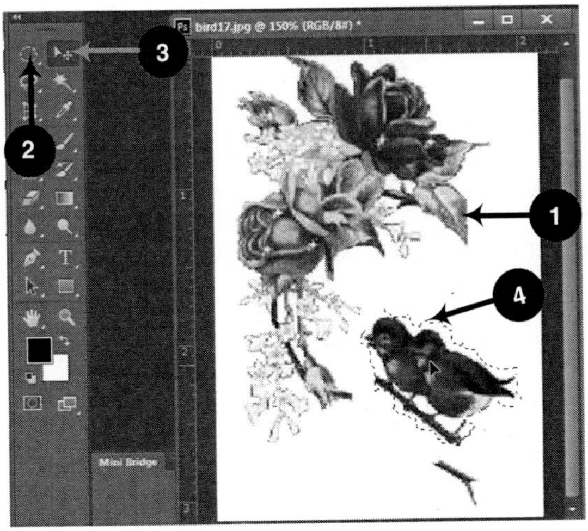

Figure 3.28 Drag to move the selection

Copy a Selection

To copy the selection in its own layer so that when we move the selected part to another location, a copy of it remains in the area from where we have moved the selection.

To copy the image within the selection, do this:

1. Open an image.
2. Make a selection using the Marquee Tool.
3. Click the **Move Tool** in the Tools panel or press the key **V** from the keyboard. The **Move Tool** will become active with black arrow.
4. Hold down **Alt** key, drag the selected portion to another location in the image. Or
5. The selection is moved, but a copy of it remains in the area from where we have moved it. A border highlights the window if you can drop the selection into it (See Figure 3.29).

Copying a Selection into Another Image

We can perform all the copy and paste operations in Photoshop CS6. You can also be dragged from one window to another by undertaking the following steps:

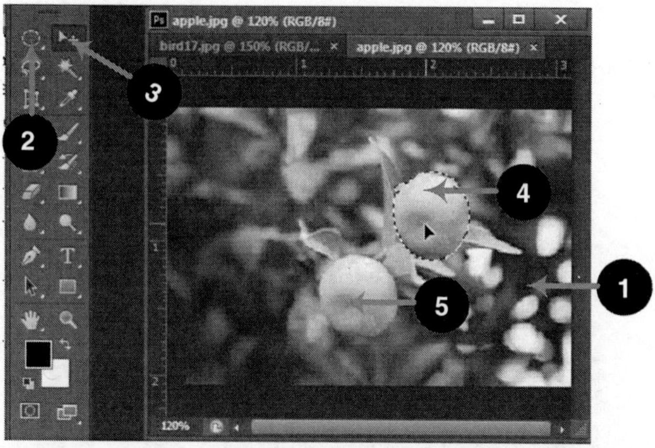

Figure 3.29 Copy a Selection to another place

To copy the selected portion into another image, do this:

1. Open an image (i.e., source image) and another image (i.e., destination image).
2. Make a selection with one of the Selection Tools in the source image as shown in Figure 3.30.
3. Click the **Edit** menu and choose **Copy** or **Ctrl+C**. Or click the Move Tool and hold down Alt key to activate the Move Tool.
4. To paste the selection into another image, open the destination image.
5. Click the **Edit** menu and choose **Paste** or **Ctrl+V**. Or drag the selection into the destination window, while you drag the arrow key changes into square plus icon and pasted in the destination window as shown in Figure 3.31.

The area selected in the source image appears in the destination image as shown in Figure 3.31.

Figure 3.30 Make a selection in the source image and select Copy command

Figure 3.31 The Source image copied to the destination image

Pasting into Selections

We can paste a copy of an image or the selection into the selection of another image. Paste Into command appears in Paste Special option pastes a cut or copied selection inside another selection in the same image or a different image.

1. Open the destination image to which you want to paste another selection.
2. Make a selection with the Elliptical Tool in the image as shown in Figure 3.32.
3. Open the source document. Select the image or a part of the image you want to paste using any of the tools, say, the Polygonal Tool as shown in Figure 3.33.
4. Click the **Edit** menu and choose **Copy** in the source document.

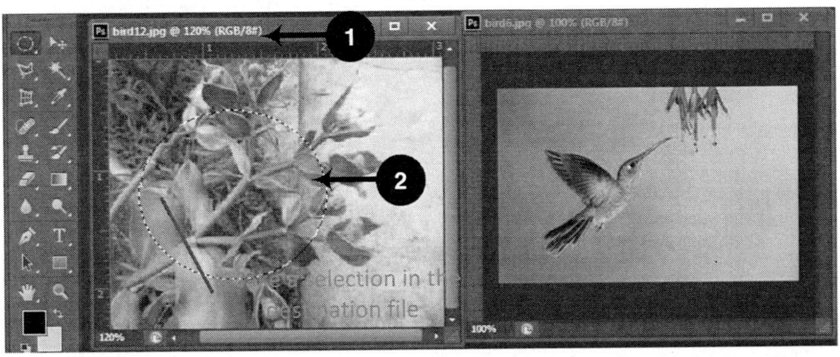

Figure 3.32 Make an Elliptical selection in the destination window

5. Now click the destination window.
6. Click the **Edit** menu, highlight **Paste Special**. A sub menu appears. Choose **Paste Into** as shown in Figure 3.34.
7. Now, the image is pasted in the destination window as shown in Figure 3.34.

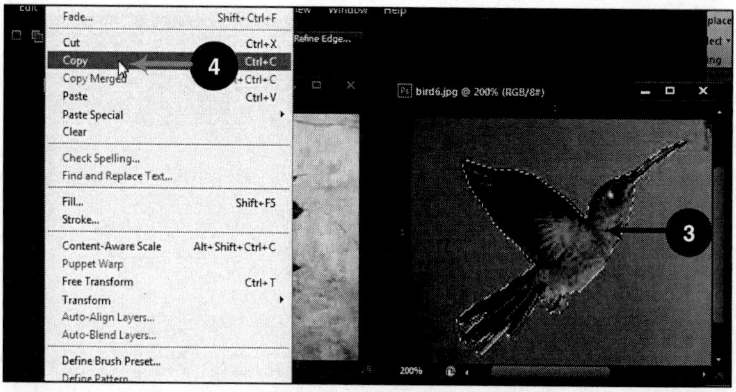

Figure 3.33 Make an Polygonal selection in the source image

Figure 3.34 Paste Into command paste to the destination image

Using Content-Aware Move and Extend

The Content-Aware Move Tool allows you to select and move or extend a part of an image and then have Photoshop automatically fill in the background using the surrounding area in the selection or the main content in the selection. This is useful when you want to move an element and replace it with details that match the surrounding area or extend an element and replace it with details that match the main content of the element.

To use Content-Aware Move Tool, do this:

1. Open an image.
2. Select the part of the image using any **Selection Tool** from Toolbox as shown in Figure 3.35. For example, here we have selected the **Elliptical Marquee Tool**. Then draw a rough selection around the content you want to move.

   Make sure the selection includes varied amounts of the background for use by Photoshop to fill in the background

3. Click the **Content-Aware Move** Tool on the toolbox.
4. Click the **Mode:** list arrow on the **Options** bar, and then click **Move** or Extend. For example, here we select the **Move** option.
5. To adjust and fine-tune how the content is filled or extended, click the **Adaptation**: list arrow on the Options bar, and then select an option: **Very Strict**, **Strict**, **Medium**, **Loose**, or **Very Loose**. For example, here we have selected **Medium** option.
6. Drag the selection to another location. You can press the **Shift** key as you drag to constrain the movement of the selection as shown in Figure 3.36.

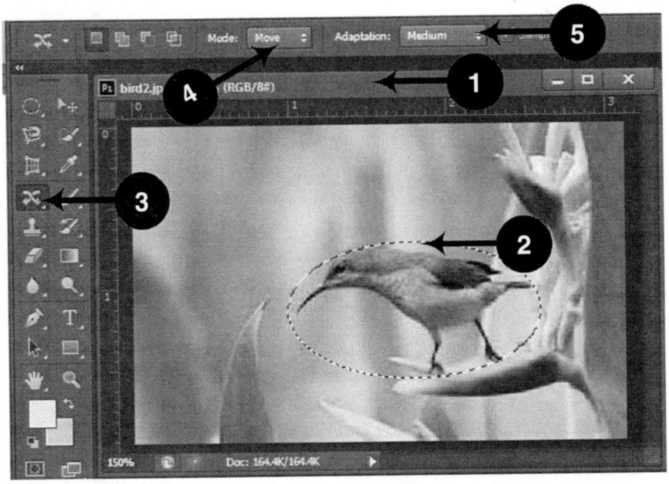

Figure 3.35 Make a selection using the Elliptical Marquee tool

Figure 3.36 Drag the selection to another location

7. A **Progress** dialog box appears showing Photoshop appears Removing as shown in Figure 3.37.

8. When you release the mouse, Photoshop uses the **Content-Aware Move Tool** adaptation setting to fill in the background or extend the content.
9. Drag to move the selection to place it in another location of the image as shown in Figure 3.37.

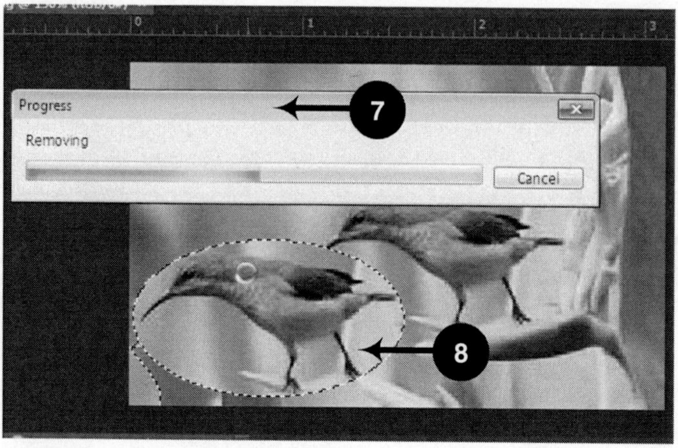

Figure 3.37 Progress dialog box and place it into another location

CHAPTER 4

Painting, Drawing and Retouching Tools

Introduction

In this Chapter, we will learn how to use the various Painting, Drawing Tools of Photoshop CS6. The Painting Tools, such as Brush, Pencil, and Paint Bucket Tools that can be used to create different kinds of painting strokes. The Drawing Tools such as Pen, Path Selection, Rectangle and Shape Tools help us to create shapes or segments.

In addition, the retouch and transform features in Photoshop let you change images to accomplish a variety of tasks. To improve a composition, correct distortions or flaws, creatively manipulate picture elements, add or remove items, sharpen or blur, or merge multiple images.

Selecting Foreground and Background Colors

There are two colored boxes in the Toolbox. Photoshop CS5 uses the foreground color to paint, fill and stroke selections. The Background color is used to create gradient fills and fill in the erased areas of an image. Some special effects filters also use the foreground and background colors.

The default foreground color is black, and the default background color is white. (In an alpha channel, the default foreground is white, and the background is black.)

Choose Colors in the Toolbox

The current foreground color appears in the upper color selection box in the toolbox and the current background color appears in the lower box (See Figure 4.1).

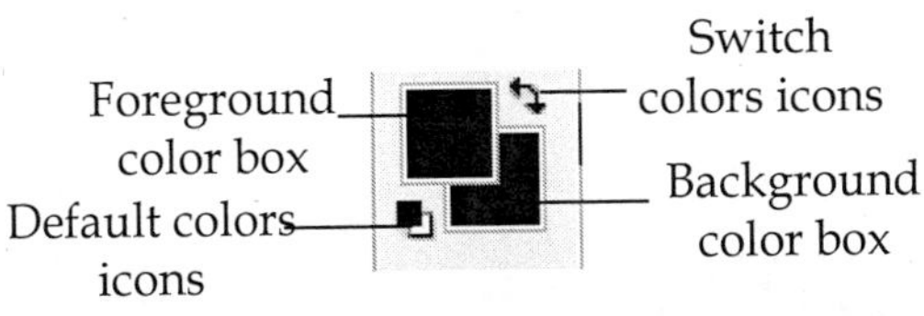

Figure 4.1 Foreground and Background color boxes in toolbox

- To change the foreground color, click the upper color selection box in the toolbox, and then choose a color in the Color Picker.
- To change the background color, click the lower color selection box in the toolbox, and then choose a color in the Color Picker.
- To reverse the foreground and background colors, click the Switch Colors icon in the toolbox.

- To restore the default foreground and background colors, click the Default Colors icon in the toolbox.

You can set the current foreground or background color using the Eyedropper Tool, the Color palette, the Swatches palette, or the Color Picker. When you click on any of the color boxes in the Tools panel, Color Picker appears. You can select and assign a new color as the current foreground or background color using Color Picker.

Using the Brush and Brush Presets Panels

Photoshop introduced the Brush and Brush Preset panels in CS6. The Brush panel allows you to create and select individual brushes, while the Brush Presets panel allows you to select and use predefined or custom brush tip sets or individual brushes.

Using the current setting options available in the Brush panel are Shape Dynamics, Scattering, Texture, Dual Brush, Color Dynamics, Transfer, Brush Pose (New), Noise, Wet Edges, Build-up (New), Smoothing, and Protect Texture—gives you control over brushes.

To use the Brush or Brush Presets panel, you first need to select a brush tool, or a tool that requires the use of a brush, such as the Eraser Tool, chosen from the toolbox, and then display the Brush or Brush Presets panel.

To display the Brush or Brush Presets, do this:

1. Click the **Window** menu, choose **Brush** or **Brush Presets** or press F5.
2. The **Brush Panel** appears as shown in Figure 4.2.

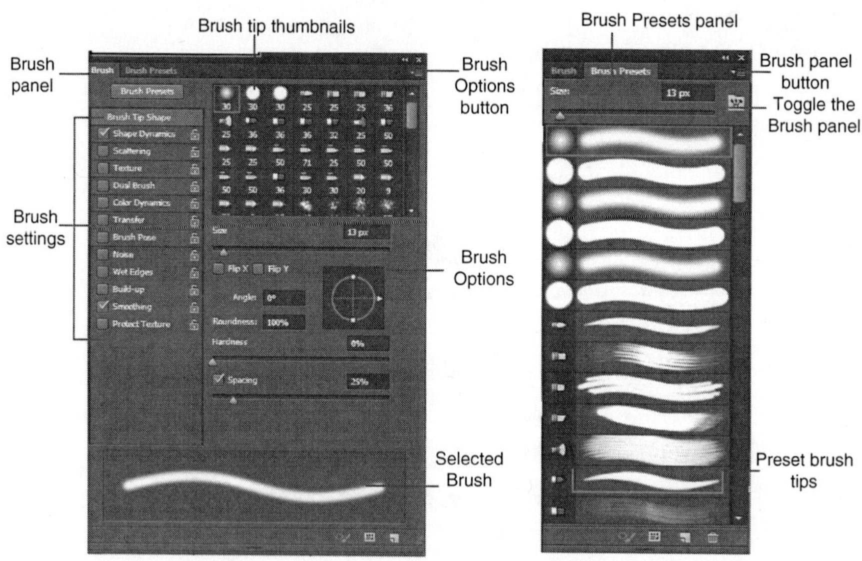

Figure 4.2 Brush and Brush Presets panel

Selecting Brush Tip Sets

The Brush Preset panel comes with a wide variety of predefined brush tip sets, including natural bristle, faux finish, and special effect brushes. Each set organizes specific brush tips by name.

To select Brush Tip Sets, do this:

1. Select a **Brush Tool** on the toolbox, and then select the **Brush Presets** panel as shown in Figure 4.3.
2. Click the **Brush Presets Options** button.
3. Click any of the predefined brush sets. For example, select **Thick Heavy Brushes** option as shown in Figure 4.3.

   A dialog box appears (Adobe Photoshop CS6 Extended) displaying Replace brushes with the brushes from Thick Heavy Brushes? as shown in Figure 4.4.
4. Click OK. This replaces the current brush tips with the selected set, or you can click Append to add them to the current set.
5. In this palette, we have to select *Flat Bristle* shape from the list.
6. The selected brush shape was applied in the image as shown in Figure 4.5.

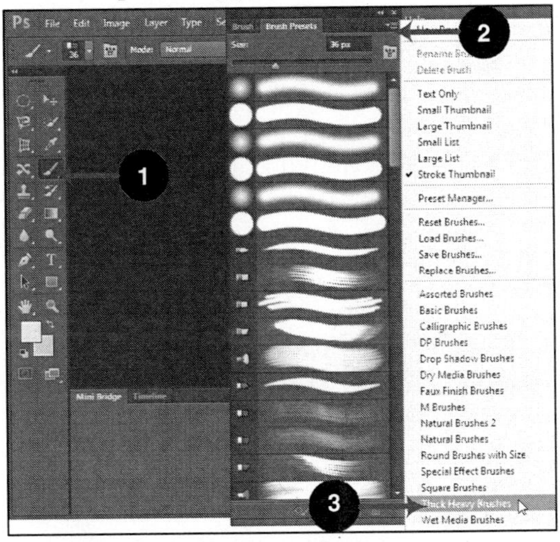

Figure 4.3 Selecting Brush Tip sets

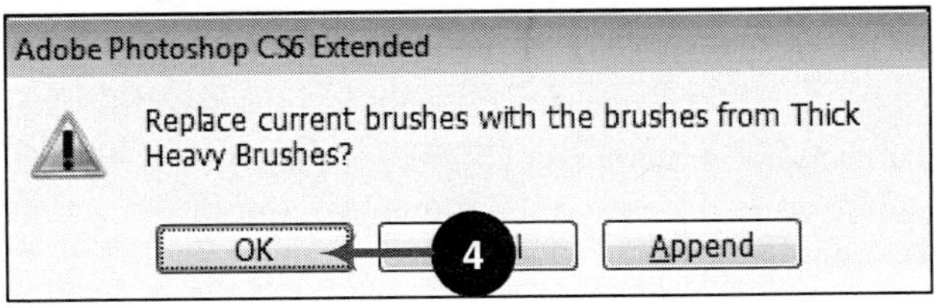

Figure 4.4 Photoshop CS6 Extended dialog box

7. We can also increase or decrease the size of diameter of the brush shape by dragging the slider of **Size:** or by entering value in the text box in pixels.

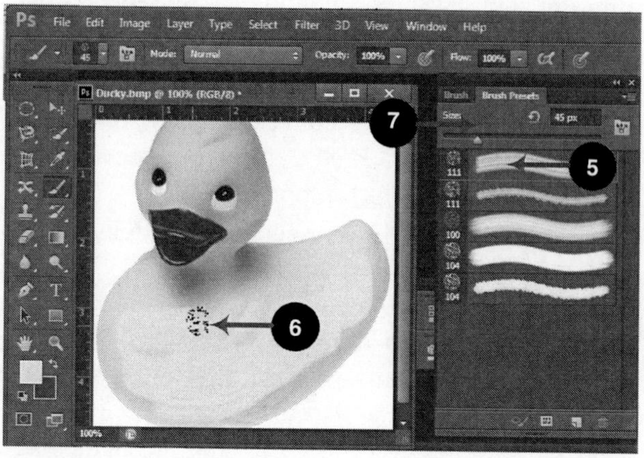

Figure 4.5 The selected brush shape applied in the image

Using Brush Options Bar

Options bar is used to find options related to the currently selected tool. It can be undocked from its position at the top of the screen and placed at the bottom of the screen. Most tools have options that are displayed in the Options bar. The Options bar is changed as different tools are selected. Some settings in the Options bar are common to several tools but some are specific to one tool.

You can also change the brush pointer to a cross-hair by pressing the Caps Lock key on the keyboard. When you select Brush Tool, the options specific to the tools appear in the Options bar as shown in Figure 4.6.

Figure 4.6 Brush Options bar

To display the Options bar, do this:

1. Click **Windows** menu and choose **Options.** After that, click a Brush Tool in the Toolbox. The **Options** bar appears as shown in Figure 4.6.

Brush Tool has the following options:

Mode: Allows you to change the blending mode for the brush stroke. Behind and Clear are the two blending modes are available on the Brush Tool.

Opacity: It controls the transparency of the brush strokes. It also specifies the maximum amount of paint coverage applied by the Brush, Paintbrush, Pencil, History Brush, Art History Brush and Paint Bucket Tools.

Flow: It controls the rate at which a Brush Tool applies the paint. By default, the Flow option is set to 100%.

Airbrush: This mode produces the spray effect. The longer you hold the mouse button, the more the point pumps out, and the wider the airbrush effect spreads.

The setting options of the selected brush tip, such as Brush size, hardness, and flow; and then paint over the area.

To paint an image using Brush Tool, do this:

1. Open a drawing in which you want to paint using Brush Tool.
2. Select **Brush Tool** on the **Tools** panel or press the **B** key as shown in Figure 4.7.

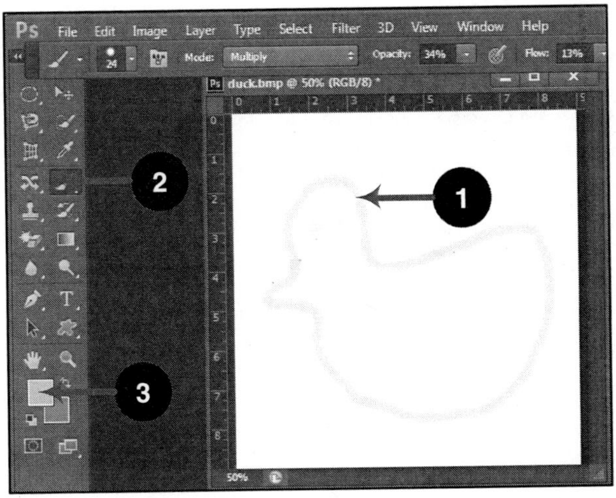

Figure 4.7 Selecting Brush Tool and set the foreground color in the Toolbox

3. Select a color in the Toolbox to **Set foreground color** that you want to paint with. In our case, we have selected **Light yellow Orange**.
4. Click the **Brush Picker** down arrow on the **Options** bar to open the Brush Preset picker.
5. Select the desired brush **size**. In our case, we have selected **37** px.
6. Select the **hardness** value for the brush. In our case, we have selected 100% as shown in Figure 4.8.
7. Paint over the parts of the drawing that you want to paint with the foreground color as shown in Figure 4.8.

The Drawing Tools

Drawing in Photoshop CS6 involves creating vector shapes and paths. In Photoshop, you can draw with any of the Shape Tools, the Pen Tool, or the Freeform Pen Tool. Options for each Tool are available in the Options bar.

The Drawing Tools of Photoshop CS6 has different Shape Tools that you use to create lines, rectangle, ellipses, and polygon. Shape Tools have their own rules in Photoshop CS6.

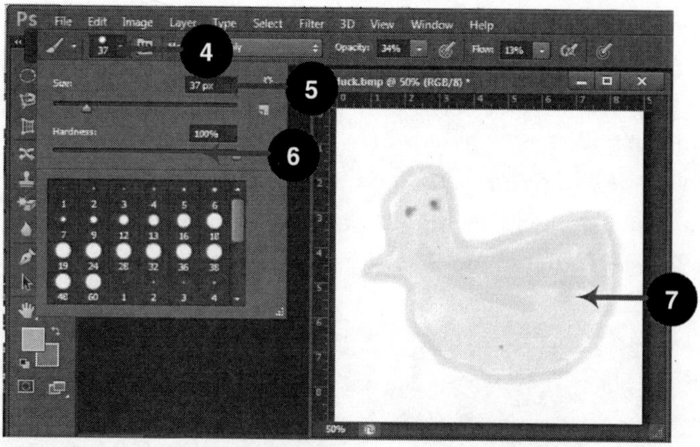

Figure 4.8 Paint over the image with the foreground color

Photoshop provides multiple Pen Tools. The Pen Tool, located in the Toolbox, has five hidden tools: the *Pen Tool, Freeform Pen Tool, Add Anchor Point Tool, Delete Anchor Point Tool,* and the *Convert Point Tool.*

Using Pen Tool to Draw a Straight Line

You can draw with the Pen Tool in a straight line, made by clicking the Pen Tool to create two anchor points. By continuing to click, you create a path made of straight line segments connected by corner points.

To draw straight lines, do this:

1. Select the Pen Tool.
2. Make sure that the Paths button is selected in the Options bar.
3. For example, to draw a star, position the Pen Tool where you want the straight segment to begin. Click to define the first anchor point (do not drag).
4. Continue clicking to set anchor points for additional straight segments.

   The last anchor point you add always appears as a solid square, indicating that it is selected (See Figure 4.9).
5. To close the path, position the Pen Tool over the first (hollow) anchor point.

   A small circle appears next to the Pen Tool pointer when it is positioned correctly. Click or drag to close the path.
6. Or continue to click the anchor point to complete the star (See Figure 4.9).

Drawing Curves with Pen Tool

You create a curve by adding an anchor point where a curve changes direction, and dragging the direction lines that shape the curve. The length and slope of the direction lines determine the shape of the curve.

To draw curves with Pen Tool, do this:

1. Select the Pen Tool.

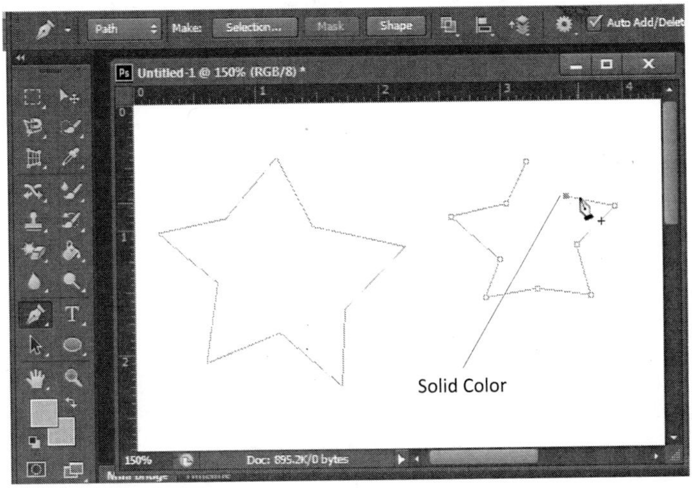

Figure 4.9 Using Pen Tool to draw Star

2. Position the Pen Tool where you want the curve to begin (See Figure 4.10).
3. The first anchor point appears. Hold down the mouse button. Click and drag the anchor point. The Pen Tool pointer changes to an arrowhead.
4. Drag to set the slope of the curve segment and then release the mouse button (See Figure 4.10).
5. Position the Pen Tool where you want the curve segment to end. For example, to create a C-shaped curve, drag in the opposite direction. Then release the mouse button.

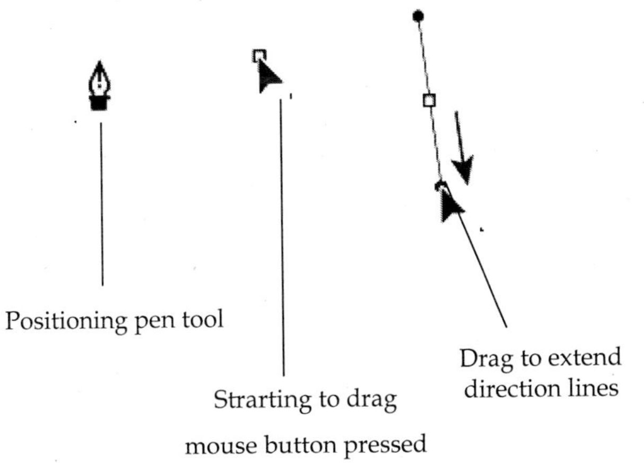

Figure 4.10 Steps to create draw a Curve

6. Again click, the anchor point continues the direction line. Drag the mouse to the opposite direction. Then release the mouse button. The S-shaped curve is drawn as shown in Figure 4.11.

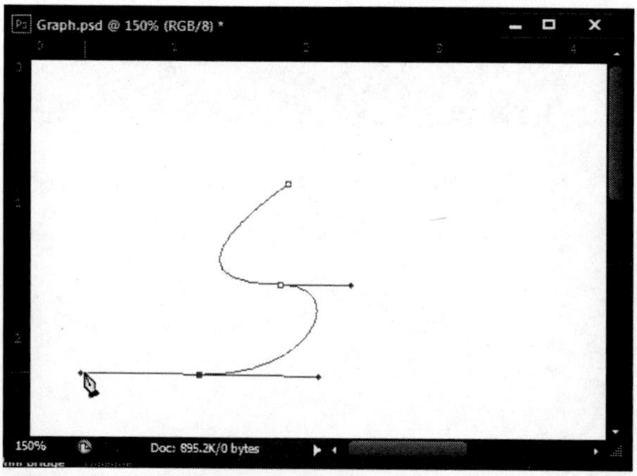

Figure 4.11 The S-shaped curve drawn using Pen Tool

Adding or Deleting Anchor Points

While creating a path, you may need to add more anchor points or you may need to remove some of the unnecessary anchor points according to your requirements. To add an anchor point, choose the Add Anchor Point Tool and click the path. A new anchor point will appear.

To delete an anchor point, choose Delete Anchor Point Tool. Click an anchor point, and the two segments connected by the point join into one. If you have selected Auto Add/Delete in the Options bar for the Pen Tool or Freeform Pen Tool, when you click at active path's line segment, a point is added, and when you click an existing point, it is deleted.

Do not use the Delete, Backspace, and Clear keys from the menu command to delete anchor points. These keys and commands delete the point and the line segments that connect to that point.

To add anchor points, do this:

1. Click and hold **Pen Tool** in the **Tools** panel.

   A plus(+) sign appears below Pen Tool, when you move the mouse-pointer above an existing path. However, outside the path, Add Anchor Point Tool appears as Direct Selection Tool.
2. To Add Anchor Point, click the Path to add an anchor point as shown in Figure 4.12.
3. Similarly, to delete anchor point, select **Delete Anchor Point Tool** from the **Pen Tool** flyout. A minus (-) sign appears below Pen Tool as shown in Figure 4.13.
4. Move the mouse-pointer over the anchor point you want to delete. In our case, we want to delete a right side corner anchor point as shown in Figure 4.13.

5. Click the existing anchor point to delete it. The anchor point is now deleted from the path as shown in Figure 4.13.

Figure 4.12 Click the path to add anchor point

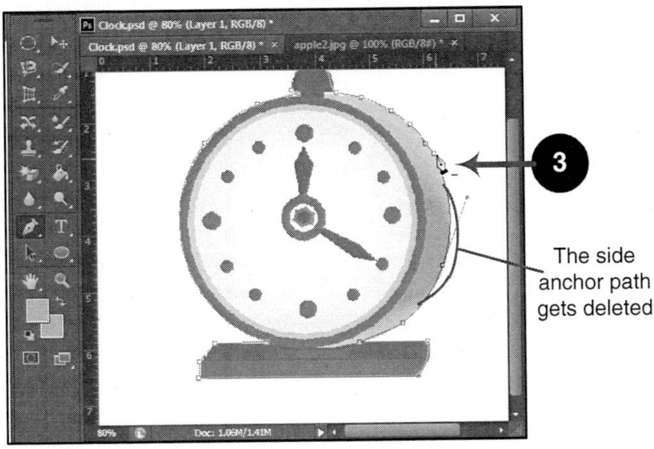

Figure 4.13 The path of the side anchor path gets deleted

The Convert Point Tool

The Convert Point Tool lets you convert a smooth curve to a sharp curve or to a straight segment, and vice versa. While you are using Pen Tool or Freeform Pen Tool you can also convert anchor point by holding down Alt key. The cursor point will turn to ⌃, arrow. Click at the point you want to convert.

Converting smooth points and corner points

1. Select the path you want to modify.
2. Select the Convert Point Tool, or use the Pen Tool and hold down **Alt** Key.

To activate the Convert Point Tool while the Direct Selection Tool is selected, position the pointer over an anchor point, press Ctrl+Alt keys together.

Position the Convert Point Tool over the anchor point you want to convert, and do one of the following:

To convert corner to smooth point, do this:

1. To convert a corner point to a smooth point, drag away from the corner point to make direction lines appear as shown in Figure 4.14.

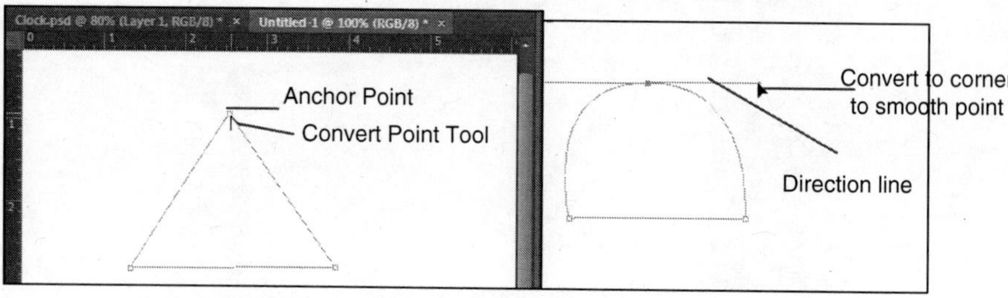

Figure 4.14 Convert corner to smooth point curve

To convert smooth to corner point, do this:

2. To convert a smooth point to a corner point, without direction lines, click the smooth point appear as shown in Figure 4.14. Or
3. Select the Direct Selection Tool. A single direction line appears, press Ctrl+Alt keys together. Click the Anchor point. It automatically converts to corner point.

Working with Retouching Tools

Photoshop CS6 provides different Retouching Tools, which can be used to improve images by performing various corrections. You can remove these and other defects from your image with the help of the Retouching Tools. The most commonly used Retouching Tools are Healing Brush Tool, Patch Tool, Eraser Tool, Blur Tool, and Sponge Tool. Some commonly used Retouching Tools are discussed in the following Sections:

Healing Brush Tool

The Spot Healing Brush Tool quickly removes blemishes and other imperfections in the image. Like the Cloning Tools, you use the Healing Brush Tool to paint with sampled pixels from an image or pattern. However, the Healing Brush Tool also matches the texture, lighting, transparency, and shading of the sampled pixels to the source pixels. When you start healing press Alt key and click to define a source point to be used to repair the image.

To use Healing Brush Tool, do this:

1. Open the image from which you want to heal the imperfections. In our case, we want to remove the rose flower using the Healing Brush Tool.

2. Select the **Healing Brush Tool** from the **Toolbox**.
3. Click the Brush size from the **Brush Preset Picker** options bar as shown in Figure 4.15.

Figure 4.15 Select the Healing Brush and selecting brush size from the brush preset picker

4. There are two types of **Sources** available, **Sampled** and **Pattern:**. It specifies the source to use for repairing pixels. If you select **Sampled** to use pixels from the current image, or **Pattern:** to use pixels from a pattern. For example, here to select the **Alt + click** to get the source point from the surrounding area to sample the pixels you want to replace over the image.
5. If you click **Aligned** check box, Samples pixels continuously, without losing the current sampling point, even if you release the mouse button. Deselect Aligned to continue to use the sampled pixels from the initial sampling point each time you stop and resume painting.
6. In **Sample:** drop-down list, select sample data from the layers. Choose any one of the following options:

   Current Layer: To sample only from the active layer, choose Current Layer.

   Current & Below: To sample from the active layer and visible layers below it, choose **Current & Below**.

   All Layers: To sample from all visible layers, choose All Layers.

   For example, here we select Current Layer from the Sample drop-down list.
7. Toggle between **Adjustment layers** icon to the right of the Sample pop-up menu. To sample from all visible layers except adjustment layers, choose **All Layers** and click the **Ignore Adjustment Layers** icon to the right of the Sample: drop-down list.
8. Drag the image. The Sampled pixels are combined with the existing pixels each time you release the mouse button as shown in Figure 4.16. In Figure

4.16 the right side of the image rose flower has been removed from the image.

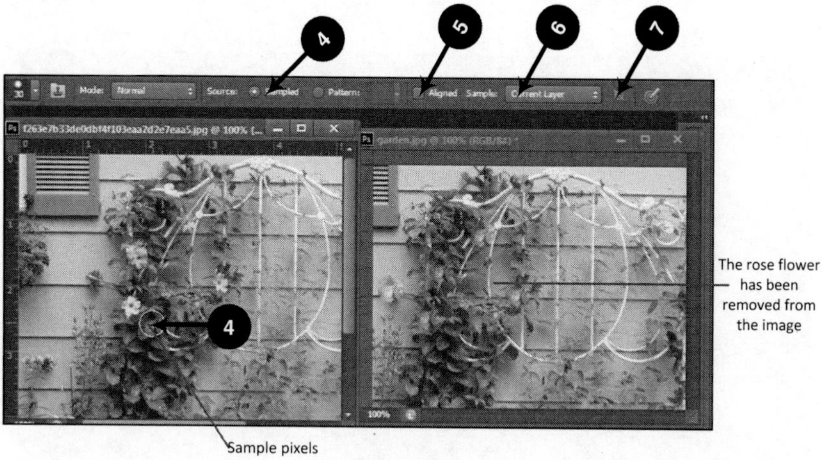

Figure 4.16 Using the sample pixels from the image the rose flower removes the image

Using the Patch Tool

The Patch Tool lets you repair a selected area with pixels from another area or a pattern. Like the Healing Brush Tool, the Patch Tool matches the texture, lighting, and shading of the sampled pixels to the source pixels. You can also use the Patch Tool to clone isolated areas of an image.

To use Patch Tool to remove imperfections, do this:

1. Open the image in which you want to retouch using Patch Tool. In our case, we have opened an image as shown in Figure 4.17.

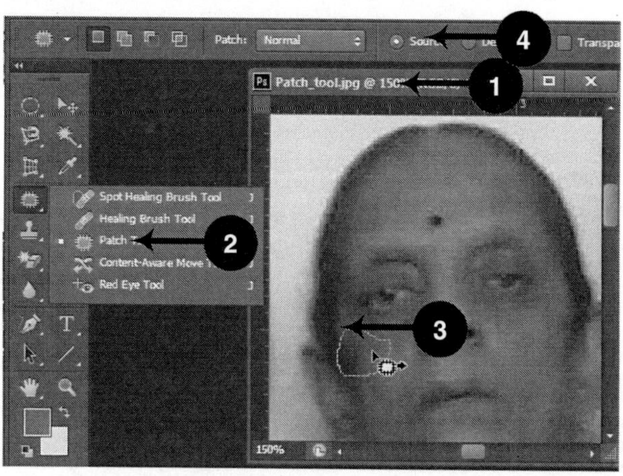

Figure 4.17 Make a selection using Patch Tool to remove damaged area

2. Select the **Patch Tool** from the **Toolbox**.
3. Make a selection around the area you want to the damaged area of the image you want to repair with Patch Tool as shown in Figure 4.17.
4. The **Source** radio button is selected in the **Options** bar. Source area is the pixels that you want to replace the existing selection. *Alternatively*, you can also use the Destination option.
5. Move into the middle of the selection marquee, and drag the selection over the area you want to repair and release. As you drag, you will see a copy of the area you are moving over appear in the original selection.
6. Release your mouse when you see the best match. The Patch Tool corrects the damaged area of the image as shown in Figure 4.18.

An arrow sign appears in the area from where the pixels are picked as sample. Similarly, you can remove the other blemishes in the image.

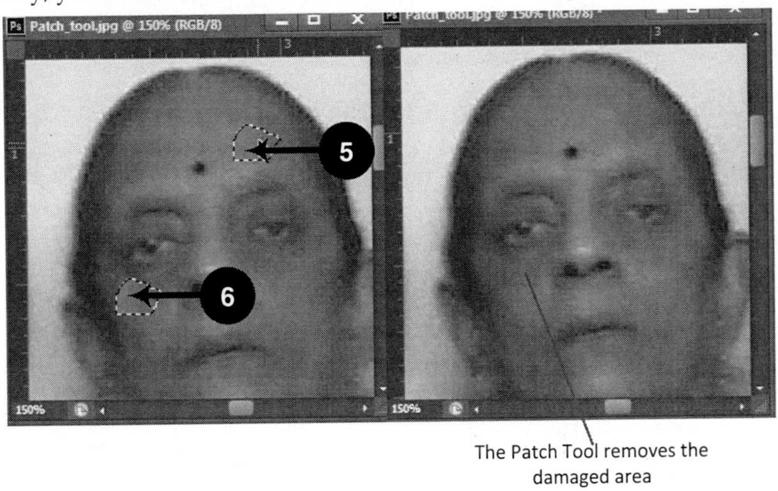

Figure 4.18 Drag the mouse-pointer over the area you want to retouch

The Clone Stamp Tool

The Clone Stamp Tool allows you to take a sample of an image, called a source point, and use that point for painting. The Source point is selected by holding down the **Alt** key and clicking with mouse at the image. As you paint, the source point moves with you. This enables you to clone a specific part of an image.

1. Open an image.
2. Select the **Clone Stamp** Tool from the **Toolbox**.
3. Click the Brush size from the **Brush Preset Picker** options bar.
4. Select a brush tip, and then select brush options, such as blending **mode**, **opacity**, and **flow**, on the Options bar as shown in Figure 4.19.
5. If you click the **Aligned:** check box, the sampled pixels flow continuously,

without losing the current sampling point even if you release the mouse button. If you Deselect Aligned check box, the sampled pixels flow from the initial point each time you stop and resume painting.

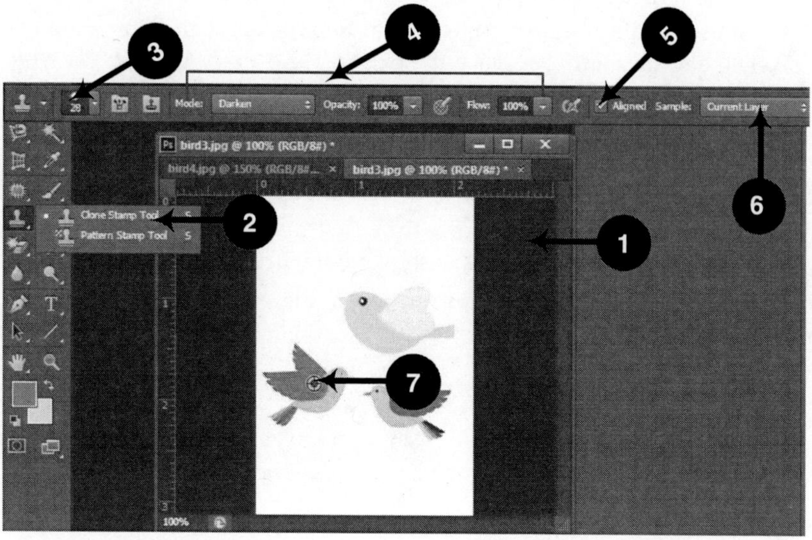

Figure 4.19 Select the Clone Stamp Tool and set the options in the Options bar

6. Click the **Sample:** list arrow on the **Options** bar, and then select the layer option you want to use to obtain sample data: *Current Layer*, *Current & Below*, or *All Layers*.
7. Set the sampling point by positioning the mouse pointer in the image. Hold down the **Alt** key and click on the part of the image to be cloned.
8. Click and drag the mouse-pointer to fill the sample of an image with the cloned pixels.

Working with the Eraser Tools

The Eraser tool contains three tools. These are Eraser Tool, the Background Eraser Tool and the Magic Eraser Tool. The Eraser Tool erases a portion of an image. This tool changes pixels to either the background color or to transparent. If you are working in the background or in a layer with transparency locked, the pixels change to the background color; otherwise, the pixels are erased to transparency.

For example, you can use the **Eraser** Tool to remove a specific color or to erase around the edge of an object. You can instruct the Eraser Tool to remove a specific color while protecting another color and at the same time, increase or decrease the tool's tolerance (the range of selection).

To use a Eraser Tool, do this:

1. Open the image.

2. Select the **Eraser** Tool from the Toolbox. The **Options** bar displays options for the Eraser Tool as shown in Figure 4.20.

Figure 4.20 Erase Tool Options bar

3. Click the Brush list arrow, and then select a **Brush tip**.
4. Choose a mode for the eraser. **Brush** and **Pencil** eraser look like circle tools. **Block** is a hard-edged, fixed-sized square with no options for changing the opacity or flow. For example, here we have selected the Brush option from the list.
5. Click the down-arrow to set the value of **Opacity** to 100% The Opacity value determines the strength of the erasure. The higher the Opacity value, the more the number of pixels erased at a time.
6. Enter a **Flow:** percentage value (1% to 100%) to determine the length of the eraser stroke. For example, we have selected 50% flow option.
7. Place the mouse-pointer on the area of the image to be erased. The pixels from the portion where we used the Eraser Tool will be removed as shown in Figure 4.21.

To temporarily use the Eraser Tool, click Erase to History in the Options bar. Hold down Alt key as you drag in the image.

Figure 4.21 Using the Eraser Tool the selected area get erased

Using the Background Eraser Tool

The Background Eraser Tool is used to erase pixels of an image to transparency. By specifying different sampling and tolerance options, you can control the range of the transparency and the sharpness of the boundaries.

1. Open the image.

2. Click the **Background Eraser Tool** in the Toolbox. The **Options** bar displays the options for the Background Eraser Tool.
3. Click the drop-down next to the **Brush:** to set brush options in the pop-up palette. Choose settings for the Size, Hardness, Spacing, Angle, and Roundness options as shown in Figure 4.22.

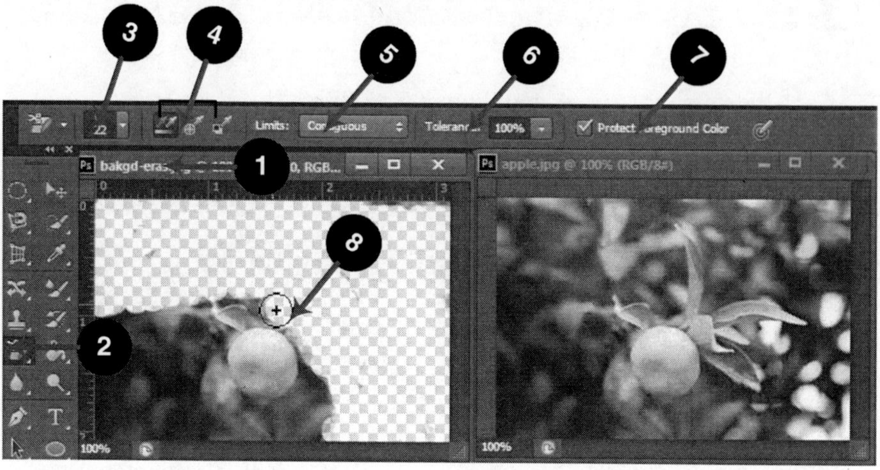

Figure 4.22 Using the Background Erase Tool

4. The Options bar of Background Eraser provides three types of Sampling which are as follows:

   Sampling Continuous: Select this option to erase colors that are sampled as you drag. The sampling color will change as you drag over various colors. (You can see the effects in the Background of toolbox.)

   Sampling Once: Select to erase color that match only the first place of your click. This will erase only the color that was sampled when you first click on the image and will not continuously sample while dragging.

   Sampling Background Swatch: Select to erase only colors that match the background color.

5. Click the down-arrow button beside the **Limits:** in the list. How far to let the erasing spread, choose any one of the options given below.

   Discontiguous: To erase similarly colored areas from non-adjacent areas.

   Contiguous: To erase similarly colored areas from adjacent areas.

   Find Edges: To erase pixels from similarly colored adjacent areas while preserving the edge contrast so that the edge boundaries of the image remain unaffected. For example, here to select the options as Discontiguous.

6. Move the mouse pointer over the down-arrow button beside the **Tolerance:** option to erase a range of similar colors. Click the left mouse-button. A slider bar appears. Drag the slider to set the Tolerance value to 100%.

7. Select **Protect Foreground Color** to prevent the erasure of areas that match the foreground color in the toolbox.
8. Place the mouse-pointer on the area of the image and drag the mouse-pointer to be erased.

Figure 4.22 shows the image before and after we use the Background Eraser Tool. The Background Eraser tool pointer appears as a brush shape with a crosshair indicating the tool's hotspot.

Using the Magic Eraser Tool

The Magic Eraser Tool is used to select similar colored areas in an image based on Tolerance setting. The Magic Eraser Tool is used to erase pixels from similar colored areas of an image. Using Magic Eraser Tool do the following steps:

1. Open the image, which you want to erase a portion.
2. Select the **Magic Eraser Tool** from the Toolbox.
3. Enter a **Tolerance:** value to define the range of colors that can be erased. A low tolerance erases pixels within a range of color values very similar to the pixel you click. A high tolerance erases pixels within a broader range.
4. Select **Anti-aliased** to smooth the edges of the area you erase.
5. To erase pixels from the areas, which are contiguous to the portion when you first clicked, click the **Contiguous** check box. If this option is deselected, then the pixels of color similar to the sampled area will be erased from the entire image.
6. Specify **Opacity:** to define the strength of the erasure. Opacity of 100% erases pixels completely. A lower opacity erases pixels partially.

Now click anywhere on the image. All the pixels similar in color to the portion when you clicked will be erased as shown in Figure 4.23.

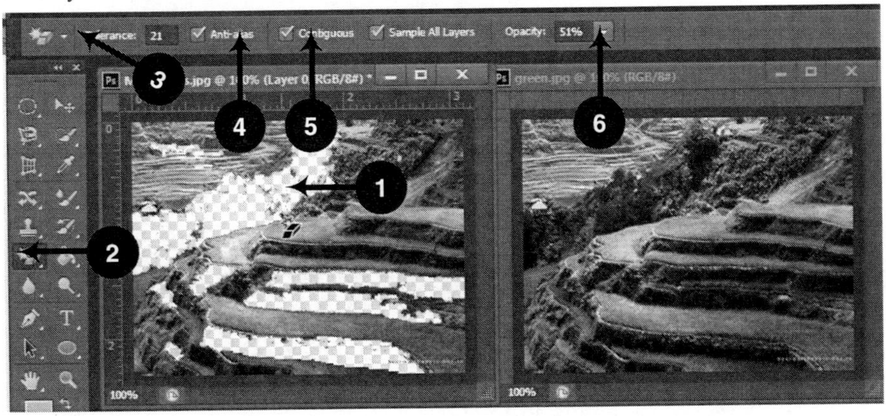

Figure 4.23 Using the Magic Eraser Tool to erase the portion of image

CHAPTER 5

Layers in Photoshop CS6

Introduction

Layers allow you to work on one element of an image without disturbing the other parts of the image. Think of layers as sheets of plain glass placed one on top of the other elements (See Figure 5.1). If there is no image on a layer, then you can see through to the layers below (See Figure 5.1).

You can also change the composition of an image by changing the order and attributes of layers. In addition, special features of layer's are adjustment layer, fill layer, layer mask, and layer effects and styles.

We can perform different functions in the layer, such as adding layers, dragging and copying layers, duplicating layers, deleting layers, merging layers as well as adjusting. These are explained further.

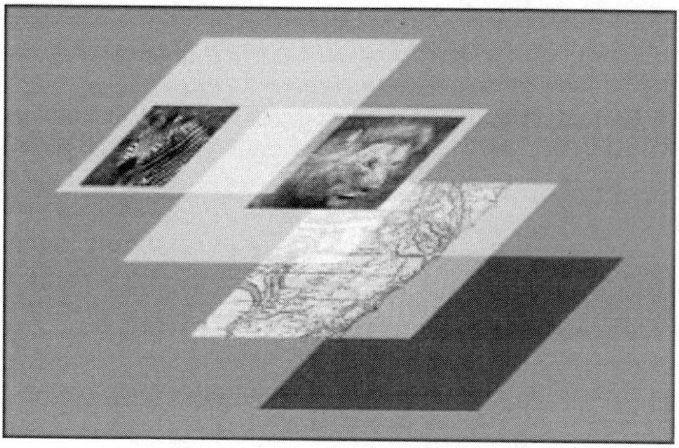

Figure 5.1 Layers are like sheets of plain glass placed one on top of other elements

Layers Palette

The Layers palette lists all layers, such as layer groups and layer effects in an image. You can use the Layers palette to show and hide layers, create new layers, and work with groups of layers. You can access additional commands and options in the Layers palette menu.

To Display a Layer's Panel, do this:

1. Click the **Window** menu and choose Layers. The **Layers** panel appears as shown in Figure 5.2.

- **Layer Filter options:** Select this option to find layers based on filter criteria, such as Kind, Name, Effect, Mode, Attribute, and Color.

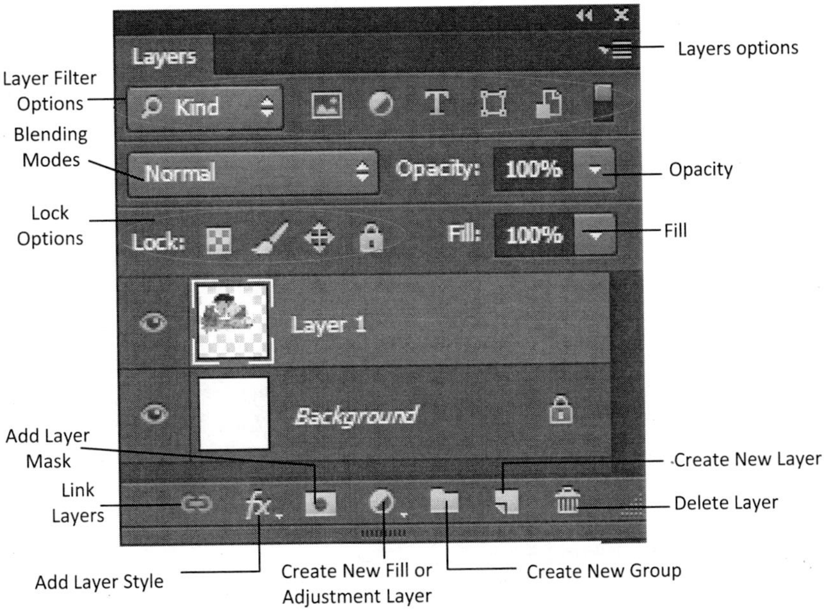

Figure 5.2 Layers Panel

- **Blending Modes:** A layer's blending mode determines how its pixels blend with underlying pixels in the image. We can create a variety of special effects using blending modes.
- **Opacity:** Drag the slider to increase or decrease the Opacity value from 0% to 100%.
- **Fill:** Select a value from 0% to 100% to change the opacity of the active layer without changing the opacity of any applied layer styles.
- **Eye:** The eye icons present on the left column of the layers palette indicate the visibility of a layer. We can show/hide a layer using this icon.
- **Lock options:** Click the Lock Transparent Pixels, Lock Image Pixels, Lock Position, or Lock All Buttons for one or more layers.
- **Link Layers:** We can link two or more layers or groups.
- **Add a layer Style:** A layer style is one or more effects applied to a layer or layer groups. Click a small black arrow at the bottom right corner of the Add a Layer Style icon. A pull-down menu appears containing a list of styles. For example, inner glow style emanates the inside edge of the layer. An icon appears near the name of the layer in the Layers palette indicating that a style has been applied to the layer.
- **Add Layer Mask:** Click this button to apply a layer mask to the active layer. Click this a second time to add a vector mask to the active layer.

- **Create New Fill or Adjustment layer:** This option is used to create a new adjustment layer. An adjustment layer lets us view the image in a different size or style without changing the image.
- **Create a New Group:** This option allows us to create a group of layers.
- **Create a New Layer:** This option allows us to create a new layer.
- **Delete Layer:** This option deletes the current layer.
- **Layers Options:** Click this button to access a menu of layer-specific commands.

Convert the Background Layers

When you create a new image with a white background or a colored background, the bottommost image in the Layers palette is called Background layer (See Figure 5.3). An image can take only one background layer. You cannot change the stacking order of a background layer, its blending mode, or its opacity. However, you can convert a background into a regular layer, and then change any of these attributes.

Convert a background into a layer 0

1. Double click the background in the **Layer panel** or choose **Layer** menu highlight **New** and then choose **Layer From Background...** .
2. A **New Layer** dialog box appears. Set layer options in the **New Layer** dialog and then click OK.
3. In the **Layers** panel, change its name from the **Background Layer-to-Layer 0**.
4. The Background layer is the locked layer. But Layer 0 is not locked and is fully editable just like any other layer in the Layers pane (See Figure 5.3).

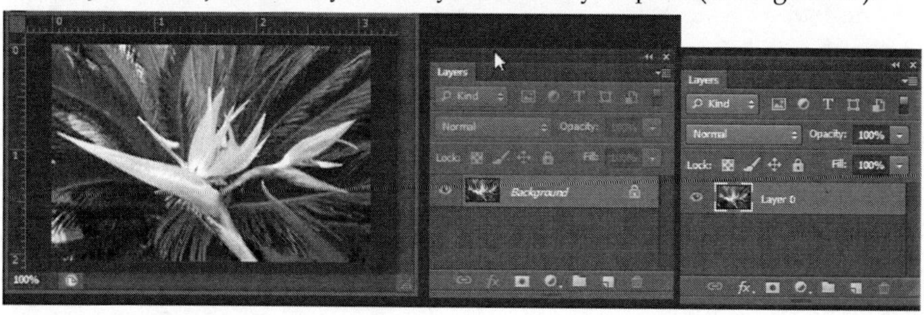

Figure 5.3 Convert Background layer into Layer 0

Convert a Layer into Background

When an image is flattened, all of the document's layers are compressed into a single layer in the Layers panel, named Background. That means no more layers, no more transparency, and no more control.

1. Select a layer in the Layers panel.
2. Choose **Layer** menu highlight **New** and then choose **Background** from layer.

Any transparent pixels in the layer are converted to the background color, and the layer drops to the bottom of the layer.

Working with Layers

Using layers let us make changes to different parts of an image, such as Create a new layer, Show/Hide a layer, Delete a layer, Sort layers, Reposition layers, Merge two or more layers and Flatten all the layers in an image into one.

Creating a New Layer

Whenever pasted on an image, it will automatically place a new layer. You can create empty layers and add contents to them. When you create a new layer, it appears either above the selected layer or within the selected layer set in the Layer palette.

To create new layers, do this:

1. Click the **Layer** menu highlight **New**. A sub menu appears. Select **New Layer...** . Or click the **Layer Panel** menu and choose **New Layer...** . *Alternatively,* press **Shift+Ctrl+N** keys together.
2. The **New Layer** dialog box appears as shown in Figure 5.4.
3. Specify the name of the layer in the **Name:** box. In our case, we have typed **Layer 1**.

Figure 5.4 New Layer dialog box

4. The first time you create a **New Layer**, the default name of the new layer, is **Layer 1** and it is being highlighted in the **Layer panel**. We can change it to any other name of our choice.
5. Click the **Use Previous Layer to Create Clipping Mask** check box. Note that base layer or bottom most layer acts as a mask for the entire group.
6. Select a color for the new layer from the **Color:** text box. In our case, we have selected **Gray**, as shown in Figure 5.4.
7. Specify the blending mode [how layer's pixel blend (mix) with underlying

pixel in the image] of the layer from the **Mode:** drop-down list. For example, the default blending mode is set to **Normal** and the **Opacity** value is set to 100%.

8. Specify the Opacity of the layer from the **Opacity:** drop-down list, in order to flow color and applied in the image.
9. Click **OK** button to apply the settings.
10. A new layer will be created as Layer 1 as shown in Figure 5.4. A blank layer colored gray appears above the selected layer in the Layers panel, as shown in Figure 5.4.

When you create a new layer, it appears below the active layer by default. If you want to create the new layer below an active layer, hold the **Ctrl** key and click the Create a New Layer button at the bottom of the Layers panel. You can copy the Background layer by dragging it onto the Create a New Layer button and work on the copied layer instead of converting it to a normal layer.

Creating a New Layer from a Selection

Photoshop knows gives you an easy way to create a selection from a layer. If you want to move a selection, you can drag the selection marquee, even if the layer is hidden.

New Layer via Cut

Layer Via Copy and Layer Via Cut commands allow us to create a new layer with the pixels of a selection.

To cut selections on to layers, do this:

1. Open an image. Make a selection on it using the **Polygonal Marquee** Tool or you can use any other selection tool to make a selection.
2. Click the **Layer** menu and choose **New**. A list of sub options appears. Select **Layer Via Cut** option as shown in Figure 5.5. *Alternatively*, press **Ctrl+Shift+J** keys together.

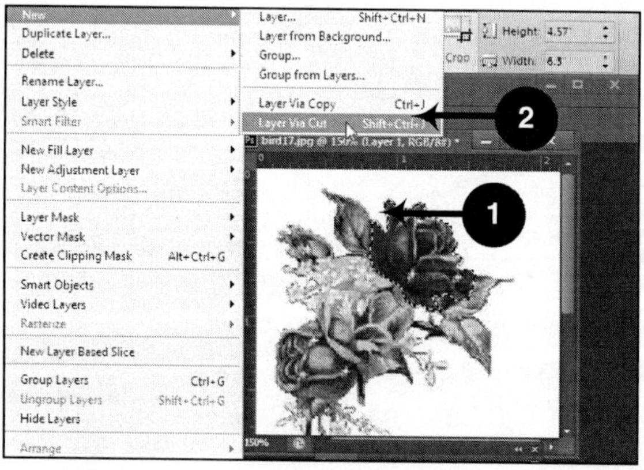

Figure 5.5 Selecting Layer Via Cut

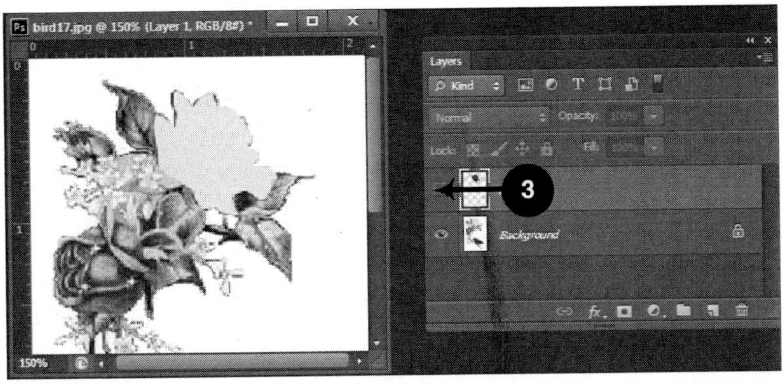

Figure 5.6 Selecting Eye icon in the Layers panel to disappear the selected layer

3. A new layer with the name, Layer 1 gets created with the selected pixels. It will remove the background layer. To see this, hide the new (Layer 1) by clicking on the Eye icon. The portion we had selected for creating the new layer will disappear as shown in Figure 5.6. The selected pixels are removed from the background layer and are moved to the newly created layers.

New Layer via Copy

This command lets us create a new layer with a copy of pixels in the selected portion of the image.

To copy selections on to layers, do this:

1. Open the image.
2. Make a selection on it using the **Quick Selection Tool** or you can use any other Selection Tool to make a selection.
3. Click the **Layer** menu and choose **New**. A list of sub options appears; select **Layer Via Copy** option.
4. From the list click on the **Layer Via Copy** option. The selected pixels are automatically copied from the Background layer (or the layer from which the selection is copied). The newly created layer is displayed in Layers panel, as shown in Figure 5.7. You can drag the selected layer and place it some other location in the document window.

Alternatively, you can press Ctrl+J keys together to create a Layer Via Copy or press Ctrl+Shift+J to create a Layer Via Cut.

Hiding/Showing Layers

When we hide a layer, the contents of that particular layer are removed from the screen, i.e., they become hidden.

To hide/show layers, do this:

1. Open an image containing more than one layer as shown in Figure 5.8.

Figure 5.7 Selected layers to be copied

2. Click on the **Eye** icon of the layer in the left most column of the **Layers** panel to hide it. In Figure 5.8, we can see an image consisting of More layers. Layer 4 contains the image of a flower.
3. When we click on the **Eye** icon of this layer in the **Layers** panel, the flower disappears from the image as shown in Figure 5.9.
4. To make this layer appear again, click on the empty box in the first column against the layer name. The flower reappears in the image.

Figure 5.8 Layers panel containing more than layers

Renaming Layers

You can also change the name of a layer of an image in Photoshop CS6. Use the Layer Properties option available in the Layer menu to rename a layer.

Figure 5.9 Flower in the image gets disappeared

To rename a layer, do this:

1. Select a layer in the Layers palette you want to rename.
2. Double-click the layer name. The layer name gets highlighted. Type a name of the layer in the text box. Here we typed a layer name as **Flower** as shown in Figure 5.10.

Figure 5.10 Double-click the layer to rename in the Layer panel

Duplicating a Layer

There are times when you will need a copy of a Photoshop layer. Duplicating a layer is a simple process that creates a pixel-to-pixel copy of the selected layer. Once the copied layer is created, it becomes a separate image within the document. You can then begin to make changes to the new layer. Duplicating a layer gives you the ability to control each layer separately and to apply non-destructive effects to your image by making them on a copy of the image instead of the original.

To duplicate a Layer, do this:

1. Select the Layers panel.
2. Select the layer you want to duplicate. For example, we have selected Background layer.
3. Click the **Layers Options** button, and then click **Duplicate Layer...** as shown in Figure 5.11.
   The **Duplicate Layer** dialog box appears as shown in Figure 5.12.
4. Enter a name for the layer in the **As:** list box.
5. To place the layer in another open document, click the **Document:** list arrow, and then select a document. Here we have selected Hide_Layer.psd document.
6. Click **OK**.

Figure 5.11 Selecting Duplicate Layer in the Layer options

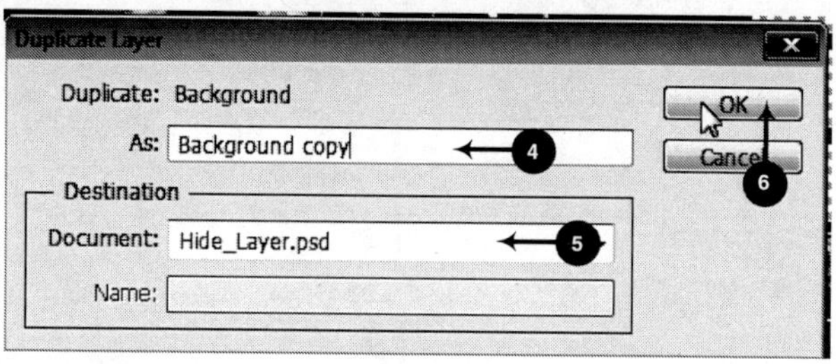

Figure 5.12 Duplicate Layer dialog box

Deleting Layers

Deleting layers refers to eliminating layers from the Layers palette. You need to delete the layers that are not required and reduce the size of an image.

To delete a layer, do this:

1. Select a layer in the Layers palette. In our case, we have selected **Brightness/Contrast** as shown in Figure 5.13.
2. Click down arrow at the top of the **Layer panel**. A list of options appears; select **Delete Layer** from the **Layer Panel Options** as shown in Figure 5.13.

Or Click the **Layer** menu and highlight **Delete**. A sub menu appears. Select **Layer** option.

3. A confirmation dialog box regarding the deletion of layer appears as shown in Figure 5.14.
4. Click the **Yes** button to delete the layer. The selected layer will be deleted.

Figure 5.13 Selecting Delete Layer in the Layer options

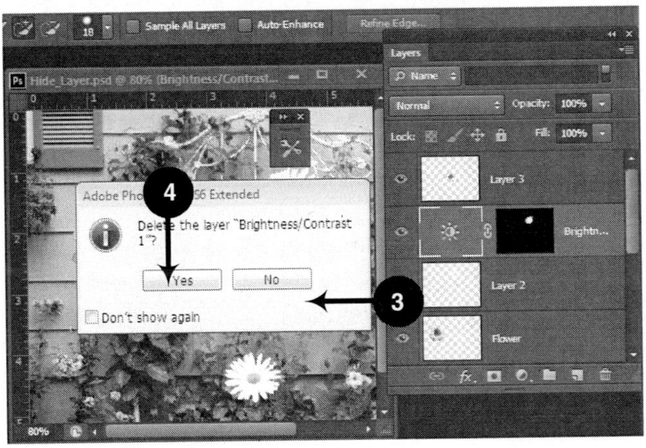

Figure 5.14 Confirmation dialog box appears to delete the layer

To delete a layer using the Delete Layer icon, do this:

1. Select the layer that is to be deleted.
2. Click on the **Delete Layer** icon at the bottom-right corner of the Layers panel. A dialog box appears confirming the deletion of the layer (See Figure 5.14).
3. Click the **Yes** button. The layer will be deleted.

Sorting Layers in the Layers Palette

We can change the order of the layers in the stack to rearrange them.

To sort Layers, do this:

1. Drag Layer **Flower 1** below Layer **Flower**. The mouse pointer changes to the shape of a hand as shown in Figure 5.15.
2. Release the mouse-button. The layer will appear in the location Flower 1 as shown in Figure 5.15. *Alternatively,* hold Ctrl+[, it shifts the layer down one level. Ctrl+] shifts the layer up one level.

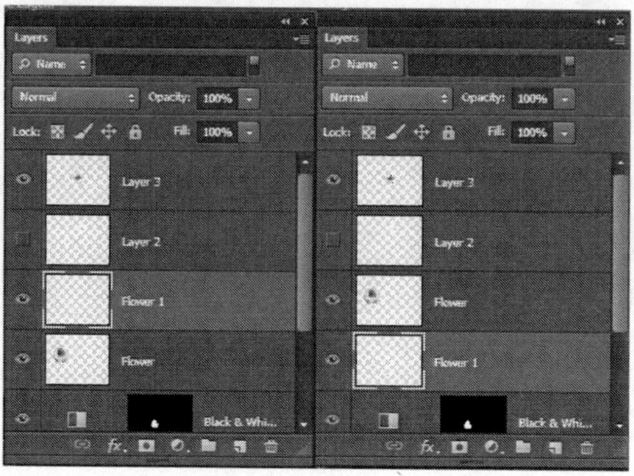

Figure 5.15 Sorting Layers from one level down to Flower

Merging Layers

The Merge Down option lets you merge one selected layer into the layer directly below it in the layer stacking order. Merged layers take on the characteristics of the layer into which they are being merged. For example, if you merge one layer into another that uses the Darken blending mode, the two merged layers will both use Darken. Or, if you merge a layer into the Background layer, the merged layer becomes a part of the Background. The Merge Visible option enables you to merge all of the layers that have the Show option enabled with just one click.

To Merge layers into a single layer, do this

1. Select the layers you want to merge. In our case, we have selected two layers, (Layer 1 and Layer 2) as shown in Figure 5.16.
2. Click the **Layers Options** button at the top right corner of the Layers panel. The Layers panel options appear, select **Merge Layers** (for multiple selection). *Alternatively,* press **Ctrl+E** keys together.
3. Photoshop merges the selected layers into the target layer (i.e., Layer 2) as shown in Figure 5.16.

Merge Down

It merges the contents of the targeted layer immediately below it into one layer. For example, merge Layer 3 with the Layer 2.

To Merge down, do this:

1. Click the **Layer 3** in the Layers panel (See Figure 5.17).

Figure 5.16 The selected Layers get merged

2. Click the right arrow button on the top right side of the Layers panel. Layers options appear as shown in Figure 5.17.
3. Click the **Merge Down** option from the Layers panel.
4. Layer 3 has merged down with Layer 2 as shown in Figure 5.17.

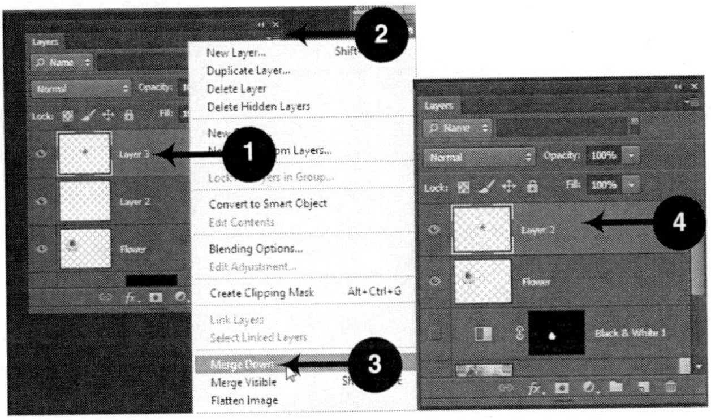

Figure 5.17 Selecting Layer 3 and Merge Down into Layer 2 using Merge Down option

Merge Visible Layers

It merges the content of all of the visible layers into one layer.

To merge visible layers, do this:

1. Click the **Show** option for all layers you want to merge (i.e., the Eye icon).
2. Click the right arrow button on the top right side of the Layers panel. Layers Options appear as shown in Figure 5.18.
3. Click the **Merge Visible** option from the list. *Alternatively,* press **Shift+Ctrl+E** keys together (See Figure 5.18).
4. Only the Visible layers in the Layers panel will be merged into a single layer.

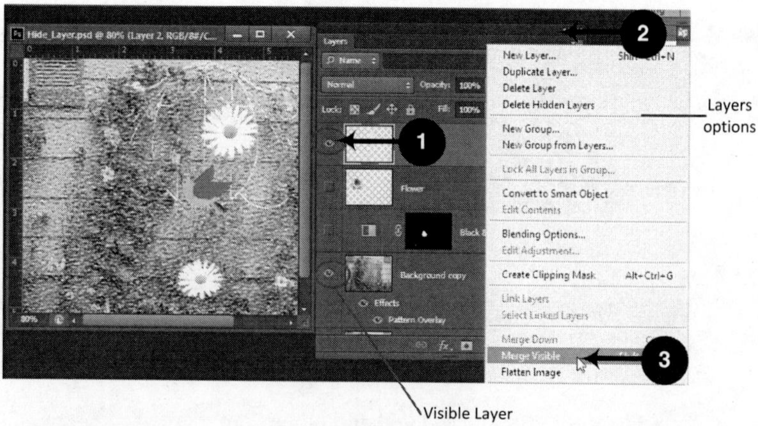

Figure 5.18 Selecting merge visible in the Layers menu

Creating a Layer Group

Photoshop layer groups give you control over all the layers within the group at one time. For example, multiple layers within a group can all be hidden or locked with one click of a button. In addition, if you click on the Group name, you can transform or move all the layer objects within the group as one unit and even add effects and adjustments to them. If you remove an item from the group, you also remove the effect or adjustment.

To create a layer group, do this:

1. Open a document that has multiple layers in a document.
2. Select the layers that you want to include in the layer group. Hold the **Shift** key down to select multiple layers as shown in Figure 5.19.
3. Click the **Layer** menu highlight **New** and choose **Group from Layers...** . Or click at the top right corner of the **Layers** panel. A list of layers options appears. Select **New Group from Layers...** option as shown in Figure 5.19.

Figure 5.19 Selecting New Group from Layers... from the Layers panel

The **New Group from Layers** dialog box appears as shown in Figure 5.20.

4. Enter the name for the Group in the **Name:** text box.
5. Select the color to assign a color to the layer in the **Color:** drop-down list. Click the **Mode:** list arrow, and then select from the available blending modes.
6. Click **OK** button as shown in Figure 5.20.

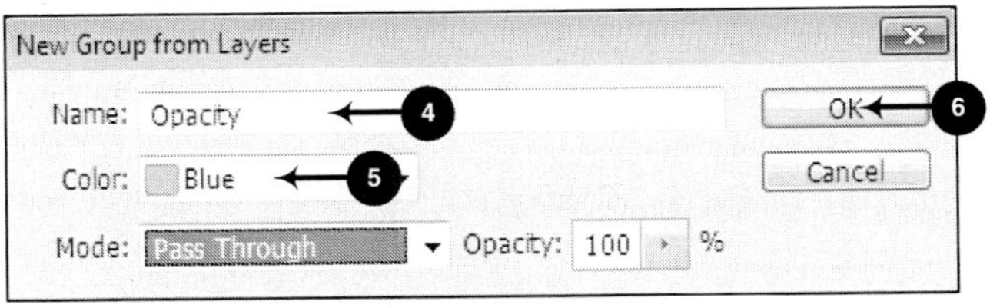

Figure 5.20 New Group from Layers

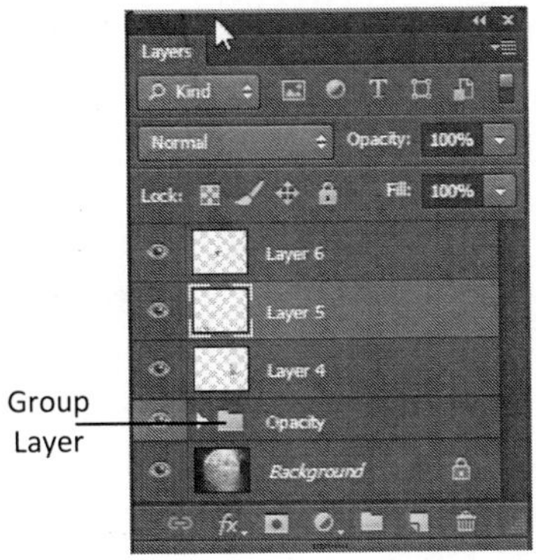

Figure 5.21 Group layer in the Layers panel

7. A new layer group appears in the Layers panel as shown in Figure 5.21.

By default, the new group layer appears in the collapsed form. You can click the right-arrow icon to expand the layer group. You can also apply masks to all the layers in the group. It is also able to collapse or expand all layer groups at the same time by clicking the right-arrow icon while holding the **Ctrl** key down.

Working with Layer Blending Modes

Layer Blending Modes are one of the most creative areas within the Layers panel. With blending modes, you can instruct Photoshop to mix the image information between two or more layers. For example, using the Multiply Blending Mode instructs Photoshop to multiply the color of one layer with that of another layer, resulting in a darker color.

To apply a blending mode to a layer, do this:

1. Open a multi-layered document. In our case, we have selected Layer 1 and Layer 2, as shown in Figure 5.22.

2. Select the **Layers** panel.
3. Click the layers you want to adjust; you can apply blending mode to one or more selected layers in the Layers panel.
4. Click the **Set the blending mode for the layer** drop-down list and select a Blend Mode from the drop-down list. In our case, we have selected **Exclusion** and **Dissolve** as shown in Figure 5.22.
5. The **Exclusion** and **Dissolve** blending modes are applied to the underlying layers as shown in Figure 5.22.

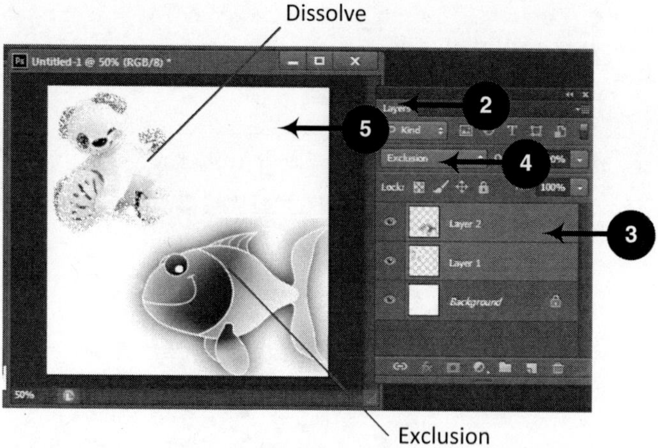

Figure 5.22 Applied blending modes in the selected layers

Types of Blending Modes

Normal: It allows each pixel to appear in its original state.

Dissolve: It works with a layer that has an Opacity setting of less than 100%.

Darken: It converts lighter pixels to transparent and retains the darker pixels unchanged.

Multiply: It darkens the colors of the layer by multiplying the color with the layers beneath the selected layer.

Color Burn: It searches for the color information in the selected layer, and darkens the layers beneath it in the Layers panel. The Blending mode increases the contrast of the image.

Linear Burn: Darkens the layers beneath the selected layer by decreasing the brightness.

Darken Color: It operates on all channels simultaneously rather than operating on one channel at a time. When blending two colors with this blending mode, only the darker color is visible.

Lighten: It inverses the effect of the Darken Blending mode.

Color Dodge: It decreases the contrast to reflect the blend color. It is the opposite of the Color Burn Blending mode.

Linear Doge: It reflects the blend color by brightening the base color. It is the opposite of the Linear Burn Blending mode.

Lighter Color: The lighter color is visible when blending two colors with this mode.

Overlay: Overlay Blending mode if you want to preserve the shadows and highlights of an image.

Soft Light: It creates a diffuse spotlight effect. The blend color with 50% or more brightness lightens the image the blend color with 50% or less brightness darkens the image.

Hard Light: The effect is similar to that of shining a Harsh spotlight on the image.

Vivid Light: It burns or hides the colors by increasing or decreasing the contrast, depending on the blend color.

Linear Light: It burns or hides the colors by decreasing or increasing the brightness, depending on the blend color.

Pin Light: If the blend color is lighter than 50% gray, pixels darker than the blend color are replaced, and pixels lighter than the blend color do not change.

Hard Mix: It applies a posterization effect based on the selected layer's opacity value.

Difference: It checks the color information in each channel and subtracts either the blend color from the base color, depending on which has a greater brightness value.

Exclusion: The effect that matches the low contract of difference blending mode.

Subtract: The color information in each channel and subtracts the blend color from the base color.

Divide: The color information in each channel and divides the blend color from the base color.

Different types of blending modes as shown in Figure 5.23.

Working with Layer Styles

Layer styles are applied to the layers in the active document. When you add a style to a layer, the results of the style are only displayed in that layer. Each layer can have its own style, and you can apply more than one style to a single layer. Layer styles can be applied to any layer except the Background.

Two of Photoshop's layer styles require both transparent and non-transparent layer elements (Drop Shadow and Outer Glow). For example, to apply a Drop Shadow to a layer, it would require a transparent area within the image to hold the shadow.

Figure 5.23 Different types of Blending modes

The various layer style options in the Layer Style dialog box are described below.

Drop Shadow: You can apply a Drop shadow effect to an image, text, or a shape contained within the layer. It allows you to specify the color, opacity, blend mode, position, size and contour of the effect.

Bevel and Emboss: The Bevel and Emboss style, creates a 3D (Three Dimensional) illusion of roundness to a flat surface. You can apply the Bevel layer style to text to get the impression of 3D text. If the layer you are applying the Bevel and Emboss to has no transparent areas, the style will be applied to the outer edge of the image.

Inner Shadow: It applies basic drop shadows to the inside boundaries of an image.

Outer Glow: It applies a circle of around an image, type or shape contained within the layer.

Inner Glow: It creates the glow effect to the inside boundaries of a layer.

Satin: It adds variations in opacity by creating waves of repeated color as defined in the contour option.

Color Overlay: It fills a layer with a solid color.

Gradient Overlay: It fills a layer with a gradient.

Pattern Overlay: It fills a layer with a pattern.

Stroke: It creates outline using color, gradient and pattern around an image.

Adding a Layer Style

To add a layer style to a layer, select the layer, and add one or more layer styles by clicking the Add a layer style button in the Layers panel.

To add a layer style to a layer, do this:

1. Open a document and select the layer on which you want to add layer styles. In our case, the layer with a Lotus layer is selected, as shown in Figure 5.24.
2. Click the **Add a Layer Style** button at the bottom of the Layers panel.
3. Select the **Drop Shadow...** option from the drop-down list. The **Layer Style** dialog box appears as shown in Figure 5.25.

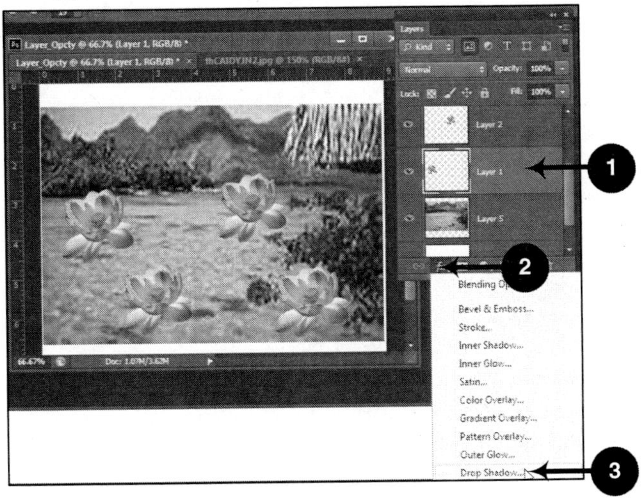

Figure 5.24 Selecting Layer style from the Layers panel

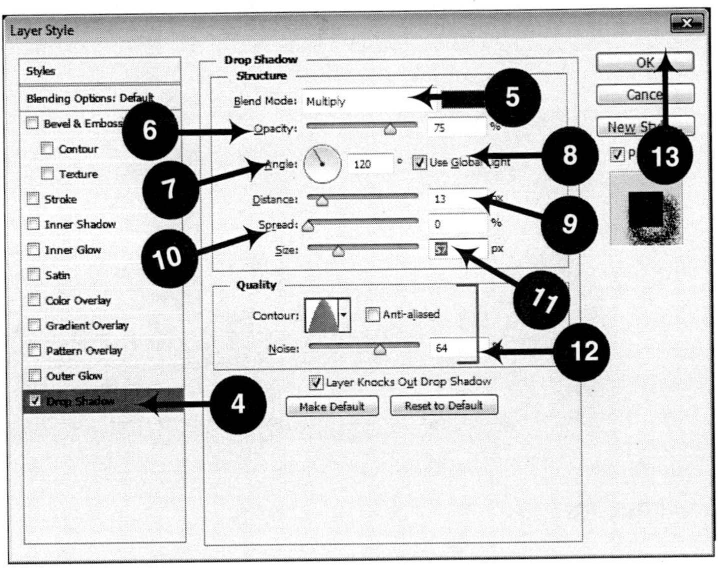

Figure 5.25 Layer Style dialog box

4. Select a layer style check box in the Styles pane. In our case, we have selected **Drop Shadow** option from the drop-down list.
5. **Blend Mode:** It determines how the layer style blends with the active layer. For example, a drop shadow blends only with the layers beneath the active layer.
6. **Opacity:** Enter or drag the slider to set the opacity of the layer effect.
7. **Angle:** It determines the lighting angle at which the effect is applied to the layer. You can drag in the document window to adjust the angle of a Drop Shadow.
8. Select the **Use Global Light** check box to conform the angle of the drop shadow to any other effects applied to other layers.
9. **Distance:** It specifies the offset distance for a shadow effect. . You can drag in the document window to adjust the offset distance.
10. **Spread:** It determines the amount of image used for the spread of the shadow (default: 0%).
11. **Size:** It specifies the amount of the size of the shadow.
12. In the **Quality** area, the following two options are displayed:

    Contour: It allows you to specify the fade.

    Noise: Enter a value or drag the slider to specify the number of random elements in the opacity of a glow or shadow.
13. After applying the **Drop Shadow** options, click **OK** button.

The effect of **Drop shadow** applied in the text layer is shown in Figure 5.26.

Drop-Shadow applied in the Lotus flower

Figure 5.26 Drop-Shadow style applied in the selected layer

Removing Layer Styles

You can remove a layer style effect permanently by clearing all of them at once, or selecting or clearing individual styles that you do not need.

To remove a layer style from a layer, do this:

1. Select the layer with layer styles applied in the Layers panel, for example we have selected Layer 1.
2. Drag the layer style (Effects) and drop on the **Delete layer** icon at the bottom of the Layers panel, as shown in Figure 5.27. Or *Alternatively*, you can select the Layer menu highlight Layer Style and choose Clear Layer Style from the Menu bar. The Clear Layer Style option removes all the layer style applied to a layer.

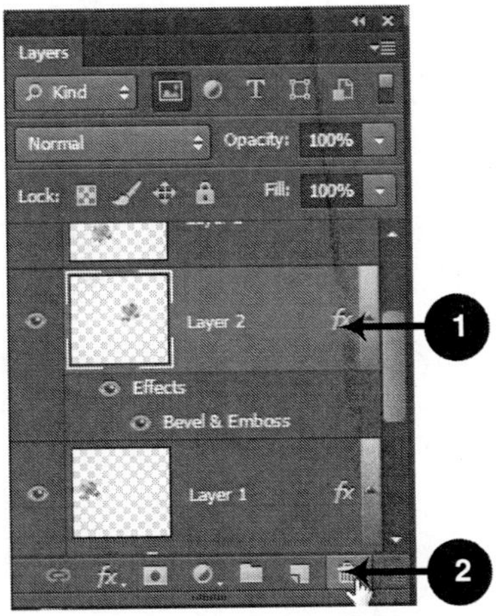

Figure 5.27 Selecting Delete icon in the Layers panel

CHAPTER 6

Working with Video and Animation

Introduction

You can use Photoshop Extended to edit individual frames of video and image sequence files. In addition to using any Photoshop tool to edit and paint on video, you can also apply filters, masks, transformations, layers styles, and blending modes. After making edits, you can save the document as a PSD file and you can playback in Premiere Pro and After Effects or you can render it as a QuickTime movie or image sequence.

Photoshop CS6 also allows you to create a timeline-based animation. The Timeline panel allows you to create and modify animation in Photoshop CS6. It also adds video and audio layers in the Timeline panel. When you insert a video, it appears in the Timeline and Layers panels. To animate layer content in timeline mode, you set keyframes in the Animation panel, as you move the current-time indicator to a different time/frame, and then modify the position, opacity, or style of the layer content.

In this Chapter, you will learn how to import video files. Next, you will learn how to create a video layer with different ways. Next, you will learn to modify the video layer by trimming and splitting. You also learn to add transition, text vector element, audio to a video layer. Finally, you will learn to work with animation, and also to create and export the animation.

Creating a Video Layer

There are different ways to create a video layer in Photoshop. You can open an existing file to create a video layer, or create a blank video layer. Click Layer menu highlight Video Layers and choose New Blank Video Layer or New Video Layer from file. Both these options are available when there is an open document.

To create a video Layer, do this:

1. Open a Photoshop document.
2. Select **Layer** menu, highlight **Video Layers** and choose **New Blank Video Layer** from the **Menu** bar to create a blank layer.
3. A new blank video layer appears in the Layers panel and appears selected by default, as shown in Figure 6.1.

Creating a New Video Project

You can also create a video project from scratch using an empty Photoshop document. It also provides the Film & Video preset to quickly create a video project.

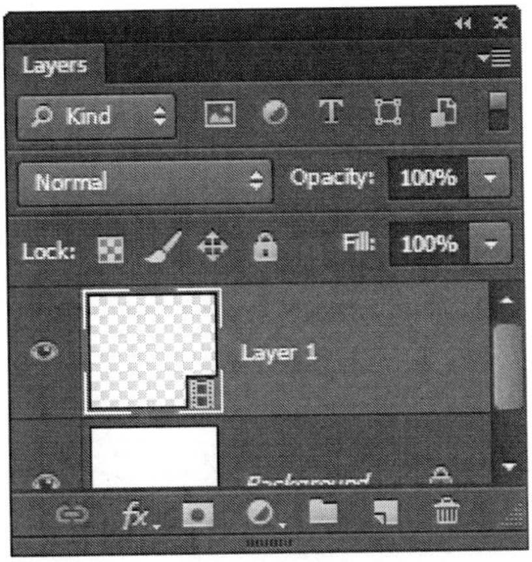

Figure 6.1 Layers panel

To create a new video project, do this:

1. Click **File** menu and choose **New...** . *Alternatively,* press **Ctrl+N** keys together. The **New** dialog box appears as shown in Figure 6.2.
2. Type the name for the project in the **Name:** text box.
3. Select the **Film & Video** option in the **Preset:** drop-down list.
4. Select **HDV/HDTV (High Definition Video/High Definition Television) 720p/29.97** in the **Size:** drop-down list as shown in Figure 6.2. The **Width:** value is 1280 pixels and the **Height:** value is 720 pixels.
5. Click the **OK** button to create a new document with specified settings.

   The new video document appears with guideslines that indicate where to place titles (text) and important parts of the video.

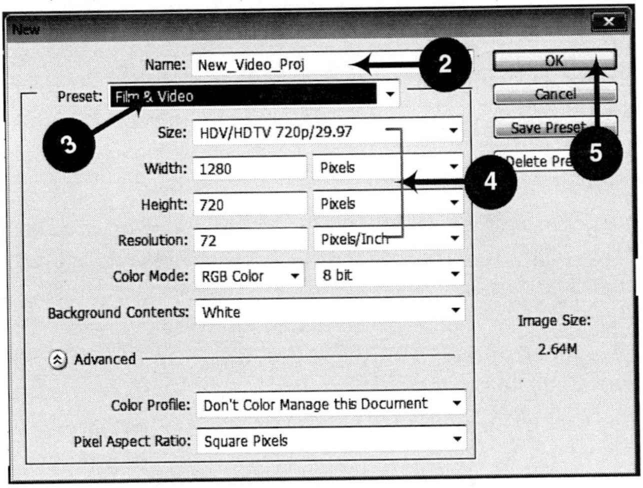

Figure 6.2 New dialog box

Importing Video Files

In Photoshop, you can start a video project by importing an existing video or creating a new document using video presets. You can import video files using the Open command in the File menu. In the Open dialog box, you can select the image Sequence check box to import image sequence. This option is enabled when you select an image sequence. It supports various video and audio formats, such as .mov, .avi, mpeg-2 and mp4. When you import a video file into Photoshop, it automatically performs a pixel aspect ratio correction on the document. To preview original pixels, turn off pixel aspect ratio correction by selecting view menu.

To import an existing video file into Photoshop, do this:

1. Open Photoshop document window.
2. Select **File** menu and choose **Open** to open a video file.
3. The **Open** dialog box appears as shown in Figure 9.3.

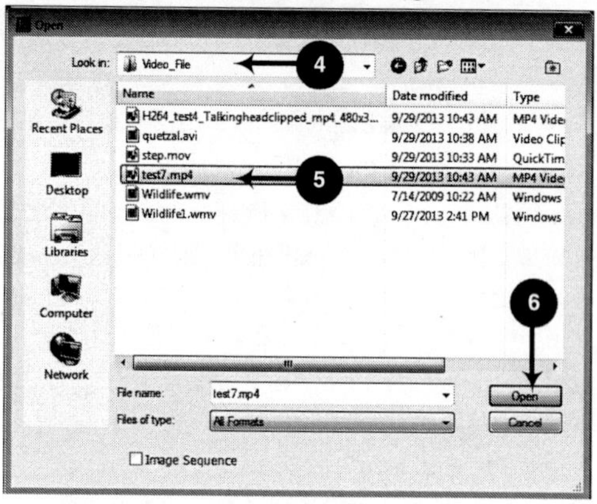

Figure 6.3 Open dialog box

4. Locate the folder that contains the video file in the **Look in:** drop-down list.
5. Select the file that you want to import. In our case, we have selected **test7.mp4**.
6. Click **Open** button.
7. Photoshop CS6 creates a new document whose size matches the dimensions of the video. The **Timeline** panel appears automatically with the video clip, as shown in Figure 6.4.
8. In our case, the first frame of the video is a black screen. You can see the **Timeline panel** appears with the video file in the **Layer 1**. In addition, a video layer is created in the Layers panel.

In our case, the first frame of the video is a black screen. You can see the Timeline panel appears with the video file in the Layer 1. In addition, a video layer is created in the Layers panel.

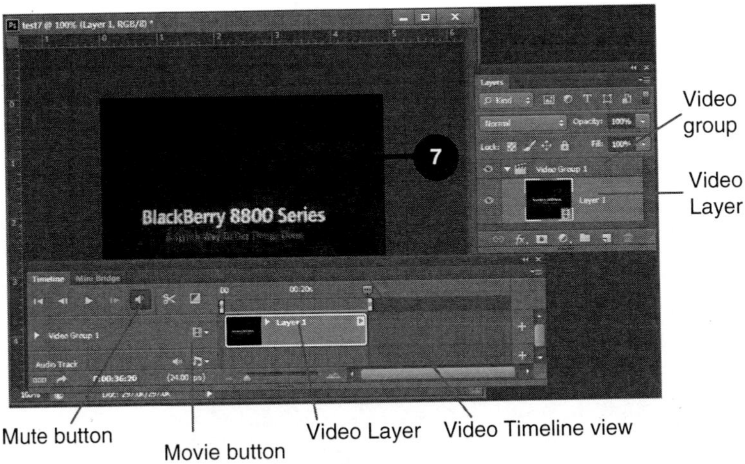

Figure 6.4 Video clip appears in black

Modifying a Video Layer

After you insert a video layer, you can modify it in Photoshop using the Timeline panel in Video Timeline view. You can zoom in and out to display the Timeline the way you want, and then drag the playhead, also known as the current-time indicator, to the time or frame number in the video where you want to start your modifications. You can change the start and stop points (also known as In and Out points), trim frames, add a fade-in or fade-out, or add animation using keyframes. A keyframe defines the location of a property change to the video layer. When you set at least two keyframes that change properties, such as position, opacity, or style, you create animation.

To modify a video Layer duration, do this:

1. Open a document with a video.
2. Select the **Timeline** panel as shown in Figure 6.5.
3. To switch to **Video Timeline view**, click the **Convert to Video Timeline** button.
4. Use any of the following methods to change the video duration:

   Start and End Work Area: Point to the ends of the work area bar, and then drag to change the position. Click the Timeline Options button, point to Work Area, and then select an option to lift (delete) or extract (crop) the work area.

   In and Out Points: Point to the start or end of the clip (cursor changes to a double-arrow), and then drag to change the duration.

   Move Position: Point to within the clip, and then drag it.
5. To delete a clip, do any of the following:

   Timeline Panel: Select the clip, and then press Delete or Backspace.

Layers Panel: Drag video or group layer to delete icon.

Figure 6.5 Modify the video layer duration

Trimming a Video File

As you add new video layers to a project, you may find that you need to trim them. Trimming a video layer consists of cutting the unwanted ends off the layer, leaving the rest of the video intact. You can trim a video clip by dragging the video clip duration bar manually, using the Timeline or by splitting the video clip. To trim by dragging the duration bar, click and drag the start or end of a video clip. The cursor appears as a square bracket with a two-headed arrow when you place it over either end of the video.

To trim a video clip in Photoshop, do this:

1. Open the document and import the video that you want to trim. In our case, we have created a document with the video preset and imported the fractogene video clip, as shown in Figure 6.6.

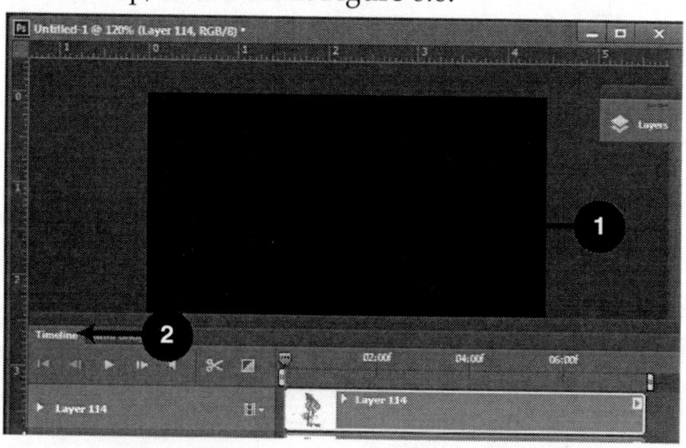

Figure 6.6 Import video clip

2. Ensure the **Timeline** panel is visible.
3. Move the playhead to the desired time/frame as shown in Figure 6.7.

   The Timeline panel displays the current time at the bottom of the panel. You can double-click the Current Time indicator to precisely set the current time.
4. Right-click the playhead. A context menu appears, as shown in Figure 6.7.
5. Select the **Trim Start of Clip** option from the context menu as shown in Figure 6.7.

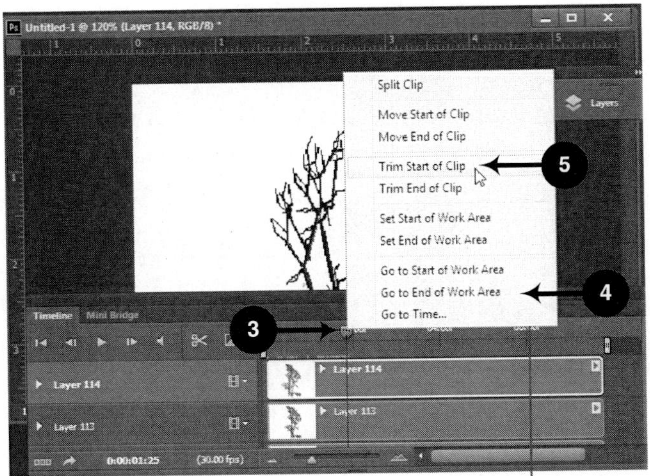

Figure 6.7 Selecting Trim Start of Clip from the context menu

6. The start of the video clip moves to the current playhead position and deletes the portion of the video clip before the playhead as shown in Figure 6.8.

Figure 6.8 Video clip trim to start

7. Move the playhead to the desired frame.
8. Right-click the playhead and select the **Trim End of Clip** option from the context menu as shown in Figure 6.9.
9. The end of the video clip moves to the current playhead position and deletes the position of the video clip after the playhead, as shown in Figure 6.10.

Figure 6.9 Selecting Trim End of Clip from the context menu

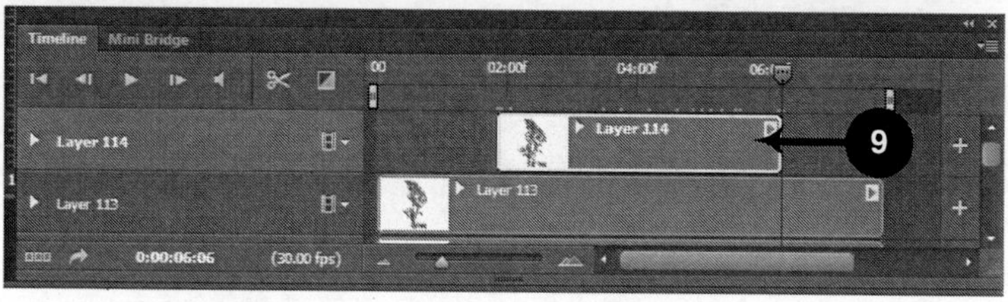

Figure 6.10 Video clip trim to end

Splitting a Video Layer

You can split a video layer into two new video layers at the specific point. To place the playhead where you want to split, drag the playhead to the time or frame number in the video track.

To split a video layer in Photoshop, do this:

1. Open the document with a video layer that you want to split.
2. Drag the playhead over the frame where you want the video layer to split.

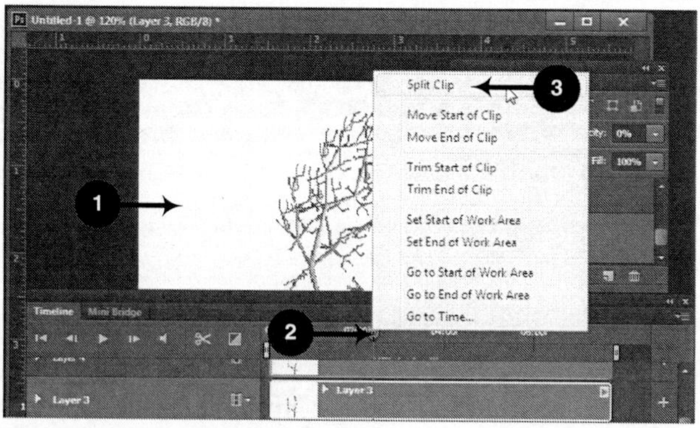

Figure 6.11 Selecting Split Clip from the context menu

3. Right-click the playhead and select the **Split Clip** option from the context menu, as shown in Figure 6.11.
4. A duplicate copy of the video layer (Layer 1 copy) appears containing the video frame current time to the end as shown in Figure 6.12.

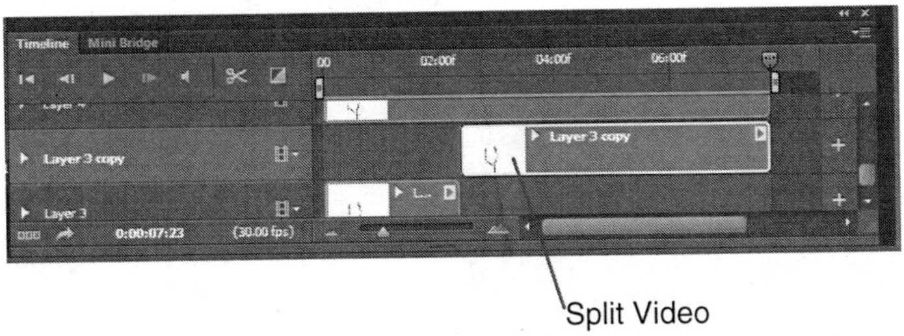

Figure 6.12 Split a video layer

Adding Text to a Video Layer

The power of Photoshop comes to the forefront when you work with video because you can add text and other elements to video just like you would with a still image. For text, you can use a Type Tool and other formatting options to create the look you want, and then adjust the position and duration in the Timeline panel.

To add Text to a Video Layer, do this:

1. Open the document with a video on which you want to add text.
2. Click the **Video icon** with a down arrow for **Video Group 1**. A drop-down list appears as shown in Figure 6.13.
3. Select the **New Video Group** option in the drop-down list.

Figure 6.13 Selecting New Video Group from the Timeline panel

4. A new video group is created (i.e., Video Group 2) and becomes active as shown in Figure 6.14. You can also notice a new video group is created in the Layers panel.

   Select a type tool on the **Tools** panel. In our case, we have added text using the **Horizontal Type Tool**.
5. Click or drag a type box on the video, and then enter the text you want to add.

6. The **Layers** panel shows the type layer (i.e., Layer 2) under Video Group 2, as shown in Figure 6.14.

   Format the text as per your requirement and place it inside the area.

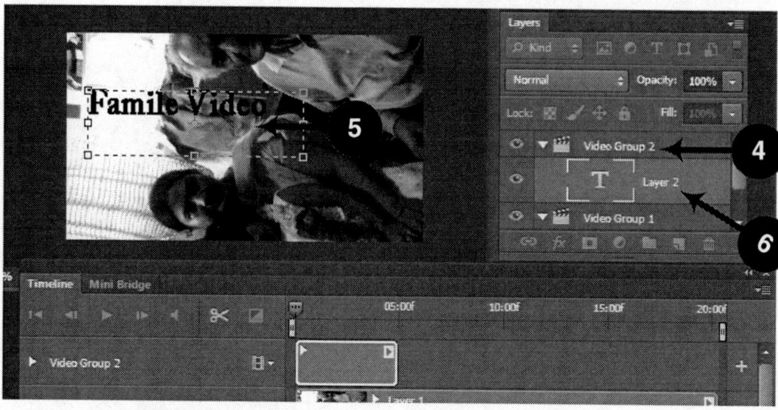

Figure 6.14 Type the text inside the video clip

7. Drag the end point of the text video track to the end of the workarea to stretch to the total duration as shown in Figure 6.15.
8. Click the **Play** button to preview the text through the video playback.

Figure 6.15 Click the Play button to preview the text through the video playback

Creating an Animation

An animation is a sequence of images, or frames, that vary slightly to create the illusion of movement over time. One of the animation formats is the animated GIF (Graphics Interchange Format). The GIF file format is used primarily for clip art, text, and line art, or for images that contain areas of solid color. You can use a sequence of individual image layers to create animation frames in Frame view in the Timeline panel, which you can save as an animated GIF. Once the image is created, you can open and use it in any application that supports the GIF file format.

To create an Animated GIF from Scratch, do this:

1. Open Photoshop. Click the **File** menu, and then click **New** as shown in Figure 6.16.
2. The **New** dialog box appears on the screen.
3. Enter a name in the **Name:** box.
4. Click the **Preset:** list arrow, and then select from the available presets. Here we have selected **Custom** option. You can enter a customized in Width, Height, and Resolution in **Width:**, **Height:** and **Resolution:** fields, respectively.
5. Click the **Color Mode:** list arrow, and then select a color mode for the image.
6. Click the **Bit Size** list arrow, and then choose a bit depth for the image (8 bit recommended).
7. Click the **Background Contents:** list arrow, and then click White, Background Color, or Transparent (animated GIF files look best using transparency).
8. Click **OK**.
9. The new file appears in the document as shown in Figure 6.17.
10. Click the **Create Frame Animation** button in the Timeline panel as shown in Figure 6.17.
11. Create the first image for the animated GIF.
12. Press **Ctrl+J** to create a copy of your first animation in a separate layer. In our case, we have placed the Duck image as shown in Figure 6.18.

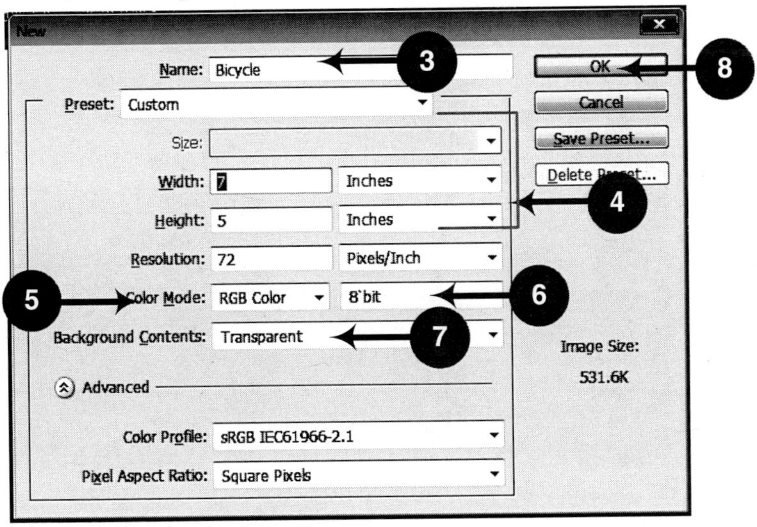

Figure 6.16 New dialog box

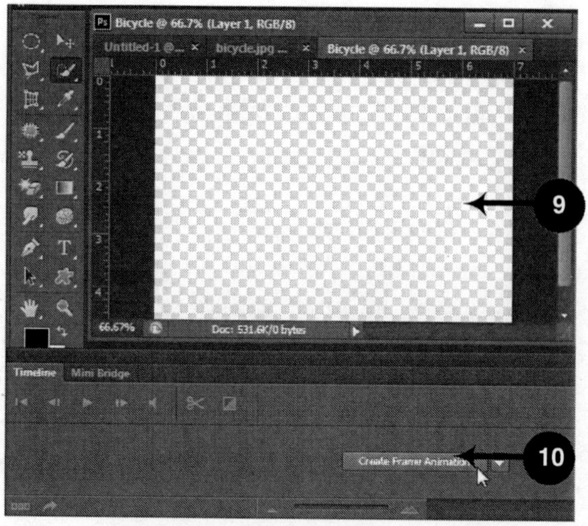

Figure 6.17 Select Create Frame Animation

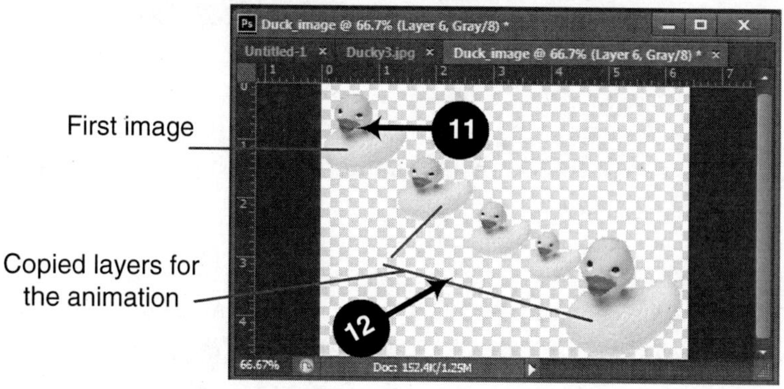

Figure 6.18 The duck image was copied in the layers

Figure 6.19 Modified the each layer by using the Freeform to resize the image

13. Modify the second image (animations are essentially the same image, modified slightly between each animation frame or each layer). Press Ctrl+T keys together to make a Free Transform to resize the image as shown in Figure 6.19.

    Repeat Steps 12 and 13 until you have enough layers for the animation.

14. Click the **Timeline Options** button on the **Timeline** panel, and then click **Make Frames From Layers** as shown in Figure 6.20.
15. Select the Frame, click the down arrow button to **select delay frame time**. A pop-up appears select the second to set each frame time at the bottom of the Timeline Options as shown in Figure 6.21.
16. In our case, we have selected 0.5 seconds. Repeat the setup continuously till the end of the frame.

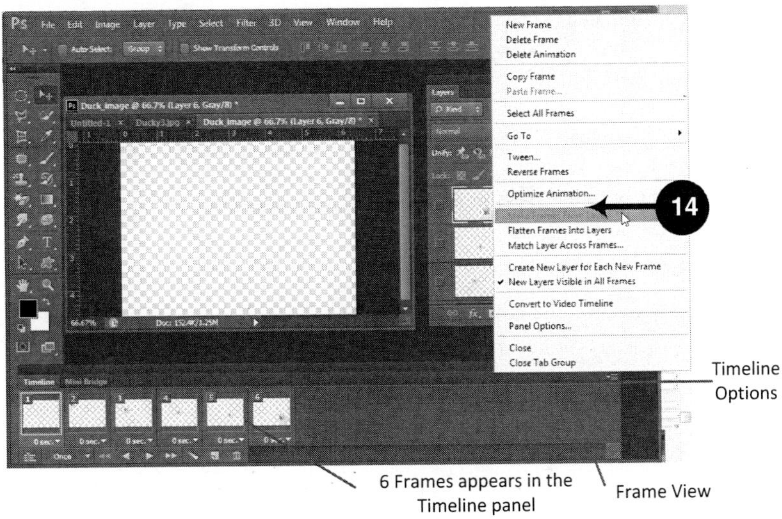

Figure 6.20 Select the Make Frames from Layers

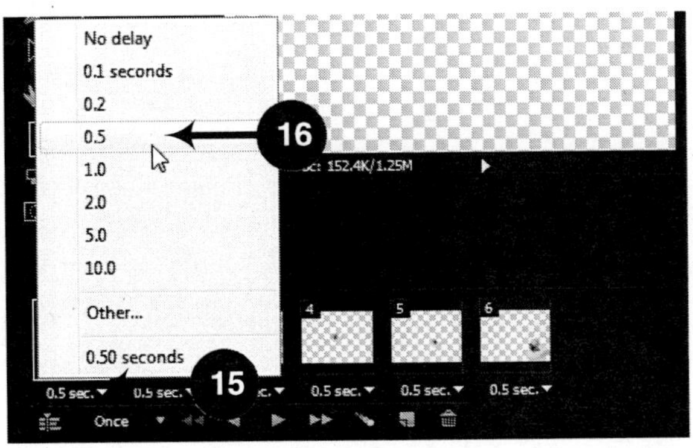

Figure 6.21 Select the frame delay time at the bottom of the Timeline options

17. Click the **Play** button to view your animation in the document window as shown in Figure 6.22.
18. Click the **File** menu and then click **Save for Web**.
19. To make fine-tune the image, use the available options.

Figure 6.22 Select the Play button to animate the image

20. Click **Save** to save the current image using the **Save Optimized As** dialog box.

CHAPTER 7

Introduction to CorelDRAW Graphics Suite X5

Introduction

CorelDRAW X5 is a very powerful graphic design package. It is used to create illustrations, page layouts, Web graphics, as well as edit photos and pictures. The application was developed by one of the world's leading software development company, Corel Corporation of Ottawa, Canada, Corel Corporation, founded by Michael Cowpland in 1985. CorelDRAW X5 offers a new and enhanced design tools that allow you to create the most intricate of illustrations and perform other graphics manipulation tasks more quickly and easily than ever before.

In this Chapter, you will learn about the various applications of the Suite and explore its new features. It also describes the components of the CorelDRAW X5 user interface. You will also learn to work with basic geometric shapes and figures using the various CorelDRAW X5 tools. It also discusses how to start the CorelDRAW X5 application and to create, save a new document and open an existing drawing in CorelDRAW. Finally, you will learn to preview a drawing, view a drawing in different views modes, work with page layout, close a drawing and quit CorelDRAW.

Understanding CorelDRAW Graphics Suite X5

The latest upgraded fifteenth version, known as CorelDRAW Graphics Suite X5, in February, 2010. This version is supported for all the Windows-based Operating systems, such as Windows XP, Windows XP and Windows 7.

Let us discuss the various applications that are included in the CorelDRAW Graphics Suite X5.

Introducing the Applications of CorelDRAW Graphics Suite X5

CorelDRAW Graphics Suite X5 is a collection of various applications, such as CorelDRAW X5, Corel Photo-Paint X5, Corel PowerTRACE X5, Corel CAPTURE X5 and Corel CONNECT. The Suite contains major enhancements, particularly related to design tools, color management, and Web graphics. The main applications of CorelDRAW Graphics Suite X5 are as follows:

CorelDRAW X5: It refers to the vector-design application used for designing page layouts.

Corel Photo-Paint X5: It refers to image-editing application, such as to adjust the color and tone of an image, retouch images and mask images.

Corel PowerTRACE X5: It lets you accurately convert Bitmap images and Vector graphics.

Corel CAPTURE X5: It provides the facility to capture a shot of the screen with one-click.

Corel CONNECT: A full-screen browser that lets you search files, templates and images from your computer and selected Websites.

Getting Started with CorelDRAW X5

After installing CorelDRAW Graphics Suite X5 on your computer, you can open the CorelDRAW X5 application and start working with a new blank page.

To start CorelDRAW, do this:

1. Click the **Start** menu, highlight **Programs**, highlight **CorelDRAW Graphics Suite X5** and then click on **CorelDRAW X5**.
2. The **Welcome** screen appears as shown in Figure 7.1.

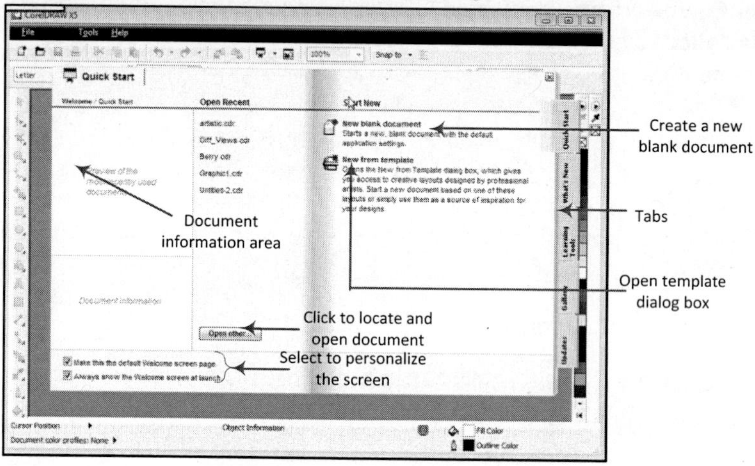

Figure 7.1 Welcome screen

3. The **Welcome** screen displays the following options:

- **New blank document:** It creates a new blank document.
- **New from template:** Enables you to choose from a list of pre-designed page templates that you can use as a basis to begin a design.
- **Open Recent:** It displays the list of recently opened documents.
- **Open Other...:** Browse and open documents other than the recently opened documents.
- **Document information area:** View information related to a document, such as size, date of creation and path of the document.
- Select tabs to view the options of the Welcome screen:
  - ➢ Start working with a new drawing in CorelDRAW X5 by clicking the Quick Start link.

- To learn the new features of CorelDRAW X5 by clicking the What's New link.
- To learn the various designing tools by clicking the Learning Tools link, such as Video tutorials, Guidebook, CorelTUTOR and Tips & tricks.
- To view a sample of predefined design patterns by clicking the Gallery link.
- Explore the updates available for the CorelDRAW X5 application by clicking the Updates link.

- Personalize the Welcome Screen.

After a brief understanding of various options in the Welcome screen of CorelDRAW X5, let us learn to create a new document in CorelDRAW X5.

Creating a New Document in CorelDRAW X5

After the Welcome screen appears, you can open a new blank document by clicking the **New blank document** under the **Start New** section in the **Welcome Screen**. The CorelDRAW window **Create a New Document** dialog box appears as shown in Figure 7.2.

To create a new document in CorelDRAW X5 by using the Create a New Document dialog box, do this:

1. Type a name of the document in the **Name:** text box. In our case, we have typed **Image-1** as shown in Figure 7.2.

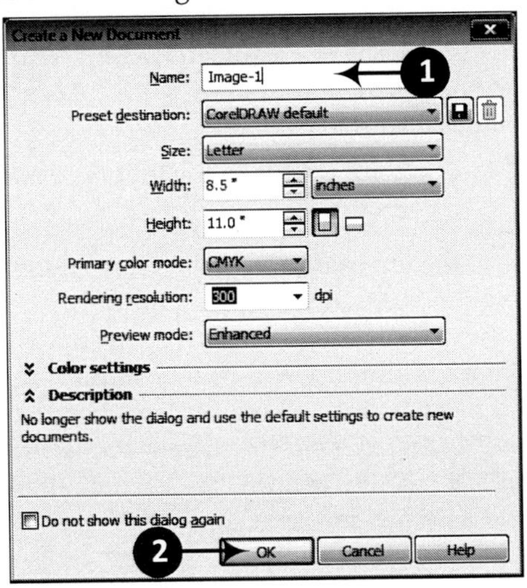

Figure 7.2 Create a New Document dialog box

2. Click the **OK** button.
3. The workspace of CorelDRAW X5 [**Untitled-1**] with a blank document appears, as shown in Figure 7.3.

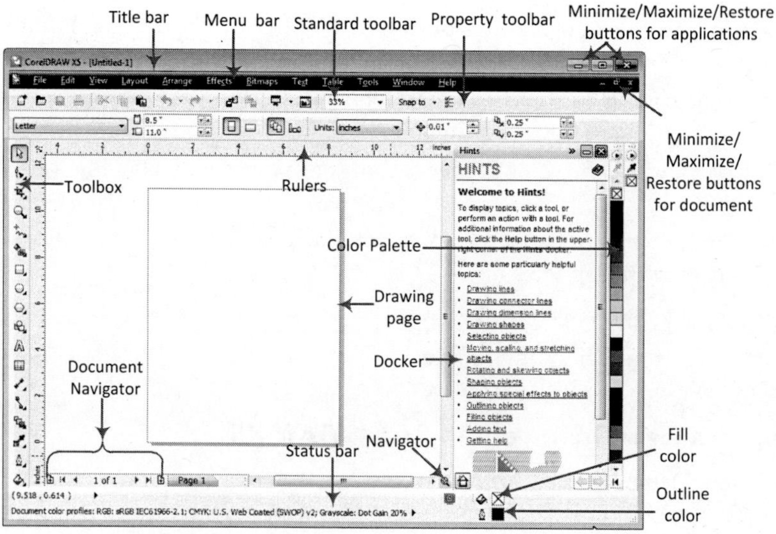

Figure 7.3 Blank document window screen

The User Interface of CorelDRAW X5

CorelDRAW X5 offers you a wide range of features and tools that help you to work with the different designing work. The user interface also includes the Toolbox, Drawing page, Status bar and Property bar that allow you to design the page settings, units and layout of the document. You can also find various application tools in the workspace area. CorelDRAW allows you to customize the workspace area so that you can keep only these tools and applications which are necessary for your daily work.

Let us discuss some of these components in the following sections:

Title Bar

The Title bar appears at the top of the CorelDRAW Window. The Title bar shows the name of the file you are currently working on. When the size of the window is less than the maximum size, you can move the entire window by clicking on the Title bar and dragging the mouse to a new position. The right side of the Title bar contains a button panel that has three buttons from left or right: **Minimize, Restore/Maximize** and **Close**. These buttons are used to minimize a CorelDRAW window, restore the size of the window to its default size or maximize the window, and close the window, respectively.

Menu Bar

The Menu bar is located below the Title Bar and contains the Pull-down menus. The Pull-down menus contain the CorelDRAW commands, such as File, Edit, View, Layout, Bitmaps and Text. Each menu opens a drop-down list from where you can select other options according to your requirement.

Standard Toolbar

The Standard toolbar is directly under the Menu bar, and it displays icons for commands like New, Open, Save, Print, Copy, and Paste, etc. Additional toolbars contain shortcuts for more specific tasks. These shortcuts appear when you move the cursor over the command on the Standard toolbar. Brief descriptions of the various buttons on the Standard toolbar are:

New: Open a new file.

Open: Activate the Open Drawing dialog box so you can open an existing file.

Save: Resaved an already saved file, or open the Save Drawing dialog box.

Print: Print a drawing.

Cut: Cut selected objects and places them in the Clipboard, from which they can be pasted.

Copy: Copy the selected objects into the Clipboard.

Paste: Paste the contents of the Clipboard into the Drawing area.

Undo: The icon undoes your last action; the drop-down list enables you to undo a series of actions.

Redo: The icon redoes the last undone action; the drop-down list enables you to redo multiple undo actions.

Import: Open the Import dialog box from which you can import non-CorelDRAW files.

Export: Open the Export dialog box. It enables you to export objects or files to other file formats.

Application Launcher: Enable you to start other CorelDRAW applications.

Welcome Screen: Open the Welcome screen.

Zoom levels: The drop-down list enables you to zoom in or zoom out on your drawing.

Snap to: Enable or disable automatic alignment for the grid, guidelines, objects, and dynamic guides.

Property Bar

The Property bar gives the information about any selected object in the Drawing window. The Property bar changes, depending on what object you select in the Drawing window. There is a special Property bar that appears when you do not have any object(s) selected. In Figure 7.3, because the Drawing window does not have any objects yet, the No Selection Property bar displays information about the Drawing page specification, such as page size, etc.

Toolbox

The toolbox is located to the left of the Drawing window and contains the tools to create and edit graphic objects. When you move the cursor over any of the tools in the toolbox, a ToolTip will appear identifying that tool.

The toolbox contains a range of tools that you can use for specific drawing and editing tasks. Some tools let you draw shapes, and other tools let you apply colors, patterns, or other types of fills to objects. Some tools belong to flyouts, which are groups of related tools. A small arrow in the lower right corner of a toolbox button indicates that the tool belongs to a flyout. The last-used tool in the flyout appears on the button. You can access the tools in a flyout by clicking the flyout arrow.

Drawing Page

The section of the Drawing window bounded by the shaded box is called the Drawing page. This is the part of the composition that prints when you send a file to the printer.

You can store graphic images that you do not want to print (but do want to save) in the area of the Drawing window outside the Drawing page. The area outside the Drawing page can be a handy storage space when, for example, if you have a file that you use as a template for a publication. You can save logos, blocks of text, etc., for use in another issue of your publication, but they would print if they are not on the Drawing page.

Document Navigator

Document Navigator is an area at the bottom of the CorelDRAW drawing window. It controls you to add pages in the document and to move between the pages. There are two + sign controls. The first control (located to the left of Document Navigator) is used to insert a page to the left of the selected page while the second control is used to insert a page to the right of the selected page.

Dockers

Docker windows are similar to conventional dialog boxes, but are more interactive. They remain on the screen, until you close them. They can be placed next to the object you are drawing. This provides quick access to the commands placed in the docker window and their subsequent execution. Dockers can be either docked or floating. Docking a toolbar attaches it to the edge of the application window. Undocking a docker detaches it from other parts of the workspace; so it can be easily placed wherever you want.

The Status Bar

The Status bar is located below the Drawing area and gives you important information about a selected object. The Status bar tells you the type of object you have selected and the type of fill. For example, in Figure 7.3, the Status bar shows that the object selected is a polygon and that the fill color is Red. This is very useful when your illustration involves hundreds of objects. The Status bar is a handy way to tell exactly what object is selected.

The Status bar identifies the location of the cursor in X and Y coordinates on the left side of the screen.

The X value (the first one) represents the distance from the left edge of the Drawing page.

The Y value (the second one) represents the distance your current point is from the bottom of the Drawing page.

Color Palette

The Color Palette is located at the right side of the CorelDRAW X5 window. It is a dockable bar which contains solid colors used for filling, outlining and highlighting objects.

Navigator

The Navigator button in CorelDRAW X5 provides a smaller display of the Drawing window, which helps to move around a drawing.

Rulers

Rulers are the measuring tools displayed on the left side and along the top of the drawing window. The rulers help you size and position the objects in your drawing.

Rulers can help you size, align and draw objects accurately. You can hide the rulers or move them to another position in the drawing window. You can also customize the ruler settings to suit your needs. For example, you can set the ruler origin and select a unit of measure.

To control the display of rulers, do this:

1. Click the View menu and choose Rulers. The ruler is displayed when a check mark appears.
2. To hide the ruler click again.

When you move any object, you can see a white dotted line on the left and top rulers. These lines help you to position your object correctly.

Drawing Basic Geometric Figures

Geometrical figures basically consist of lines. Therefore, if you want to create designs in CorelDRAW, you need to begin by creating simple geometrical figures. Basic figures include line, rectangle, ellipse, polygon and star. To draw these shapes on the drawing page, you need to be practiced in handling the mouse. There are number of tools that you can use to draw basic shapes. For example, there is the Freehand Tool, which is used to draw to simple lines, Ellipse Tool to draw ellipse and Spiral Tool to draw spirals. Let us begin by learning the Freehand Tool.

Drawing a Line

A line is a path between two points. Lines can consist of multiple segments, and the line segments can be curved or straight. The line segments are connected by nodes, which are depicted as small squares. CorelDRAW provides various drawing tools that let you draw curved and straight lines, and lines containing both curved and straight segments.

To draw a line by using the Freehand Tool, do this:

1. Create a new blank document.
2. Click the **Curve** flyout from toolbox, and choose the **Freehand** Tool.
3. Click to specify the starting point of the line on the Drawing page.
4. Drag the mouse pointer, and click a location to specify the endpoint of the line as shown in Figure 7.4.

   As you click, a straight line is created by joining the two points.

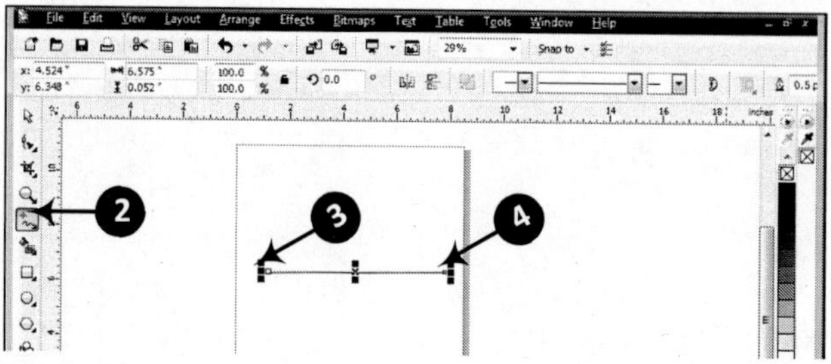

Figure 7.4 Using Freehand tool to draw a straight line

Draw a Rectangle

The Rectangle Tool is used to draw rectangles, such as round, scalloped, and chamfered corners. After drawing the rectangle, you can resize it by using the handles on its boundary or specify its height and width on the Property bar.

To draw a rectangle, do this:

1. Select the **Rectangle** Tool from the **Toolbox**.
2. Click and drag the mouse pointer to draw a rectangle on the Drawing page as shown in Figure 7.5.

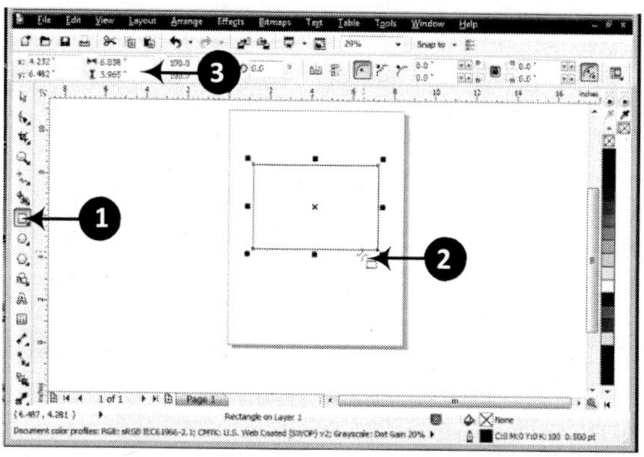

Figure 7.5 Draw a rectangle

3. Type some values in the **Object size** text boxes on the **Property bar** to specify the width and height of the rectangle.

Drawing a Spiral

You can draw two types of spirals: symmetrical and logarithmic. Symmetrical spirals expand evenly so that the distance between each revolution is equal. Logarithmic spirals expand with increasingly larger distances between revolutions. You can set the rate by which a logarithmic spiral expands outward.

To draw a spiral, do this:

1. Click the Object flyout and choose Spiral Tool.
2. Specify the number of revolutions you want in the Spiral revolutions spin box on the Property bar. In our case, we have set the value, which is 8 (See Figure 7.6).
3. Click and drag in the drawing window till the spiral is of the desired size (See Figure 7.6).
4. If you do not want the spiral to be symmetrical, click on the Logarithmic Spiral button in the Property bar.
5. Set the spiral expansion factor by dragging the slider on the Property bar.
6. The spiral is created as shown in Figure 7.6.

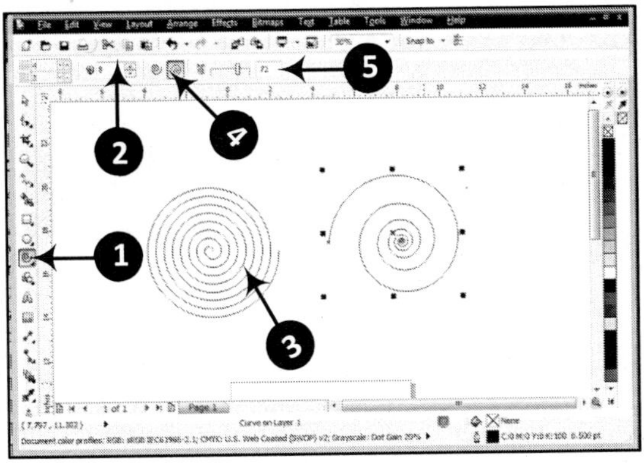

Figure 7.6 Two types of Spiral

Saving a Drawing in CorelDRAW X5

Once a document is created in CorelDRAW, you would like to save it for future use, so that you can open and work on it later according to your requirements. Documents are saved as files with the name and format specified by you.

To save a CorelDRAW document, do this:

1. Click **File** menu and choose **Save As**. The **Save Drawing** dialog box appears as shown in Figure 7.7.
2. Navigate the location where you want to save your document. In our case, the location is **New_DTP_Course** folder as shown in Figure 7.8.
3. Type a name for the document in the **File name:** drop-down list. In our case, we have typed the name **Berry**.

4. Click the **Save** button to save the document as shown in Figure 7.8. The name of the document and its location appears on the **Title** bar.

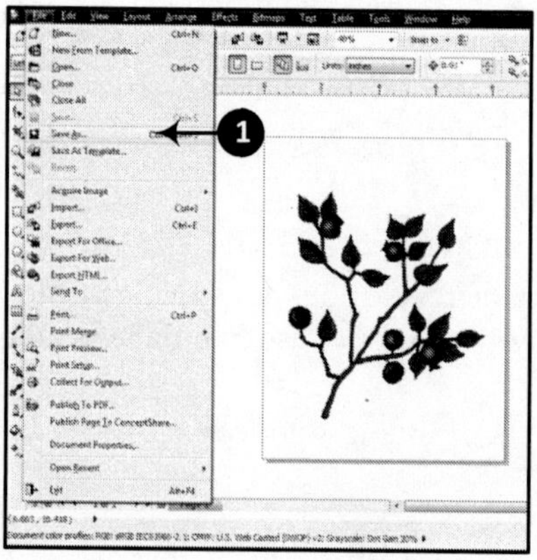

Figure 7.7 Selecting Save As… from the File menu

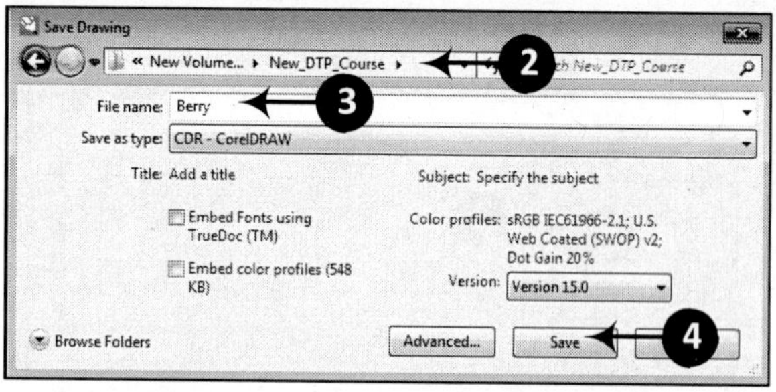

Figure 7.8 Save Drawing dialog box

After saving the document, let us learn to open an existing document in CorelDRAW X5.

Opening an Existing Document

You can also open and use existing documents. Documents in this application are saved in the .cdr format by default. In this section, we are opening the document, which we saved in the previous section.

To open an existing CorelDRAW file, do this:

1. Select **File** menu and choose **Open...** . The **Open Drawing** dialog box appears.
2. Navigate the location where the document you want to open is stored, in the Navigation pane. In our case, the location is **New_DTP_course** folder.
3. Click the file name that you want to open from the location. In our case, we select the **Berry** file as shown in Figure 7.9.
4. Click the **Open** button in the **Open Drawing** dialog box as shown in Figure 7.9.

5. The selected document is opened as shown in Figure 7.10.

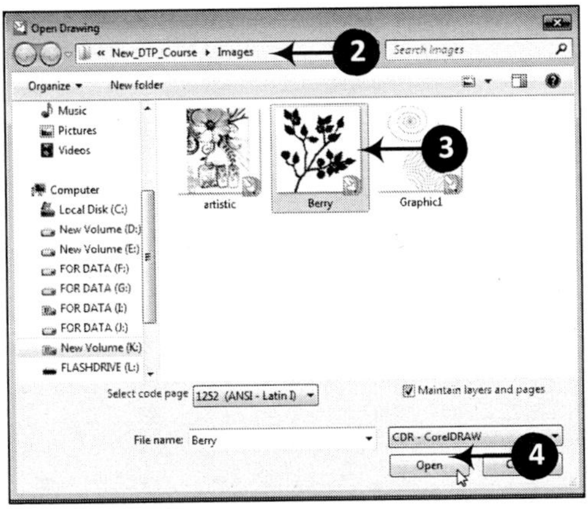

Figure 7.9 Open Drawing dialog box

Figure 7.10 The selected document is opened

Previewing a Drawing

Before printing or exporting a drawing, you can preview the drawing to see how it looks. When you preview a drawing, all the objects in the drawing on the drawing page area are displayed. While previewing an object, the remaining objects of the drawing are hidden.

Previewing a Drawing in the Full Screen Preview Mode

In the Full Screen Preview mode, a preview of the Drawing page appears in the full screen. This mode allows you to view all objects on the Drawing page. You can return to the CorelDRAW window by pressing any key from the keyboard.

To preview a drawing in the Full Screen Preview mode, do this:

1. Click the **View** menu and choose **Full Screen Preview** as shown in Figure 7.11.

2. The drawing page appears in the **Full Screen Preview** mode as shown in Figure 7.12.

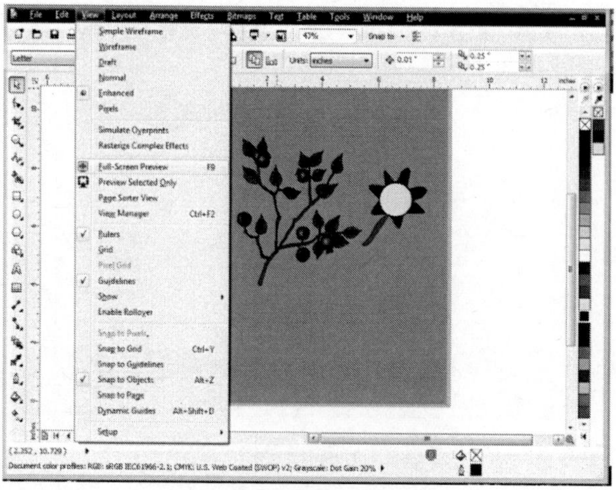

Figure 7.11 Selecting Full Screen Preview in the View menu

Figure 7.12 Full screen preview mode

Viewing a Drawing in Different Views

You can control how you see and work with a page by selecting from six view options. These view modes apply certain predefined values to various elements in your drawings, such as color, toning, linings, contrast and shades effects. When you fill a screen with objects, editing can be slow. Lower quality views can speed up that process. View quality settings from lowest to highest are:

- **Simple Wireframe**—It displays an outline of the drawing by hiding fills, extrusions, contours, drop shadows, and intermediate blend shapes. It also displays the bitmapped images in monochrome.
- **Wireframe**—It displays an outline of the drawing by hiding fills only.

- **Draft**—It displays a drawing's fills and bitmapped images using a low resolution.
- **Normal**—It displays the drawing without postscript fills and without high-resolution bitmapped images.
- **Enhanced**—It displays the drawing with postscript fills and high resolution.
- **Pixel preview**—It displays a pixel-based rendition of the drawing which allows you to zoom in on an area of an object, then position and size the object more precisely. This view also lets you see what the drawing will look like when it is exported to a bitmap file format.

Figure 7.13 shows the different views of the same drawing. The view you select affects the time it takes to open or to refresh a drawing.

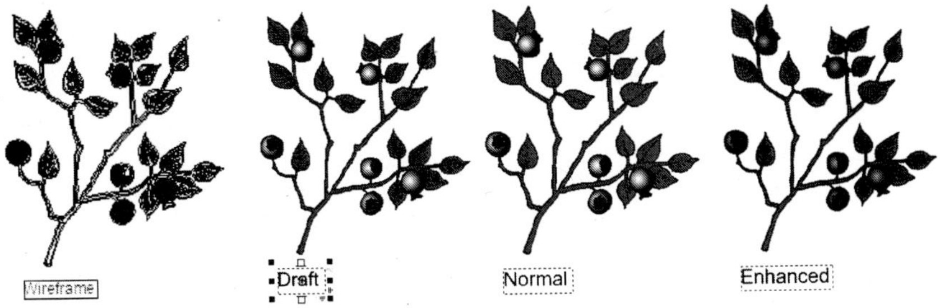

Figure 7.13 Different views of an image

Working with Page Layout

CorelDRAW X5 allows you to specify the size, orientation, unit of scale and background of the page of drawing. You can customize and display page grids and guidelines to help you to organize objects and place them exactly where you want. Also, you can add and delete pages of the document.

Modifying the Size and Orientation of a Drawing Page

CorelDRAW provides two ways to define the size of the Drawing page by selecting a preset page size, and by creating a custom page size by specifying the dimensions of the page. You can also adjust the page size and orientation settings to match the standard paper settings for printing.

To modify the size and orientation of a page, do this:

1. Click the **Paper Type/Size** down arrow button, it shows a list of options appears as shown in Figure 7.14.
2. Select a paper type option from the drop-down list. In our case, we have chosen a **Custom** option as shown in Figure 7.14.
3. Type a value in the **Page dimensions** spin boxes to specify the height and width for the Drawing page. In our case, we have type 8.0″ as the width and 10.0″ as the height of the page as shown in Figure 7.15.

4. Type a value in the Zoom level combo box to specify the level of zoom you want.
5. Click anywhere on the Drawing page to apply changes.

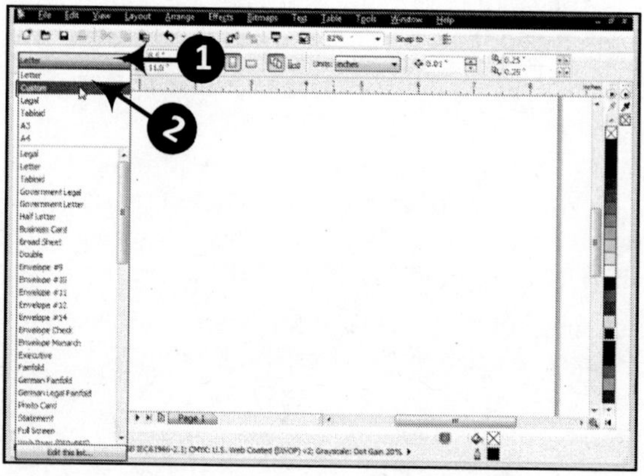

Figure 7.14 Selecting custom size from the Property bar

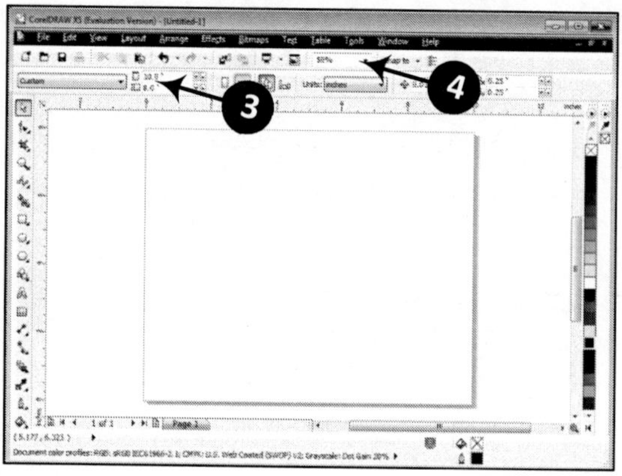

Figure 7.15 Type a value in the page dimensions

Setting the Background of a Drawing Page

You can set the background color of a page. You can apply a solid color for background if you want a uniform background to the page or you can even apply a bitmap image as a background for your page.

To set the background color of a drawing page, do this:

1. Click **Layout** menu and choose **Page Background...** .

   The **Options** dialog box appears as shown in Figure 7.16. It is divided in two panes, namely the left pane and the right pane. The left pane shows different categories and the right pane displays the options related to the selected category.

2. Click the (+) key besides the **Document** category from the left pane of the Options dialog box. The selected category expands to display various subcategories.
3. Select the **Background** subcategory. The related options to set the background of the Drawing page are displayed on the right pane.
4. Click the **Solid** radio button. The list box located beside the Solid radio button is activated.
5. Click the down arrow button of the list box. A **Color palette** appears as shown in Figure 7.16.
6. Select the desired color you want to set as a background from the Color palette.
7. Click the **OK** button. The selected color is applied as a background to the Drawing page.

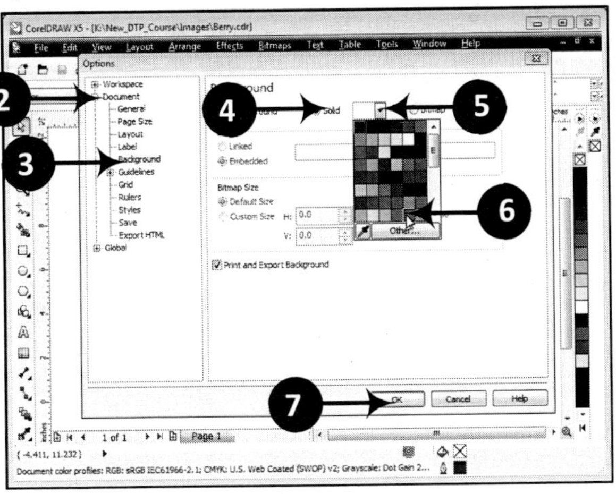

Figure 7.16 Options dialog box

Adding, Renaming, and Deleting Drawing Page in a Document

The Drawing page you add is named Untitled-1 by default. The pages inserted can be renamed according to your requirement for easy reference and can also be deleted.

Adding a Drawing Page

You can add any number of Drawing pages in the document. The inserted pages can be added before or after the current page.

To add a Drawing page in the document, do this:

1. Select the location where you want the new page to be inserted in the document, from **Document Navigator**. In our case, we have selected **Page 1**.
2. Click on the **Layout** menu, and choose **Insert Page...** as shown in Figure 7.17. The **Insert Page** dialog box appears as shown in Figure 7.18.

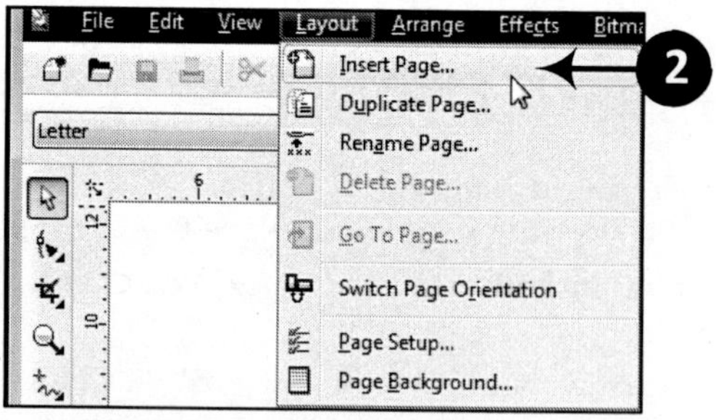

Figure 7.17 Selecting Insert Page

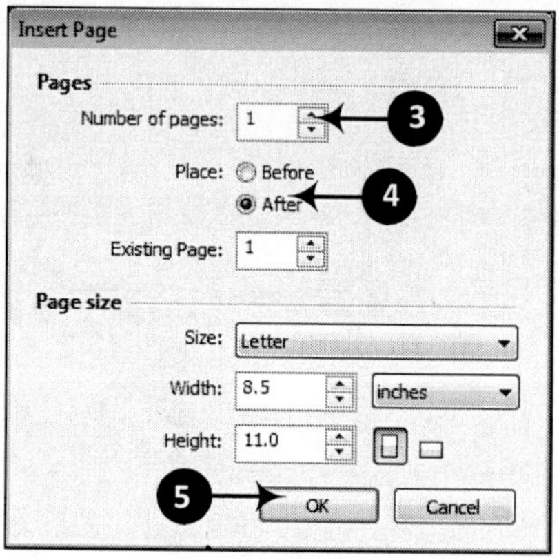

Figure 7.18 Insert Page dialog box

3. Specify how many pages you want to insert in the **Number of page:** spin box. In our case, we have typed 2.
4. Select a radio button beside the **Place** option, to specify where you want the new page(s) to appear in the document. In our case, we have selected the **After** radio button as shown in Figure 7.18.
5. Click the **OK** button in the **Insert Page** dialog box.

   Two pages are inserted at the specified location (i.e., after page 1) and displayed on Document Navigator.

Renaming a Drawing Page

You can rename the Drawing page to your requirements.

To rename a page, do this:

1. Select the page that you want to rename from **Document Navigator**. In our case, we have selected Page 3 as shown in Figure 7.19.
2. Click the **Layout** menu and choose **Rename Page...** .
3. The **Rename Page** dialog box appears as shown in Figure 7.20.
4. Type the new name for the **Drawing page** in the text box under the **Page**

name: option. In our case, we have typed the name **Graphi-1** as shown in Figure 7.20.

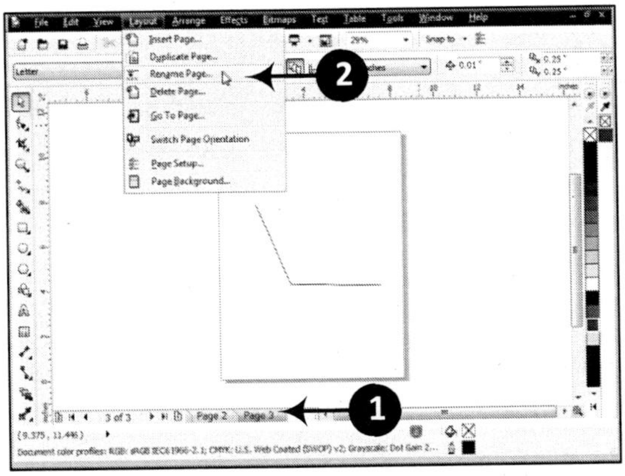

Figure 7.19 Selecting Rename page

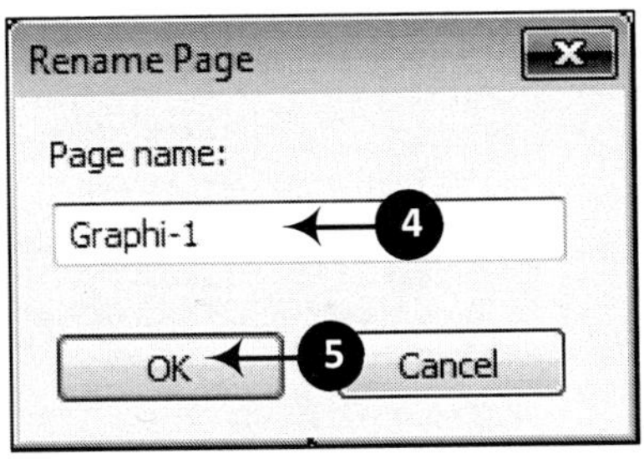

Figure 7.20 Rename Page dialog box

5. Click the **OK** button in the **Rename Page** dialog box, as shown in Figure 7.20.
6. The Drawing page will be renamed with this new name, and can be viewed in the Document Navigator.

Deleting a Drawing Page

You can delete an individual Drawing page or a range of Drawing pages from the document by using the Delete Page option.

To delete a Drawing page, do this:

1. Select the page you want to delete from the Drawing page. In our case, we have typed Page 3.
2. Click the **Layout** menu and choose **Delete Page...** .
3. The **Delete Page** dialog box appears.
4. Type the page number of the page you want to delete, in the, **Delete page:** option spinner box.

5. To delete multiple pages, click the **Through to page:** spinner box, and set the page number up to which you want to delete, in the spinner box.
6. Click the **OK** button in the **Delete Page** dialog box.
7. The selected Drawing page is deleted in the Document Navigator.

Closing a Document and Quitting CorelDRAW X5 Application

After you have finished working in CorelDRAW, you can close the application. However, before you must save the drawing and then close it. This is important because saving helps to retain the changes made in a document, so that next time you open the document, you can continue working with all the changes intact. In case, you forget to save your files and attempt to quit the CorelDRAW window, a message box appears, asking you whether you want to save changes made in the documents. You need to ensure that all opened documents are saved and closed before quitting the CorelDRAW application.

To close a drawing, do this:

1. Click the **File** menu and choose **Close** option.

To quit CorelDraw application, do this:

2. Click the **File** menu and choose **Exit**.

CHAPTER 8

Working with Lines

Introduction

Lines are the basic elements of drawing. Lines are used to create different shapes, which can be either regular, enclosed geometric shapes, such as rectangles and squares. The boundary of a shape is also known as its outline. You can edit the outline of the object to change its shape. CorelDRAW X5 provide a number of drawing tools, such as Freehand, Bezier, Artistic Pen and Polyline, which you can use to create lines, outlines shapes and curves.

In this Chapter, you learn about drawing lines using various tools, drawing calligraphic liens and changing the appearance of line and outlines. In addition, you also learn about some advanced editing tools, such as the Fillet, Scallop and Chamfer tools.

Let us begin by learning to draw a simple curve from a line.

Drawing Curves using Lines

A line is a path between two points. Lines can consist of multiple segments, and the line segments can be curved or straight. The line segments are connected by nodes, which are depicted as small squares. CorelDRAW provides various drawing tools that let you draw curved and straight lines, and lines containing both curved and straight segments. You can also draw a curve using various tools, such as the Freehand, Bezier, Artistic Media, Pen, Polyline, 3 Point Cuvre and Dimension tools. The Freehand Tool is a default tool is selected on the Curve Tools flyout in the Toolbox.

To draw a curve by using the 3-Point Curve tool, do this:

1. Click the **Curve** flyout, and then select **3-Point Curve** tool from the toolbox.
2. On the Drawing page, click where you want to start the curve, and drag to where you want the curve to end as shown in Figure 8.1.

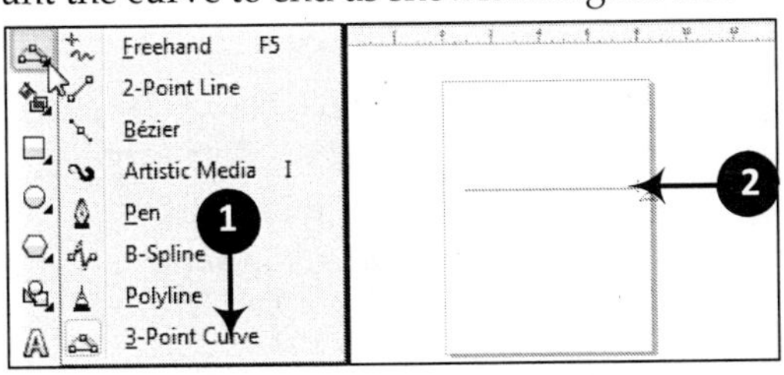

Figure 8.1 Draw a curve by using the 3-point curve tool

3. Release the mouse button, and click where you want the center of the curve to be upward or downward on the Drawing page as shown in Figure 8.2.
4. A curve drawn by specifying width and height is shown in Figure 8.3.

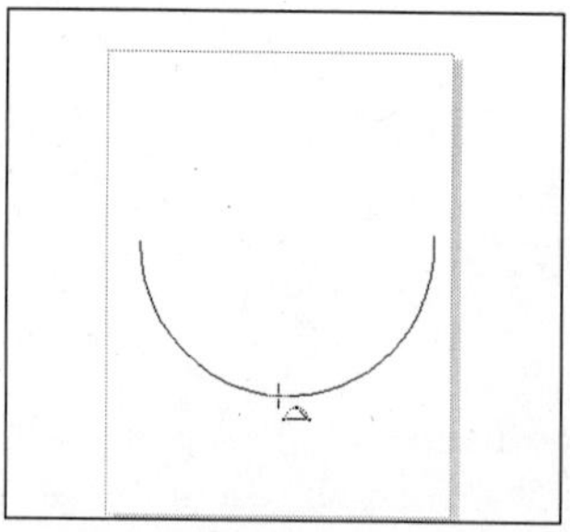

Figure 8.2

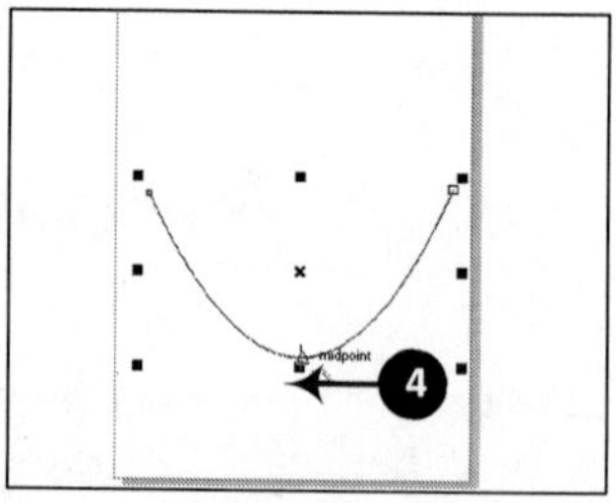

Figure 8.3

Drawing a Calligraphic Line

Calligraphic lines are similar to lines drawn using a calligraphic pen. Such lines change their thickness according to the direction of the line. Line's thickness also varies depending upon the angle of the pen nib.

To draw a Calligraphic line, do this:

1. Click the **Curve** flyout and choose the **Artistic Media Tool** from the Toolbox.
2. Click the **Calligraphic** button on the Property bar as shown in Figure 8.4.

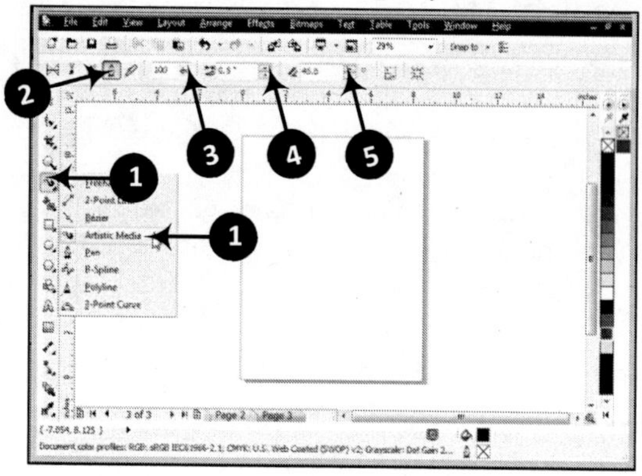

Figure 8.4 Selecting Artistic media tool

3. If you want to smoothen the edges of the line, type a value in the **Freehand Smoothing** spinner box on the Property bar. If Property bar is not visible, right click the tool in the toolbox, and check Property bar.
4. Type the value in the **Stroke Width** spinner box on the Property bar, to specify the width of the stroke for the calligraphic line. In our case, we have typed the value 0.6" as shown in Figure 8.4.
5. Type a value in the **Calligraphic Angle** box on the Property bar, to specify the angle for the stroke in the calligraphy.
6. Click and drag the mouse-pointer to make a desired shape from the line. A Calligraphic line appears as shown in Figure 8.5.

Now, let us learn to draw pressure-sensitive lines in CorelDRAW X5.

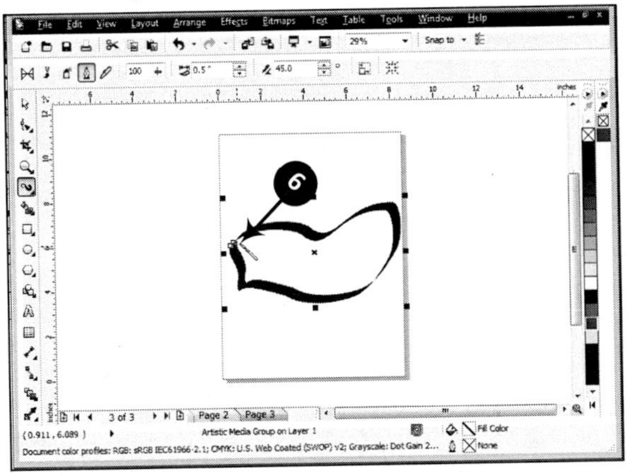

Figure 8.5 Calligraphic curved line

Drawing Pressure-sensitive Line or Curve

Pressure-sensitive lines are those lines with curved edges that vary in width or thickness along a path. This effect can be created using mouse or a pressure sensitive pen.

To draw a pressure-sensitive line or curve, do this:

1. Click the Curve flyout and choose **Artistic Media** Tool.
2. Click the **Pressure** button on the Property bar as shown in Figure 8.6.

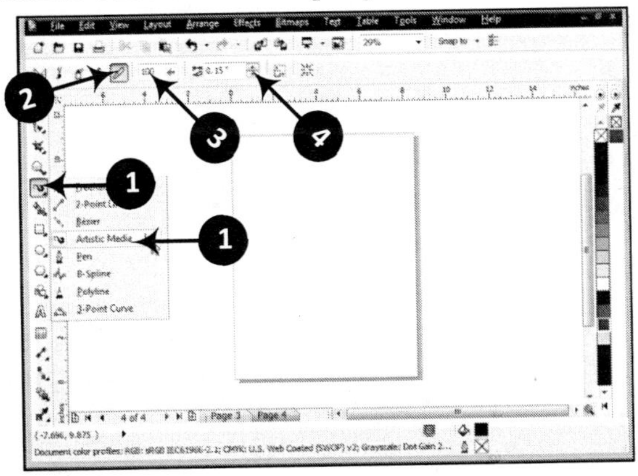

Figure 8.6 Selecting Artistic Media Tool

3. To smooth the edges of the line, type a value in the **Freehand Smoothing** spinner box on the Property bar.
4. Type the value in the **Stroke Width** spinner box on the Property bar, to specify the width of the stroke for the line. In our case, we have typed the value **0.15"** as shown in Figure 8.7.

5. Click and drag until the line is of the shape you want. Figure 8.7 shows a pressure-sensitive line.

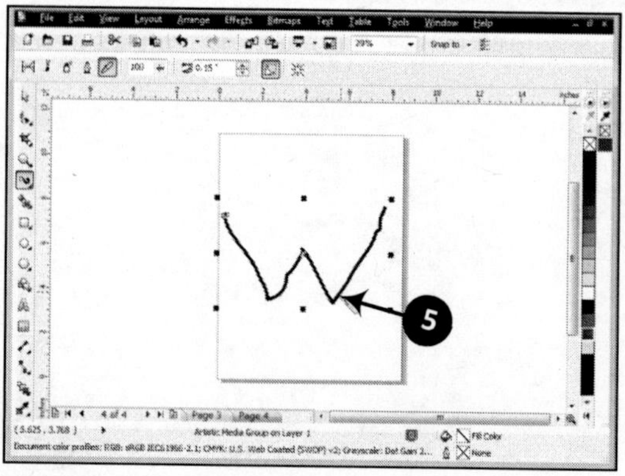

Figure 8.7 Drawing a Pressure Sensitive shape

Working with Outlines

In CorelDRAW, the Outline Pen Tool is used to change the thickness and color of the boundary or outline of an object. You can assign and apply formatting to outlines of all objects in CorelDRAW X5. You can quickly define outlines from the Property bar or in more detail from the Outline Tool flyout. You can set the width, style, color and attributes of outlines using the outline pen flyout. The Outline Color tool, which allows you to create your own custom colors, add the colors to the Color palette, and apply them to the outlines.

Define Outline Settings

To set the outline details you will need to use the Outline Pen dialog box. Outline dialog box offers many features for outlining objects.

To specify outline settings, do this:

1. Open a document containing shapes. In our case, we have opened the document named **Berry**, which contains Polygon.
2. Select the **Pick** Tool from the toolbox.
3. Select the object for which you want to define settings.
4. Click the Outline Tools from the Toolbox. A flyout appears as shown in Figure 8.8.
5. Select the Outline Pen Tool from the flyout.

   The Outline Pen dialog box appears as shown in Figure 8.9.
6. In the Ouline Pen dialog box, click the down arrow beside the **Color:** option and select the desired color from the Color palette for the outline. In our case, we have selected the **Sky Blue** color in Color: option.
7. Type a value in the **Width:** drop-down list and choose a width and unit of measurement for drawing the outline.

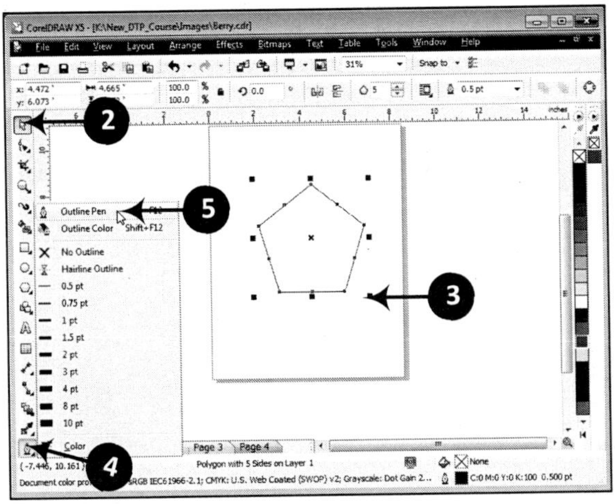

Figure 8.8 Selecting Outline Pen Tool

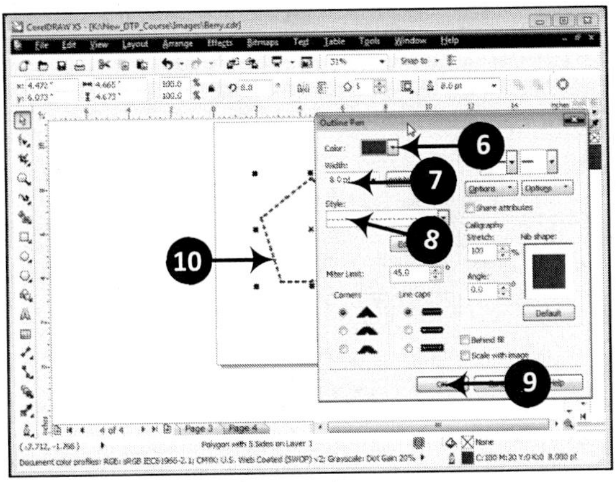

Figure 8.9 Drawing a Pressure-sensitive shape

8. Click the down-arrow below the **Style:** option, and select a style option from the outline. In our case, we have selected *Solid*, *Dash* like or *dot* like line styles from this list.
9. Click the **OK** button to apply the values set in the **Outline Pen** dialog box, as shown in Figure 8.9.
10. The Outline of the Polygon changes as you have set in preceding steps, as shown in Figure 8.9.

Creating a Calligraphic Outline

Calligraphic lines are similar to the lines drawn using a calligraphic pen. Such lines change their thickness according to the direction of the line. Line's thickness also varies depending upon the angle of the pen nib.

To create a calligraphic outline, do this:

1. Select an object using the Pick Tool. In our case, we have selected an ellipse.
2. Click the arrow on the bottom-right of the Outline Tool. The Outline Tool flyout appears as shown in Figure 8.10.

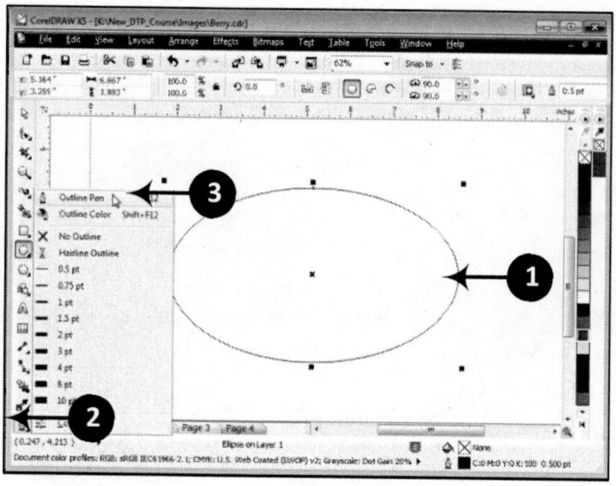

Figure 8.10 Selecting Outline Pen Tool

3. Select the **Outline Pen** Tool on the flyout, as shown in Figure 8.10. An **Outline Pen** dialog box appears, as shown in Figure 8.11.

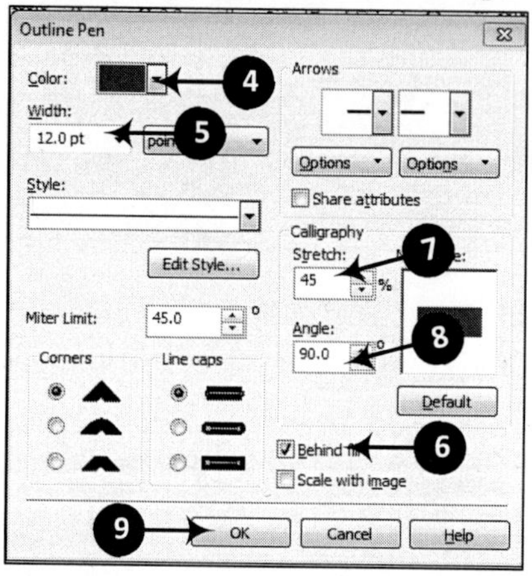

Figure 8.11 Outline Pen dialog box

4. In the **Outline Pen** dialog box, click the down arrow beside the **Color:** option and select the desired color from the Color palette for the outline. In our case, we have selected the **Sky Blue** color.
5. Type a value in the **Width:** drop-down list and choose a width and unit of measurement for drawing the outline.

6. Select the **Behind fill** check box if you want the outline color behind the object.
7. Type a value in the **Stretch:** spinner box under the **Calligraphy** group to apply a stretched effect on the outline. In our case, we have typed the value 45 as shown in Figure 8.10.
8. Type a value in the **Angle:** spinner box to specify the angle of rotation of the pen. In our case, the calligraphic angle is 90.
9. Click the **OK** button.
10. The outline of an ellipse changes to show the calligraphic effect according you set in the **Outline Pen** dialog box as shown in Figure 8.12.

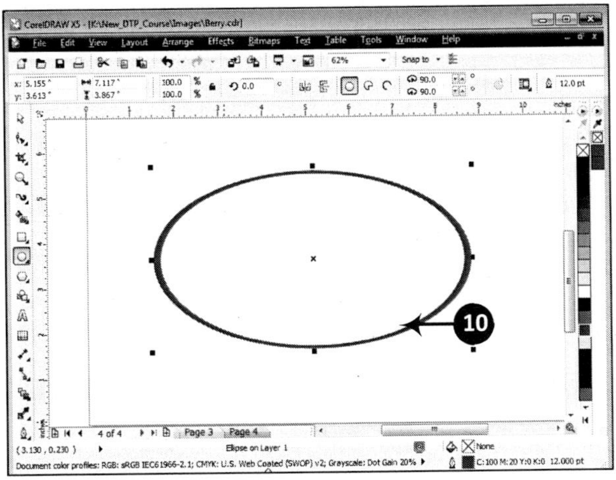

Figure 8.12 Applied Calligraphy settings

Adding an Arrowhead

CorelDRAW X5 lets you define outlines in the form of arrows to your objects. A wide variety of arrows are available and you can choose an arrow style of your choice from the exhaustive range available.

To add an arrowhead to a line, do this:

1. Create a line by using the **Freehand** Tool from the toolbox.
2. Open the **Outline Pen** tools flyout and select the Outline Pen Tool, as shown in Figure 8.13.

   An **Outline Pen** dialog box appears.
3. Type a value in the **Width:** drop-down list to specify the width of the arrow and the line. In our case, we have typed the value 8.0.
4. Click the down-arrow button under the **Arrows** section to open the drop-down list.
5. Click the desired shape of the arrowhead in the drop-down list, to define the shape at the **starting point** of the line as shown in Figure 8.13.

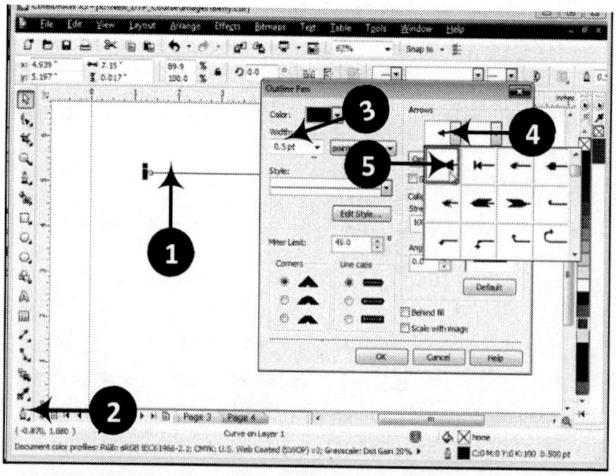

Figure 8.13 Outline Pen dialog box

6. Click the down-arrow button, to open the adjacent drop-down list.
7. Click a shape of the arrowhead in the drop-down list, to define the shape at the **ending point** of the line as shown in Figure 8.14.
8. Click the **OK** button to set all the changes made in the Outline Pen dialog box, as shown in Figure 8.14.
9. The line appears with the selected start and end arrowheads as shown in Figure 8.15.

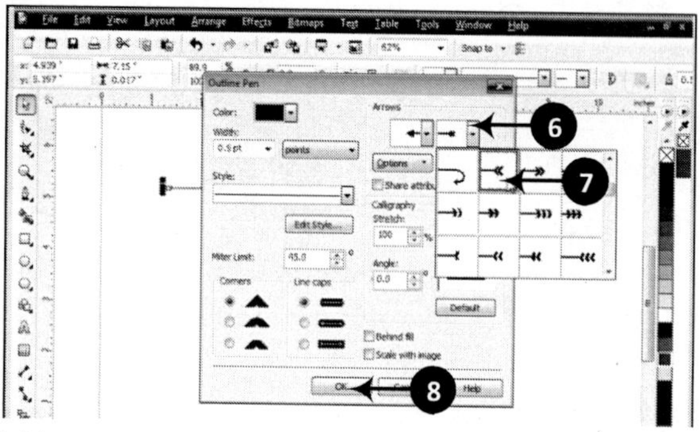

Figure 8.14 Selecting arrow head in the Outline Pen dialog box

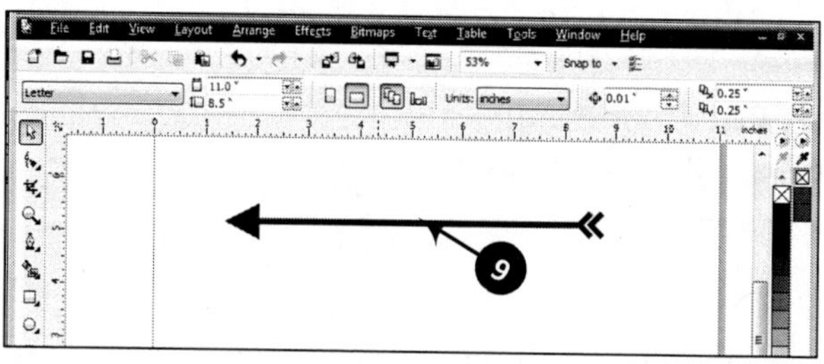

Figure 8.15 The line has been changed to arrowhead

Modifying Basic Shapes

In CorelDRAW, the most complex shape you create begin as simple shapes, such as square, rectangle, ellipse, polygon and start. These basic shapes are the fundamental to the process of creating the final shape. In this Section, you will learn to modify the basic shapes, as well as change one shape into another shape.

Rounding the Corners of a Rectangle or a Square

Creating shapes includes changing or editing one shape to another until you have the shape of your choice. For example, you can edit a shape of a rectangle by rounding its corners to create a round square.

To change the corners of a rectangle or square to a round shape, do this:

1. Select the **Rectangle Tool** from the **toolbox** and draw a rectangle or square on the Drawing page as shown in Figure 8.16.
2. Type values in the corner radius spinner boxes on the Property bar to specify the roundness of the corners of the rectangle.
3. The rectangle appears with rounded corners as shown in Figure 8.16.

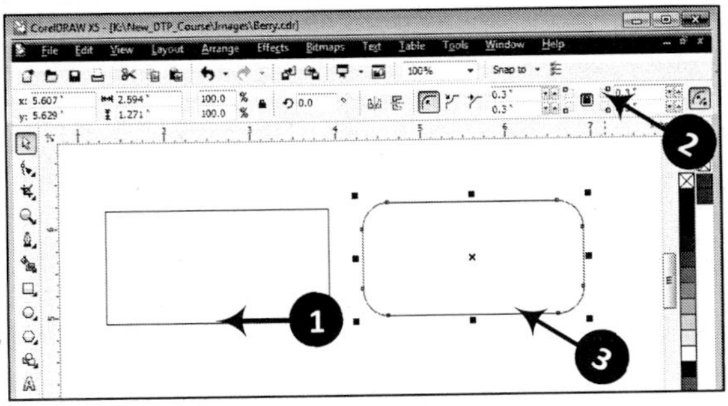

Figure 8.16 Changing the corners of a rectangle to a round shape

4. Type values in the **corner radius** spinner boxes on the Property bar to specify the roundness of the corners of the rectangle.
5. The rectangle appears with rounded corners as shown in Figure 8.16.

Converting an Ellipse into a Pie

The small square points at the end of a line or a curve segment are called nodes. These nodes can be dragged or pulled anywhere to change the shape of a line, curve or other shapes. In this Section, you learn to change an ellipse to a pie.

To convert an ellipse into a pie, do this:

1. Select the Ellipse Tool from the toolbox and draw an ellipse on the document.
2. Click the arrow on the right side of the Shape Edit Tools from the toolbox.
3. Click the Shape Tool from the flyout.
4. Select the node that appears on the outline of the ellipse as shown in Figure 8.17.

5. Drag and release the selected node till the shape of ellipse changes to a pie of the desired shape as shown in Figure 8.17.
6. The desired shape of the pie appears as shown in Figure 8.17.

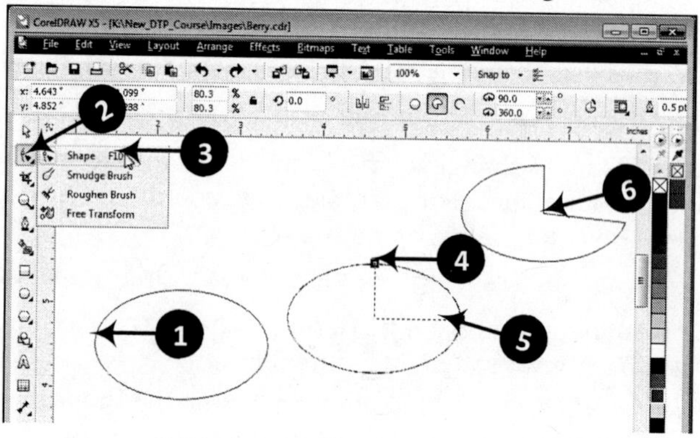

Figure 8.17 Convert ellipse to pie shape

Modifying the Lines of a Shape

CorelDRAW provides various tools to modify the lines of shapes. Some of these tools are Cropping, Splitting and Erasing tools. The Crop Tool helps to remove unwanted areas from an object. The Splitting Tool enables you to break the objects into two parts. The Eraser Tool let you to delete unwanted portions from the objects.

Cropping Objects

When cropping objects, you define a rectangular area (cropping area) that you want to keep. Object portions outside the cropping area are removed. You can specify the exact position and size of the cropping area, and you can rotate and resize it. You can also remove the cropping area.

To crop an object, do this:

1. Select the objects that you want to crop.
2. Click the **Crop Tool** from the toolbox as shown in Figure 8.18.

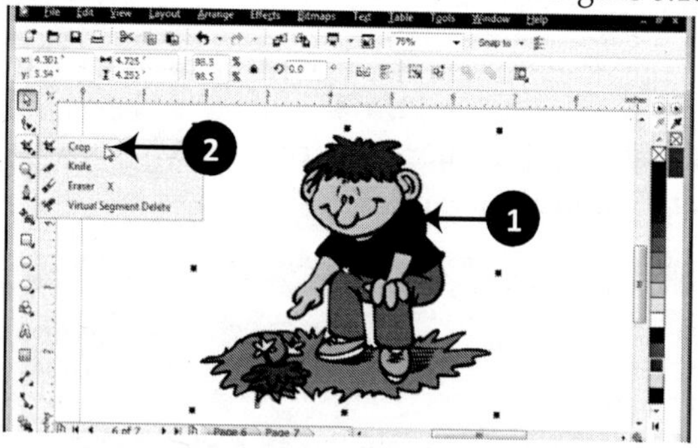

Figure 8.18 Selecting Crop tool

3. Click and drag the mouse pointer to define a cropping area. The entire drawing window, excluding the cropping area, turns gray as shown in Figure 8.18.
4. Press Enter key or double-click inside the cropping area. The cropped object appears and the gray highlight disappears, as shown in Figure 8.19.

Figure 8.19 Cropped an image

Splitting Objects

You can split a bitmap or vector object in two and reshape it by redrawing its path. You can split a closed object along a straight or jagged line. CorelDRAW lets you choose between splitting an object into two objects, or leaving it as one object composed of two or more subpaths. You can specify whether you want to close paths automatically or keep them open.

To split object, do this:

1. Select the objects that you want to cut. In our case, the Polygon is selected. Splitting is always performed on a selected object.
2. Select the **Knife Tool** from the flyout as shown in Figure 8.20.

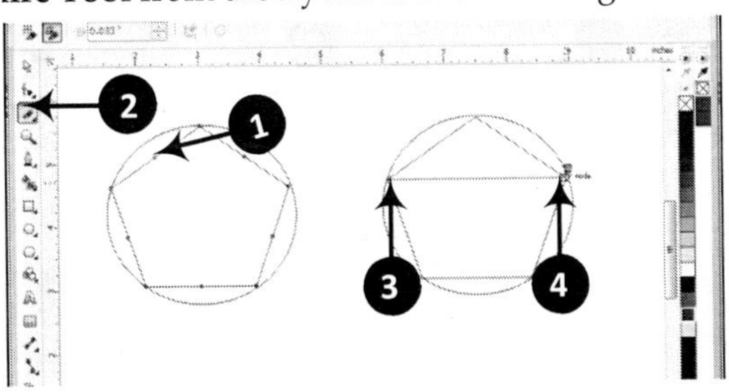

Figure 8.20 Selecting Knife tool

3. Position the Knife Tool over the object's outline where you want to start cutting.
4. Position the Knife Tool over the object's outline where you want to stop cutting, and click again.

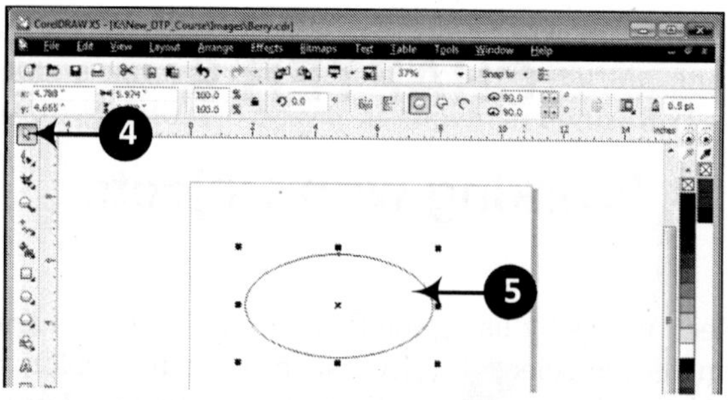

Figure 9.2 Selecting object with Pick Tool

Deleting an Object

Deleting means removing or erasing an object. Deletion helps you to remove unwanted objects from the Drawing window.

To delete an object from the Drawing page, do this:

1. Select the **Pick** Tool, and then select the object you want to delete. In our case, we have selected an Ellipse as shown in Figure 9.3.
2. Select **Edit** menu on the **Menu** bar. A drop-down menu appears as shown in Figure 9.3.
3. Select **Delete** option. Or press the **Del** key from the keyboard.
4. The selected object is deleted from the Drawing page.

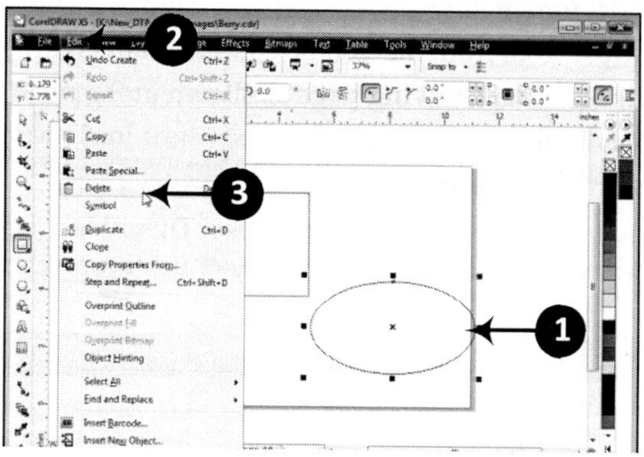

Figure 9.3 Selecting Delete option from the Edit menu

Sizing and Scaling Objects

CorelDRAW lets you size and scale objects. In both cases, you change the dimensions of an object proportionally by preserving its aspect ratio. You can change the dimensions of an object by specifying values on the Property bar or by dragging the control handles around the object. When you scale an object, you change its dimensions by a specified percentage from the Transformation docker or by dragging the object from its edges.

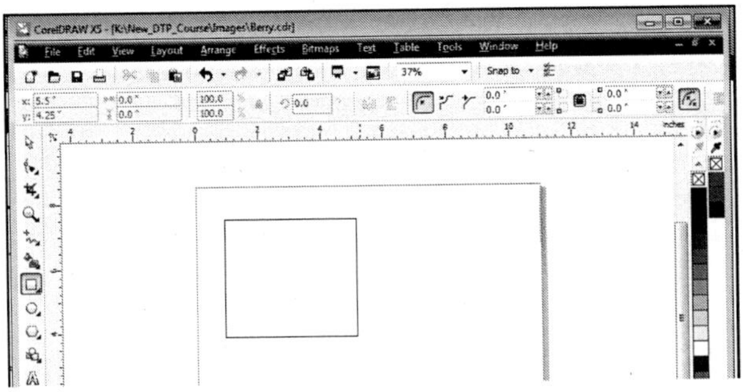

Figure 9.4 The selected object gets deleted

change the dimensions of an object by specifying values on the Property bar or by dragging the control handles around the object. When you scale an object, you change its dimensions by a specified percentage from the Transformation docker or by dragging the object from its edges.

Sizing an Object

Sizing an object refers to the process of changing the dimensions of the object. You can also size an object to multiples of its original size. For this, press the left mouse button and the **Ctrl** key, and drag one of the corner selection handles on the selected object. After the desired size of the object, release the mouse button.

To size an object from its corner, do this:

1. Select an object by using the Pick Tool from the Toolbox.
2. Click any of the corner selection handles that appear around the complex star, as shown in Figure 9.5.
3. Drag and release the selected corner handle to re-size the object when the desired size of the start shape as shown in Figure 9.6.

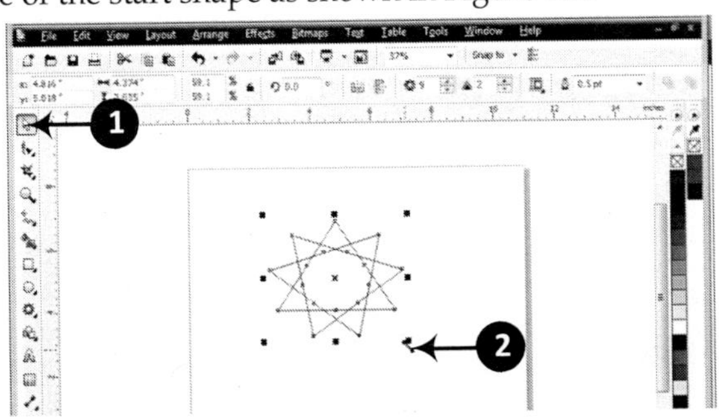

Figure 9.5 Selecting corner handles to size the object

Scaling an Object

Scaling refers to changing the dimensions of an object by a specified percentage. It also changes to the dimensions of the object are made proportionally so that its aspect ratio is preserved.

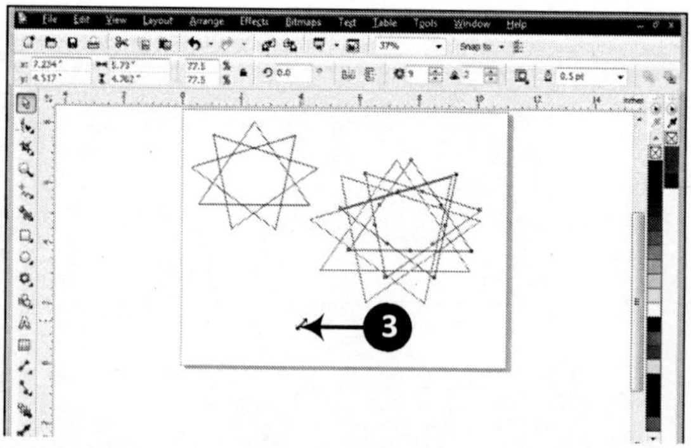

Figure 9.6 The selected object gets deleted

To scale an object, do this:

1. Select the object you want to scale by using the **Pick** Tool from the Toolbox.
2. Click **Window** menu and then select **Dockers**. A sub menu appears.
3. Select **Transformations** and then choose **Scale** from the sub menu as shown in Figure 9.7.

   The Transformation docker appears at the right side of the Drawing window as shown in 9.7.
4. Clear the **Proportional** check box.
5. Type the value in the **H:** spinner box under the Scale: section. In our case, we have typed the value 100.
6. Type the value in the **V:** spinner box under the Scale: section. In our case, we have typed the value 150.
7. Click **Apply** button to apply the changes.

The scale of the object changes according to the values applied in the Transformation docker, as shown in Figure 9.8.

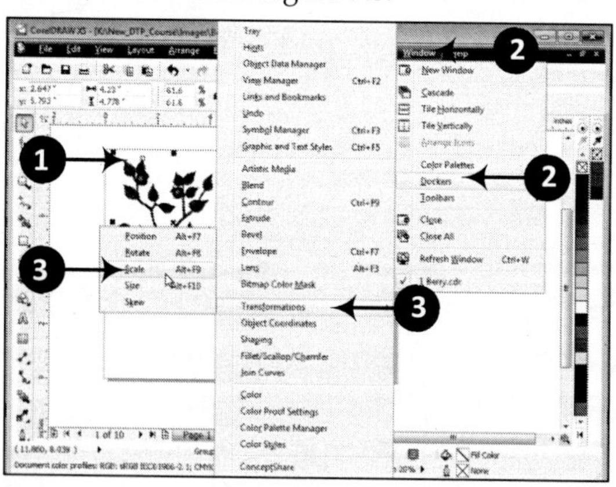

Figure 9.7 Selecting Scale option from the window menu

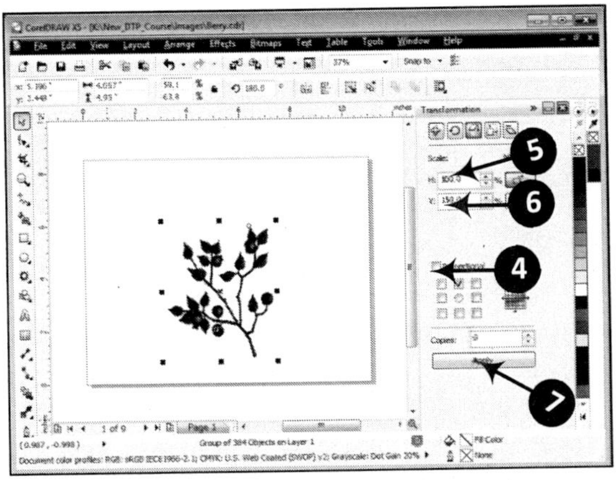

Figure 9.8 Scaling an object in the Transformation docker window

Rotating an Object

CorelDRAW lets you rotate and create mirror images of objects. You can rotate an object by specifying horizontal and vertical coordinates. A negative value for the angle of ration causes the object to rotate clockwise, while a positive value causes an anit-clockwise direction. You can move the center of rotation to a specific ruler coordinate or to a point that is relative to the current position of the object.

Mirroring an object flips it from left to right or from top to bottom. By default, the mirror anchor point is in the center of the object.

To rotate an object, do this:

1. Select the object you want to rotate by using the **Pick** Tool form the Toolbox.
2. Select **Rotate** button in the **Transformation** docker window as shown in Figure 9.9.

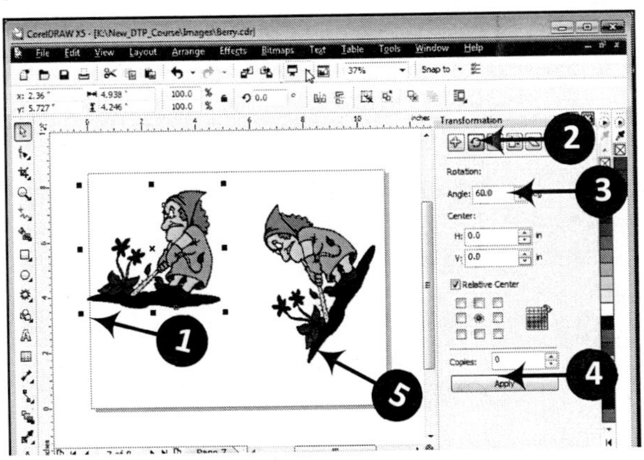

Figure 9.9 Selecting rotate option from the window menu

3. Type a value in the **Angle:** text box to specify the angle by which you want to rotate. Or

   Use rotation handles to rotate an object or drag a rotation handle clockwise or counterclockwise on a selected object.
4. Click **Apply** button to apply the changes as shown in Figure 9.9.
5. The object rotates by the specified angle as shown in Figure 9.9.

Mirroring an Object

Mirror an object refers to the flipping of the object from left to right or from top to bottom. By default, the anchor point of a mirrored object appears at the center of the object.

To mirror an object, do this:

1. Select the object by using the Pick Tool from the Toolbox.
2. In the **Transformation docker** window, select the **Vertical** mirror button in the Mirror category as shown in Figure 9.10.
3. Click **Apply** button to apply the changes.
4. The object, with the mirror effect applied on it, is shown in Figure 9.10.

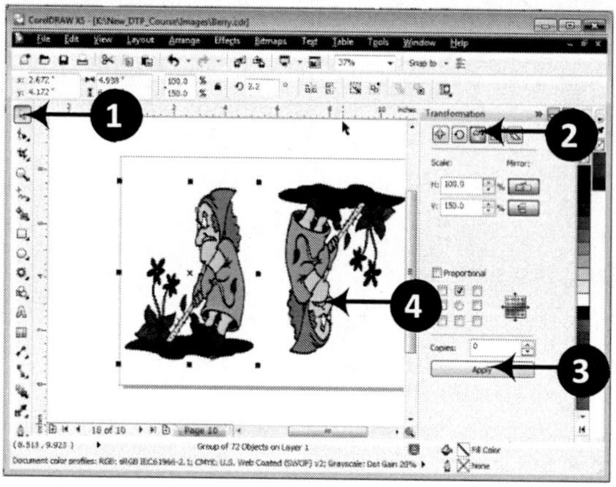

Figure 9.10 Mirror an object in the Transformation docker window

Aligning and Distributing Objects

CorelDRAW X5 lets you align and distribute objects in a drawing. You can align objects with each other and with parts of the drawing page, such as, center, edges. And you can also align multiple objects with the center of the drawing page horizontally or vertically. Single or multiple objects can also be arranged along the edge of the page.

Distributing objects automatically adds spacing between objects, on their width, height and center points. You can distribute objects so that their center points or selected edges (for example, top or right) appear at equal intervals. You can also distribute objects so that there is equal space between them. You can distribute objects over the extent of the boundary box surrounding them or over the entire drawing page.

Aligning an Object with Other Objects

You can align objects with each other and with parts of the drawing page, such as the center, edges, and grid. When you align objects with objects, you can line them up by their centers or by their edges.

To align an object with other objects in a document, do this:

1. Select the objects with a **Pick Tool** from the Toolbox.
2. Click **Arrange** menu. Choose **Align and Distribute**. The sub menu options appears, click **Align and Distribute...** .

   The **Align and Distribute** dialog box appears as shown in Figure 9.11. The **Align tab** is selected by default.

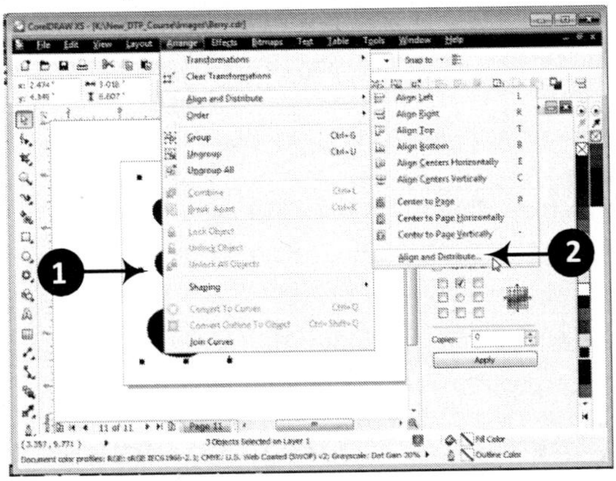

Figure 9.11 Selecting Align and Distribute from the Arrange menu

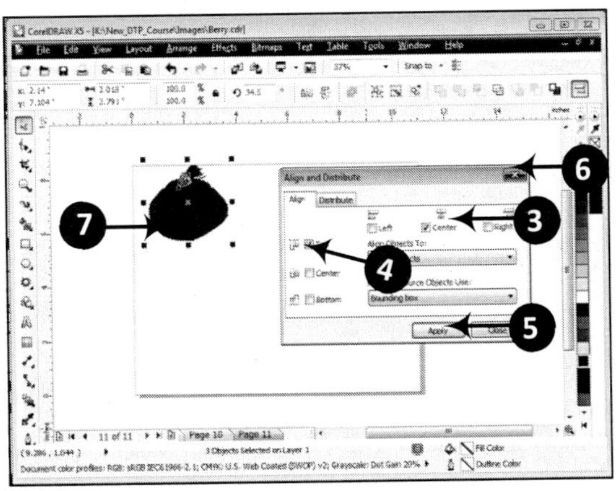

Figure 9.12 The object align at top and center aligned

3. Select the **Center** check box in the Align tab to align object vertically.

4. Select the **Top** check box in the Align tab to align object horizontally.
5. Click the **Apply** button to apply the changes you have made as shown in Figure 9.12.
6. Click the **Close** button to close the **Align and Distribute** dialog box.
7. The objects, after alignment, are as shown in Figure 9.12.

Distributing Objects

CorelDRAW allows you to distribute objects horizontally or vertically at equal spacing with respect to their center points, widths and heights.

To distribute objects, do this:

1. Select the objects with the **Pick** Tool. Click **Arrange** menu. Select **Align and Distribute** option. Then select **Align and Distribute...** option from the sub menu. The **Align and Distribute** dialog box appears on the screen.
2. In the **Align and Distribute** dialog box, click the **Distribute** tab as shown in Figure 9.13.
3. To distribute the objects horizontally, click **Left** check box option from the top-right row.
4. To distribute the objects vertically, click **Top** check box option from the column on the left as shown in Figure 9.13.
5. Select the **Extent of page** check box in the **Distribute to** group.
6. Click the **Apply** button to apply the changes.
7. Click the **Close** button to close the Align and Distribute dialog box.
8. The objects, after distribution, are shown in Figure 9.14.

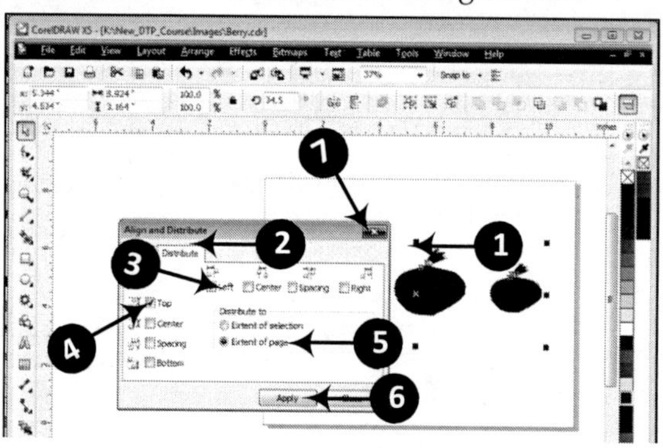

Figure 9.13 Selecting Distribute tab of Align and Distribute dialog box

Grouping in CorleDRAW

When you group two or more objects, they are treated as a single unit but retain their individual attributes. Grouping lets you apply the same formatting, properties, and other changes to all the objects within the group at the same time. In addition, grouping helps prevent accidental changes to the position of an object in relation to other objects. You can also create nested groups by grouping together existing groups.

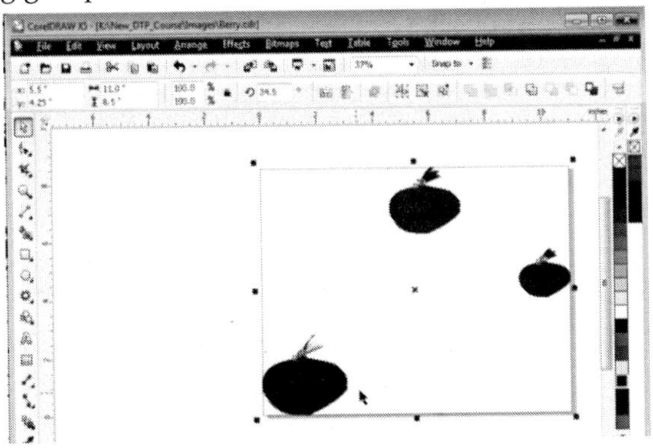

Figure 9.14

To group two or more objects, do this:

1. Open a document containing two or more objects.
2. Select the objects by using the **Pick** Tool from the **Toolbox**.
3. Select **Arrange** menu and choose **Group** as shown in Figure 9.15.
4. The selected objects form a group. This is confirmed by the text **Group of 3 Objects on Layer 1** that appears at the Status bar as shown in Figure 9.16.

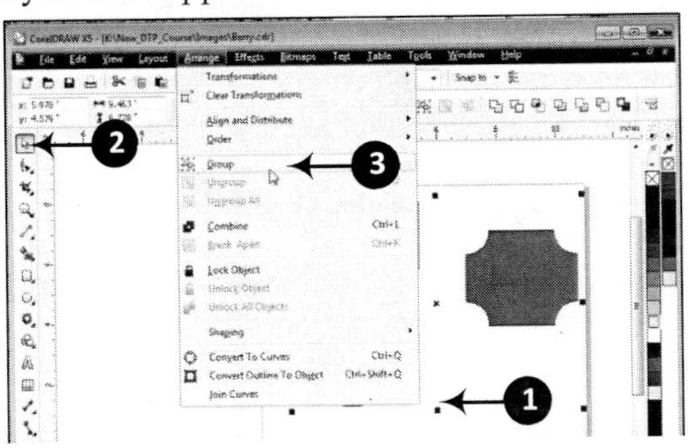

Figure 9.15 Selecting Group option from the Arrange group

Ungrouping Objects

In CorelDRAW, ungrouping objects means to removal of objects from a group. You can ungroup a single group as well as multiple groups into individual objects.

To ungroup objects, do this:

1. Open a document containing one or more group of objects.
2. Select the group by using the **Pick Tool** from the Toolbox.
3. Select **Arrange** menu and choose **Ungroup**.

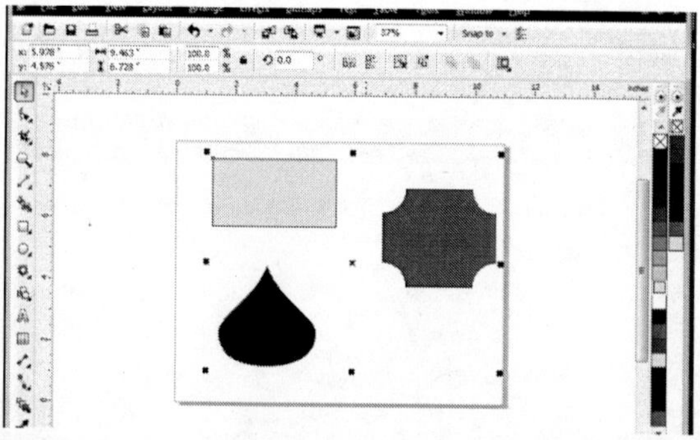

Figure 9.16 The selected objects form a group

4. The objects in the group break apart into individual objects, as shown in Figure 9.17.

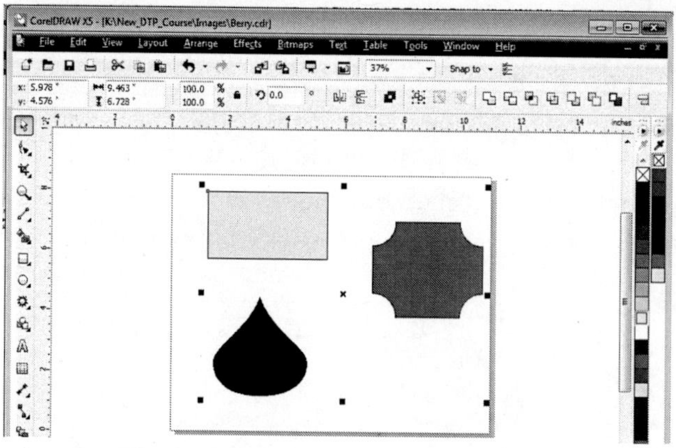

Figure 9.17 Ungrouped objects

5. After ungrouping the objects, the Status bar displays the notification **3 Objects Selected on Layer 1**, which confirms that the objects have been ungrouped.

Selecting the Color of an Object

You can choose both fill and outline colors by using the default color palette. The selected fill and outline colors appear in the color swatches on the Status bar. You can choose fill and outline colors by selecting a color from the Document palette, custom color palettes, palettes from the Palette libraries, color viewers, color harmonies, or color blends. When you want to use a color that already exists in an object or document, you can sample the color by using the Color Eyedropper Tool to achieve an exact match.

Selecting a Color using the Default Color Palette

CorelDRAW X5 provides Color palette, which contains a wide range of colors that you can use in objects. These colors appear as swatches, which you can apply an objects by using the Pick Tool. The default color palette is based on the primary color mode of the document. The default color palette contains colors from the Cyan, Magenta, Yellow and Black (CMYK) color mode. However, if color modes do not match your requirements, you can also create custom colors of your own.

To select a color from the default Color palette, do this:

1. Select an object which, you want to apply color, by using the Pick Tool.
2. Select a color swatch from the default Color palette as a fill color for the selected object. In our case, we have selected the Blue color as shown in Figure 9.18.
3. The object is filled with the selected color, as shown in Figure 9.18.

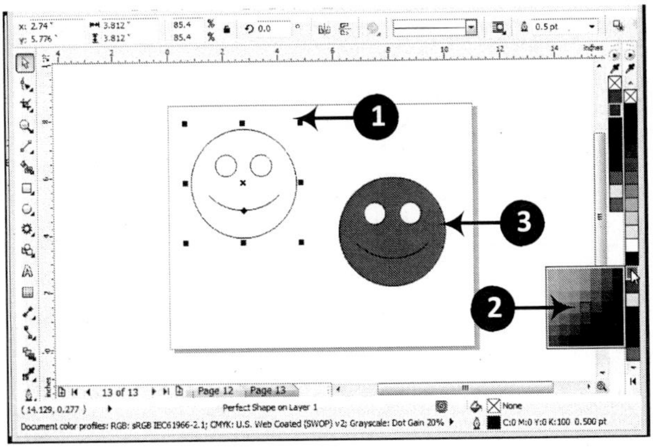

Figure 9.18 The object is filled with selected color

Creating a Custom Color Palette by Selecting Colors Manually

Custom Color palettes are useful when you want to work with a specific set of colors. The custom Color palette can be created by selecting each color manually, or by using the colors in an object. The colors can be added manually to a Color palette by selecting a color model, such as Red, Green, Blue (RGB) and CMYK, and then changing the color composition of the selected model.

To create a custom Color palette, do this:

1. Select **Window** menu highlight **Color Palettes** and then select **Palette Editor** as shown in Figure 9.19.
2. The **Palette Editor** dialog box appears as shown in Figure 9.20.
3. Click the **New Palette** button in the **Palette Editor** dialog box, as shown in Figure 9.20.

   The **New Palette** dialog box appears as shown in Figure 9.21.
4. Type the name in the **File name:** text box to specify a name for the custom Color palette you want to create. In our case, we have typed **Cust_Col_Palette**.

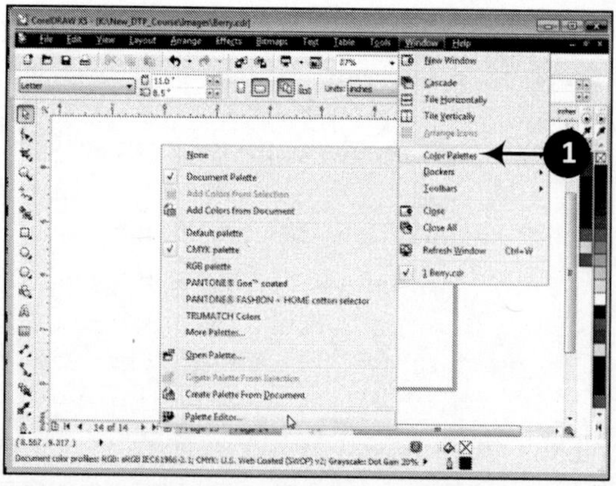

Figure 9.19 Selecting Palette Editor

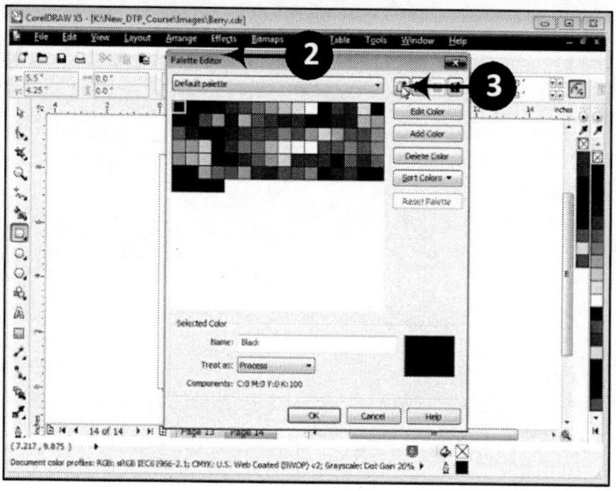

Figure 9.20 Palette Editor dialog box

5. Click the **Save in:** drop-down and select a desired location from the drop-down list. In our case, we have selected the default location, which is the **My Palettes** folder, to save our Color palette.
6. Click the **Save** button in the **New Palette** dialog box, as shown in Figure 9.21.
7. Again, the **Palette Editor** dialog box appears, click **Add Color** button as shown in Figure 9.22.
8. The **Select Color** dialog box appears, displaying the **Models** tab selected by default as shown in Figure 9.23.
9. Type values for the **C, M, Y** and **K** text boxes. In our case, we have typed the values **75, 5, 25,** and **20,** respectively in the four text boxes. The newly selected color displayed in the New color swatch of the **Select Color** dialog box.

10. Click the **Add To Palette** button in the **Select Color** dialog box to add the selected color in the **Cust_Col_Palette**.
11. Click **OK** button to close the **Select Color** dialog box. The selected color whose **CMY** and **K** values you specified get added in the **Palette Editor** dialog box.

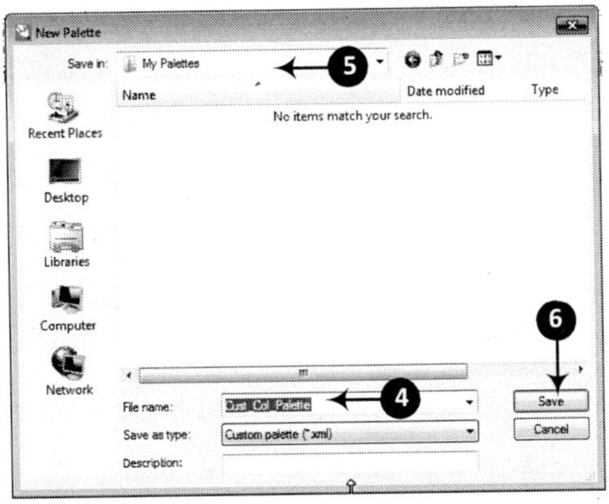

Figure 9.21 New Palette dialog box

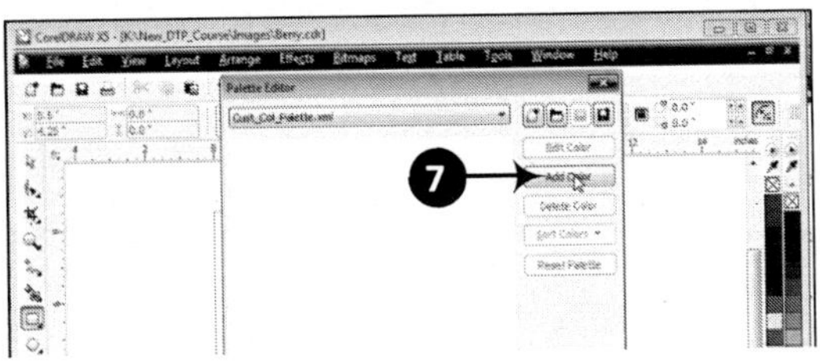

Figure 9.22 Selecting Add Color in the Palette Editor dialog box

12. Click the **OK** button to close the **Palette Editor** dialog box. The file name **Cust_Col_Palette** will act as Color palette in which you add custom colors of choice.

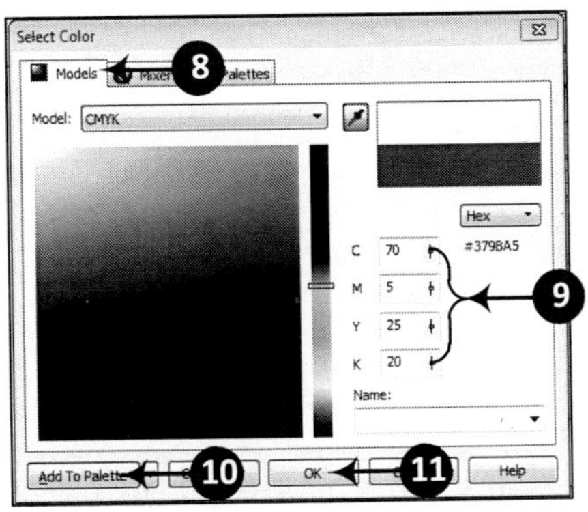

Figure 9.23 Select Color dialog box

Filling Objects

You can add colored, patterned, textured, and other fills to the inside of objects or other enclosed areas. You can customize a fill and set it as a default, so that each object you draw has the same fill. There are a number of tasks that are common to all types of fills.

Using Uniform Fills

You can apply a uniform fill to objects. Uniform fills are solid colors that you can choose or create by using color models and color palettes. You can apply a uniform fill to an object by using Interactive Fill Tools and Uniform Fill Tools on the Toolbox.

To apply uniform fills to an object, do this:

1. Select the object by using the **Pick Tool** from the **Toolbox.**
2. Click the arrow on the right side of the **Fill** tools from the Toolbox. A flyout appears as shown in Figure 9.24.
3. Select the **Uniform Fill** Tool from the Flyout.

   The **Uniform Fill** dialog box appears, displaying the **Models** tab selected by default as shown in Figure 9.25.
4. A small square appears, using the mouse click and select the color. The values of **C, M, Y** and **K** change, respectively as you select the color.
5. Click the **OK** button in the **Uniform Fill** dialog box.
6. The object is filled with the uniform colors, as shown in Figure 9.26.

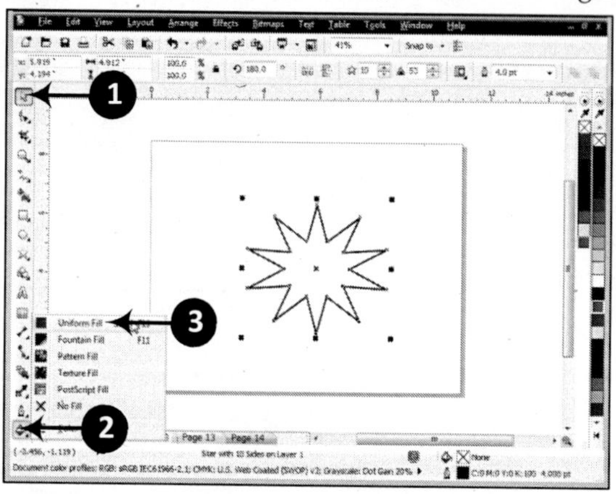

Figure 9.24 Selecting Uniform Fill from the Fill flyout

Using Pattern Fills

Pattern fills are used to fill the entire object with repeating patterns. You can fill objects with various Pattern tiles. Patterns can be two-color, full-color or bitmapped pattern fills. Two-color Pattern Fills consist of two colors which you

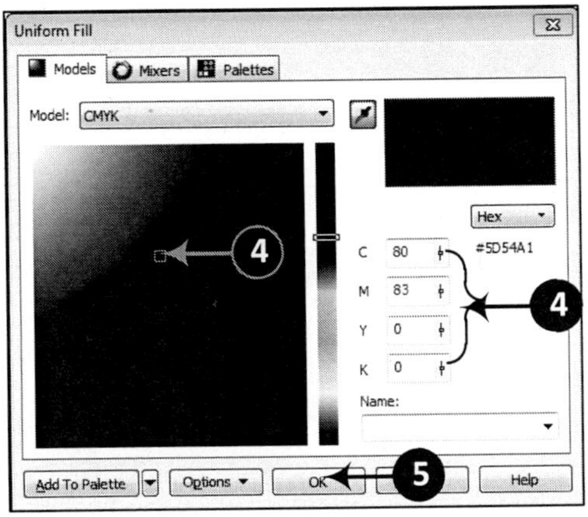

Figure 9.25 Uniform Fill dialog box

can select. Full Color Pattern Fills are made of a complex vector graphics that can be composed of lines and fills. The Bitmap Pattern Fill is created from the selected a bitmap image.

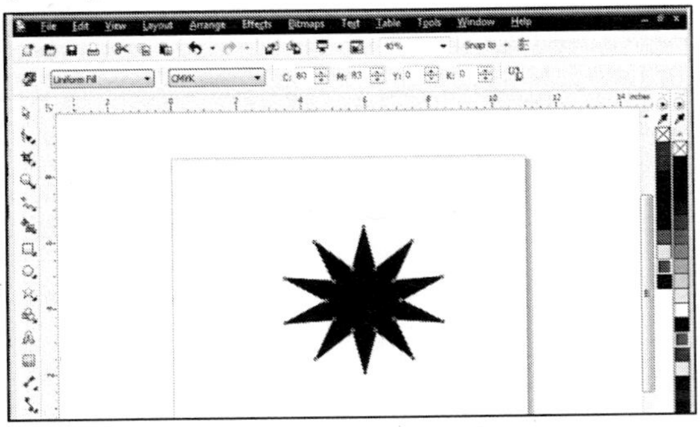

Figure 9.26 Object is filled with uniform fill tool

Using the 2-Color Pattern Fill

In the 2-color pattern fill, two colors are used to create the pattern fill. The Pattern Fill Tool enables a 2-color pattern fill mode in which you can select the front color, and the back color to fill the pattern. You can also change the tile size of the pattern filled.

To apply a 2-color pattern fill to an object, do this:

1. Select the object using the **Pick** Tool.
2. Click the arrow on the right side of the **Interactive Fill** Tools on the Toolbox. A **flyout** appears.
3. Select the **Interactive Fill** Tool from the flyout as shown in Figure 17.27.

As soon as you select the Interactive Fill Tool in the Toolbox, the various options related to the selected Tool changes on the Property bar.

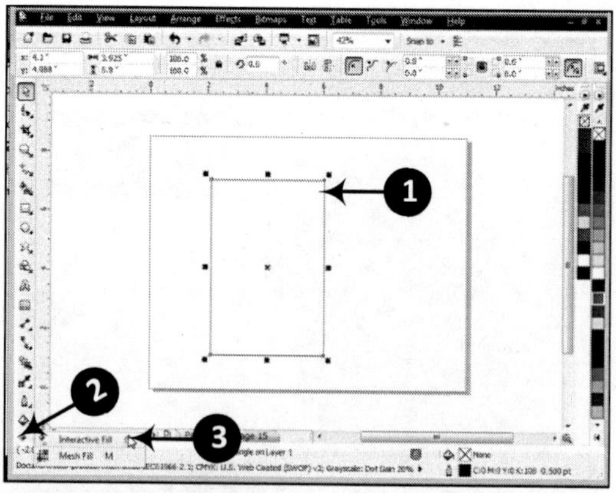

Figure 9.27 Selecting Interactive Fill Tool

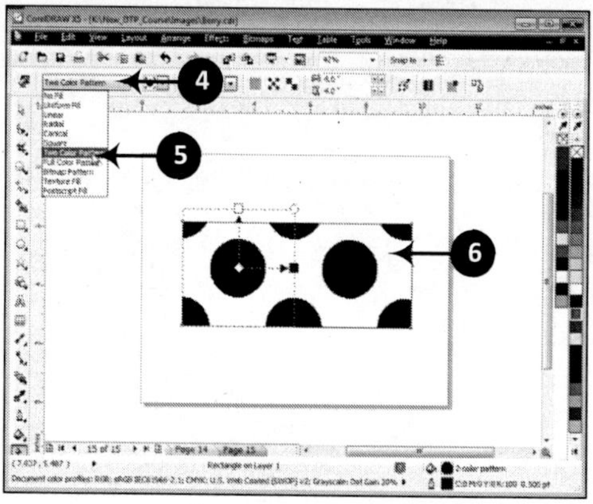

Figure 9.28 The selected pattern is applied in the object

4. Click the **Fill Type** list box from the **Property bar**. A drop-down list of pattern fill types appears as shown in Figure 9.28.
5. Select the **Two Color Pattern** from the drop-down list.
6. The selected pattern on the drop-down list as shown in Figure 9.28.
7. Click the **First Fill Color** list box in the **Property bar**. A drop-down list of pattern appears.
8. Select a pattern on the drop-down list as shown in Figure 9.29. The pattern is applied to the selected object.
9. Click the **Front Color** drop-down arrow on the **Property bar**. A **Color palette** appears as shown in Figure 9.30.
10. Select the desired color from the **Color palette** to select the front or foreground color for the selected pattern as shown in Figure 9.30. In our case, we have selected cyan color.

11. Click the down-arrow button of **Black color** on the **Property bar**. A **Color palette** appears as shown in Figure 9.31.
12. Select a desired color from the Color palette, which you want to set as the back or background color for the selected pattern. In our case, we have selected **White** color, as shown in Figure 9.31.

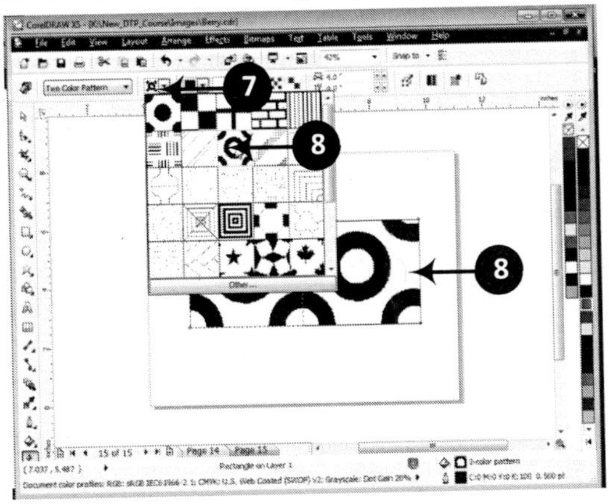

Figure 9.29 Selecting Interactive Fill Tool

Figure 9.30 The selected pattern is applied in the object

You can change the size of the tiles for pattern using one of the three buttons, such as **Small Tile, Medium Tile** and **Large Tile** for pattern that are available on the Property bar.

Using Fills to Areas

The Fill Tools that are useful to apply fills only to the large areas of an object but the enclosed areas were left out. The Smart Fill Tool helps you to apply a fill to an enclosed area. The Smart Fill Tool detects the edges of an area and creates a

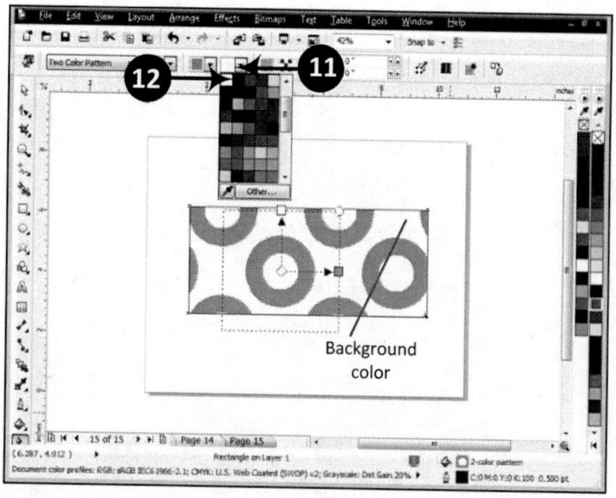

Figure 9.31 Selecting Background for pattern

closed path so that it can fill that area. For example, spirals object intersect each other at a number of point, to create enclose areas. You can fill these enclosed areas by using the Smart Fill Tool.

To fill the enclosed area in an object by using the Smart Fill Tool, do this:

1. Select the document that contains an object by using the **Pick** Tool. In our case, we have selected three spirals.
2. Click the arrow on the right side of the **Smart Fill Tools** from the **Toolbox**. A flyout appears as shown in Figure 9.32.
3. Select the **Smart Fill** Tool from the Flyout as shown in Figure 9.32.

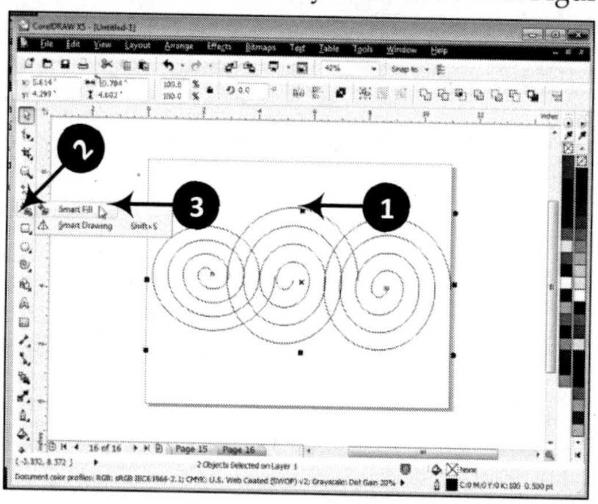

Figure 9.32 Selecting Smart fill tool

4. Click the **Fill color** drop-down arrow button on the **Property bar**. A **Color palette** appears as shown in Figure 9.33.

5. Select the desired color from the **Color palette** flyout. In our case, we have selected **pink** color.

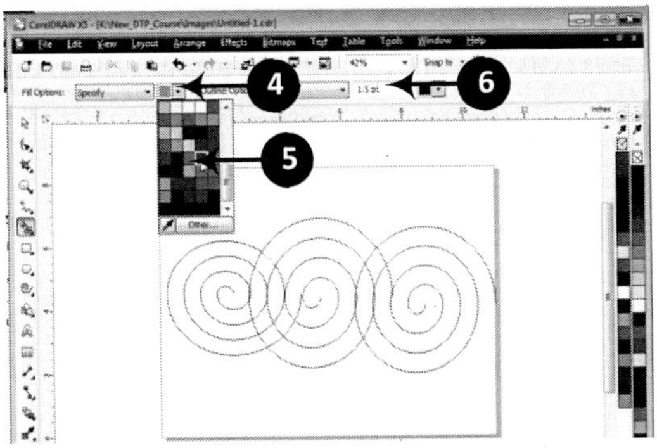

Figure 9.33 Selecting fill color to fill the object

6. Type a value in the Outline width drop-down arrow in the Property bar to specify the width for the outline of selected object. Here, we have selected 1.5pt to specify the width.
7. Click the object where you want to fill color. The first click fills the object as shown in Figure 9.34.
8. Click another portion to fill, as shown in Figure 9.34.

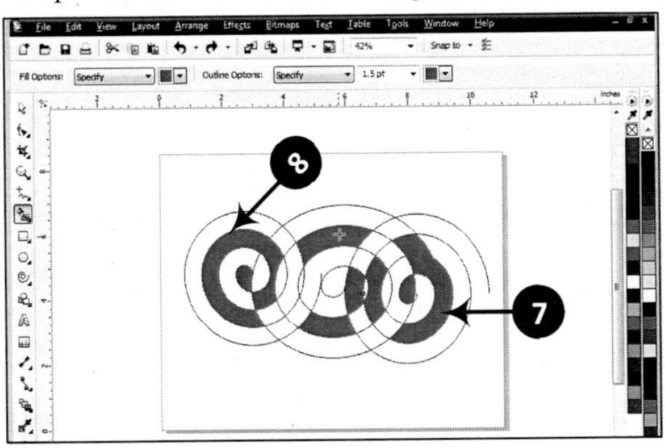

Figure 9.34 Select the area to fill the color

CHAPTER 10

Working with Text

Introduction

In graphic and layout designing applications, text plays an important role in CorelDRAW X5. Using Text Tool, you can apply various formatting options to the text, such as changing the font type, font size and font style or aligning and spacing of text in the Drawing page according to your requirements. In addition, you can also apply effects, such as fitting text to a path.

In this Chapter you will learn how to create two types of text: artistic and paragraph. You will also learn how convert text into a curved object, as well as applying different text effects and formatting methods, such as font size, font face and alignment.

Types of Text

In CorelDRAW, you can create two types of text, such as Artistic and Paragraph, using the Text Tool. When you create artistic text, you simply type the text in the Drawing page. However, when you create a paragraph text, you have to first create a text frame and then type the text within the frame. The two types of text can be briefly explained below.

Artistic Text: Artistic text is a type of text to add short lines of text, such as titles, and to apply graphic effects, such as fitting text to a path, creating extrusions and blends, and creating all other special effects.

Paragraph Text: Paragraph text allows you to apply formatting options and directly edit large blocks of text. In the Paragraph type of text, the text is created in frames and you can use various paragraph formatting features, such as Bullets Lists, Tabs, Indents and Drop Cap.

Let us learn about preparing a layout for using the text.

Creating Artistic Text

When you create an artistic text, you can make a graphic image that can be edited like any other graphic in CorelDRAW. You can easily resize or reshape artistic text, edit the graphical aspects, and also the text content and format. You can add artistic text along an open or closed path.

Use artistic text for smaller blocks of text, such as newsletters headings, master heads, and other text applications with few characters.

To add artistic text, do this:

1. Click the **Text** Tool in the Toolbox.
2. Click anywhere in the drawing window using the Text Tool. The shape of the mouse-pointer changes to the text cursor, as shown in Figure 10.1.

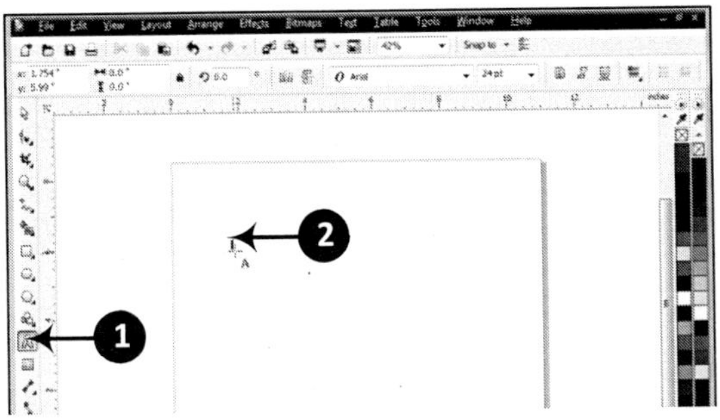

Figure 10.1 Selecting the Text Tool to create artistic text

3. Type the required text on the Drawing page. In our case, we have typed **Artistic Text** as shown in Figure 10.2.
4. After you finish typing text, select the **Pick** Tool. The text will be surrounded with eight small, square black handles as shown in Figure 10.2. These handles can be dragged to change the size and shape of the Text.

Now let us learn to create the paragraph text type.

Figure 10.2 The text surrounding by using Pick Tool

Creating Paragraph Text

For creating paragraph text, you must create a text frame for the text, and then type the text within the frame.

To create paragraph text do this:

1. Click the **Text Tool** on the Toolbox.
2. Click and drag the mouse the mouse pointer on the Drawing page to specify the location of the paragraph frame, as shown in Figure 10.3.
3. Type the text inside the paragraph frame in the Drawing page, as shown in Figure 10.3.

Converting Text from One Type to Another

If you have typed your text in the artistic mode and want to change it to the paragraph mode or vice-versa, you can do it easily.

1. Select the Pick Tool in the Toolbox.

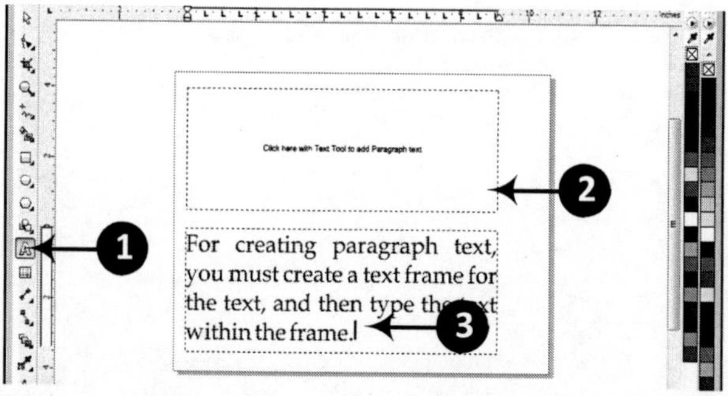

Figure 10.3 Showing entered text in the paragraph text frame

2. Select the text frame in the Drawing page by using the Pick Tool, as shown in Figure 10.4.
3. Select **Text** menu and choose **Convert To Artistic Text** from the Text menu bar as shown in Figure 10.4.
4. The selected text appears on the Drawing page without the frame, which indicates that the text is converted to artistic text as shown in Figure 10.5.

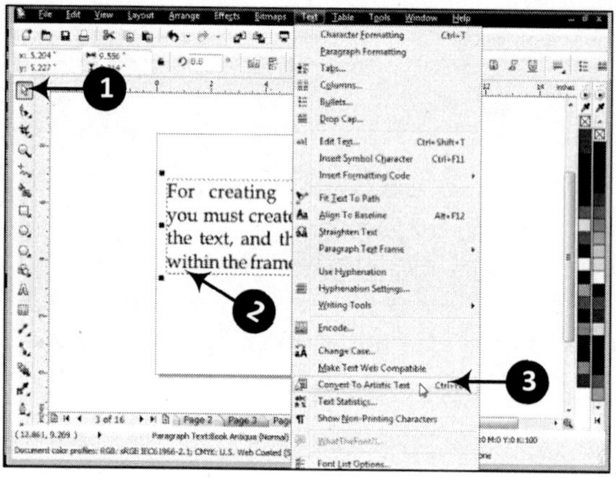

Figure 10.4 Selecting Convert To Artistic Text option in Text menu

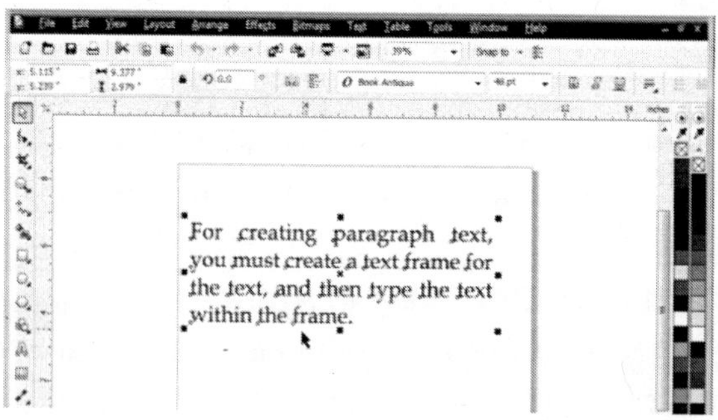

Figure 10.5 The selected text converted to artistic text

Similarly, for converting Artistic text to Paragraph text, select the Pick Tool in the Toolbox and then select the Paragraph text that you want to convert. Next, Select Text menu and choose Convert To Paragraph Text option from the Text menu.

Now, let us learn to change the appearance of text.

Changing the Appearance of Text

CorelDRAW X5 provides to change the appearance of the text in a document. For example, you can change the font of the text, the font size and the color of the text. You can also align the text and changing the spacing of the text in the Drawing page.

Changing the Font Style and Font Size of Text

You can change the Font style as well as Font size of the text to make it more attractive.

To change the font style and size of text in a CorelDRAW document, do this:

1. Select the Text Tool on the Toolbox.
2. Keeping the left mouse pressed, drag the mouse-pointer to select the text. The text appears highlighted as shown in Figure 10.6.

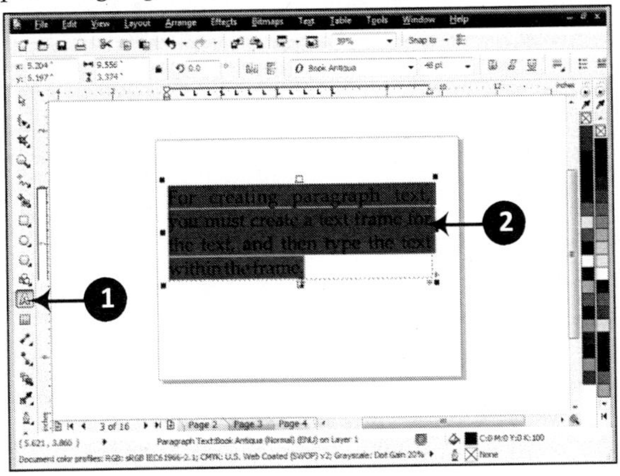

Figure 10.6 Selecting text

3. Click the down arrow of the **Font list** drop-down list on the **Property** bar. A drop-down list appears as shown in Figure 10.7.
4. Select the Font type for the selected text from the drop-down list. For example, we have selected **Book Antique Normal**, as shown in Figure 10.7.
5. The font of the text changes to the selected font style as shown in Figure 10.7.
6. Click the down arrow of **Font size** drop-down list on the Property bar. A drop-down list appears as shown in Figure 10.8.
7. Select the font size you require on the selected text. For example, in our case, we have selected **36 pt**, as shown in Figure 10.8.

8. The size of the text changes to the selected font size, as shown in Figure 18.8.

After changing the font style and size of the text in CorelDRAW, let us learn how to change the font color.

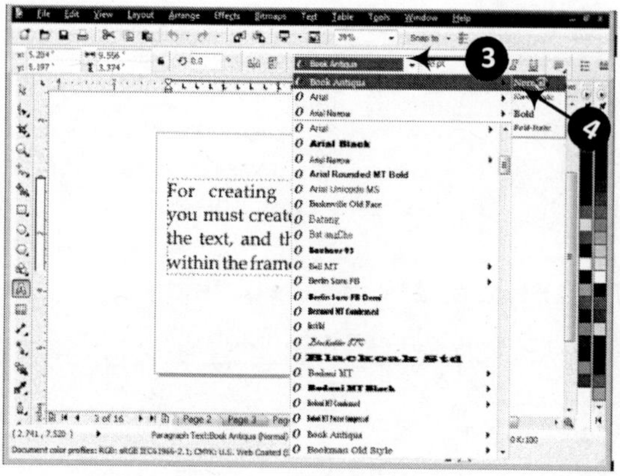

Figure 10.7 Selecting Font list

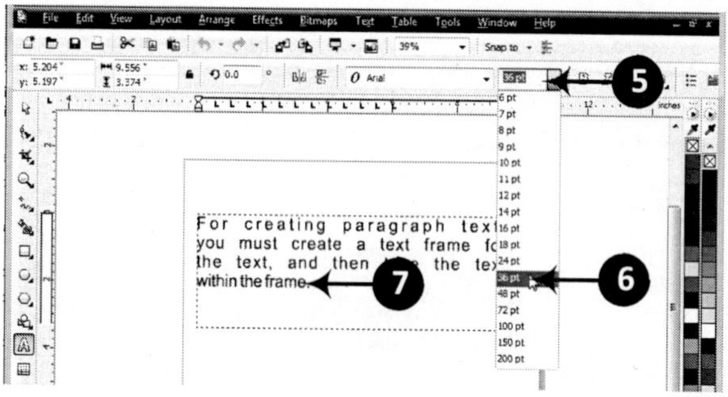

Figure 10.8 Selecting Font Size

Changing the Font Color of the Text

You can change the font color of the text in your document to make it more presentable. The default color is black, but you can change the any desired color of your choice.

To change the color of the font of the text in a CorelDRAW document, do this:

1. Click the Text Tool on the Toolbox to select it.
2. Keeping the left mouse pressed, drag the mouse-pointer to select the text. The text gets highlighted as shown in Figure 10.9.
3. Click the color for the text from the default Color palette located at the left of the Drawing page. For example, in our case, we have selected the red color, as shown in Figure 10.9.
4. The color of the text changes into the selected color, as shown in Figure 10.10.

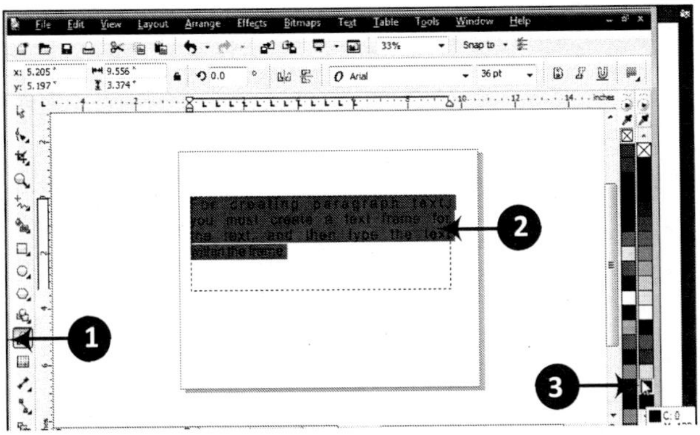

Figure 10.9 Color is to be changed for the selected text

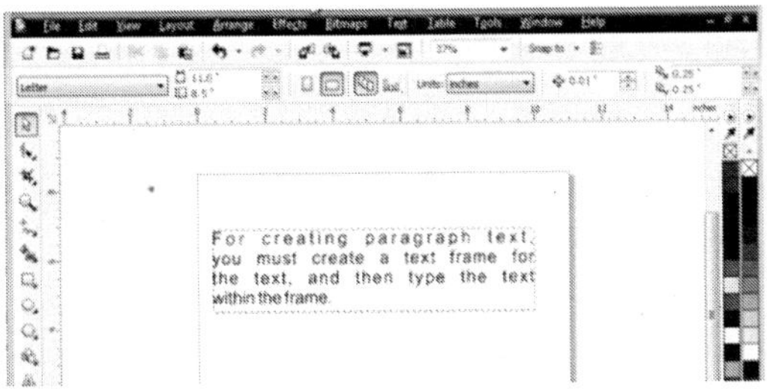

Figure 10.10 The selected text changed to into red color

Now, let us change the alignment of text in CorelDRAW.

Changing the Alignment

You can align both paragraph text and artistic text horizontally. By default, the text is horizontally aligned in the left direction but you can align it to the center or right direction. With paragraph text, you can also align the text vertically to the top, bottom or center of the text frame, according to the height and width of the text frame.

Aligning Artistic Text Horizontally

To align artistic text horizontally, do this:

1. Select the Text Tool on the Toolbox.
2. Type some text in the text box, which you want to align to the existing text as shown in Figure 10.11.
3. Click the **Text Alignment** button on the **Property** bar. A drop-down list appears as shown in Figure 10.11.
4. Select the desired alignment option from the drop-down list. In our case, we have selected the **Center** option. The text aligns itself to the center of the text frame as shown in Figure 10.11.

Let us now learn to align the paragraph text.

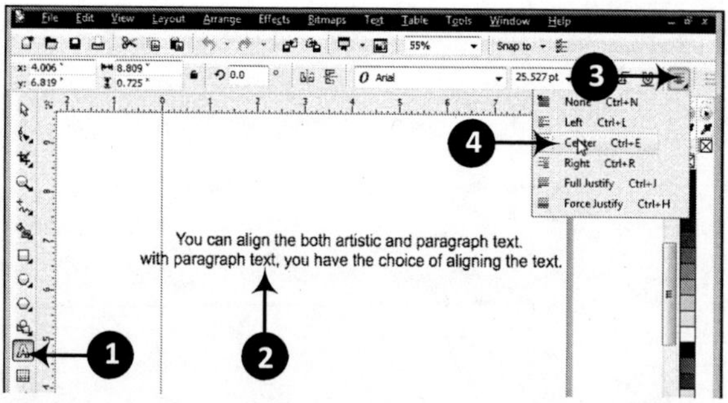

Figure 10.11 Aligning artistic text horizontally

Aligning Paragraph Text Vertically

To align the paragraph text vertically, do this:

1. Select the paragraph text frame.
2. Click the **Text** menu and choose **Paragraph Formatting** from the menu bar as shown in Figure 10.12.

   A **Paragraph Formatting** docker appears on the right side of the Drawing window as shown in Figure 10.13.
3. In the **Paragraph Formatting** docker, under the **Alignment** group, click the down arrow button beside the **Vertical** option. A drop-down list appears as shown in Figure 10.13.
4. Select the alignment option for your text from the drop-down list. In our case, we have selected **Center**. The text aligns to the **Center** of the text frame as shown in Figure 10.13.

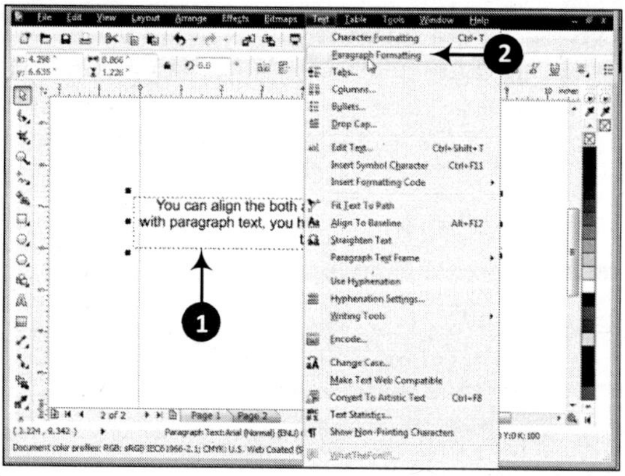

Figure 10.12 Selecting Paragraph Formatting option in Text menu

Changing Text Spacing

You can change character spacing and word spacing in selected paragraphs, or in an entire paragraph text frame or artistic text object. Changing the space between characters is also known as "tracking" or "letter spacing." You can change the spacing between characters in an entire block of text or in a small group of characters. You can also change the spacing before and after paragraphs in paragraph text.

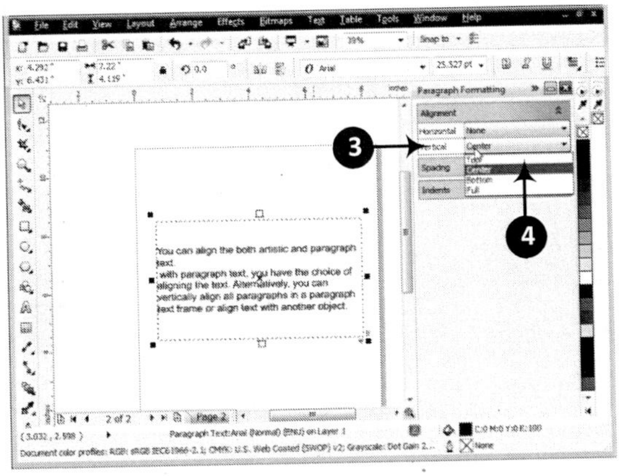

Figure 10.13 Selecting Center vertical alignment

To change the text spacing, do this:

1. Select the text to which you want to change the text spacing.
2. Click the **Spacing arrow** button in the **Paragraph Formatting** docker window as shown in Figure 10.14. A drop-down list appears.

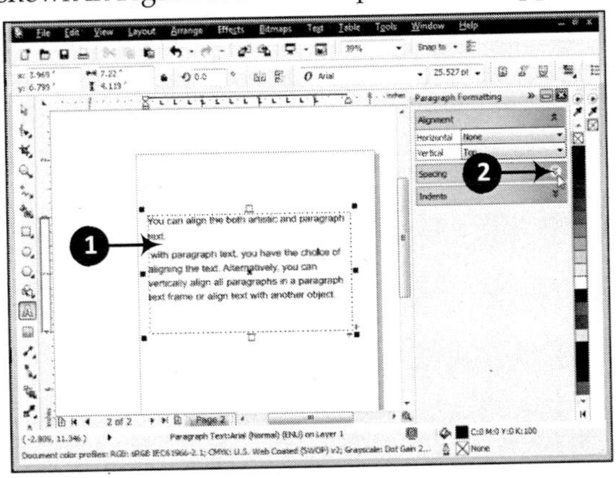

Figure 10.14 Select the Spacing button in the Paragraph Formatting docker window

3. Type a percentage value in the **Before Paragraph** spinner box in the **Paragraph and Line** category in the **Paragraph Formatting** docker, to specify the spacing before the paragraph within the bounding frame of the paragraph text. For example, in our case, we have typed typed 160% as shown in Figure 10.15.

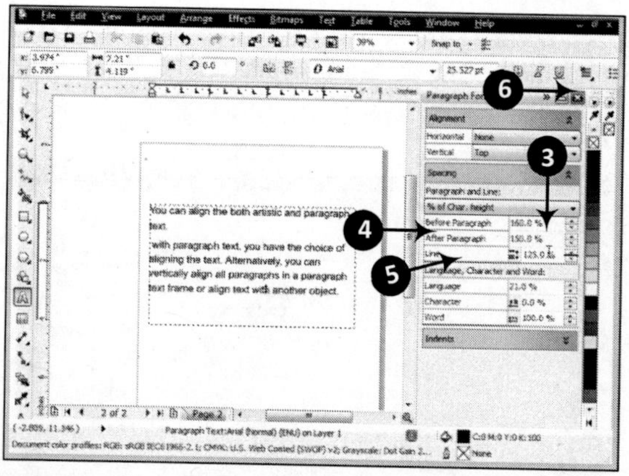

Figure 10.15 Selecting Center vertical alignment

4. Type a percentage value in the **After Paragraph** spinner box in the **Paragraph and Line** category in the **Paragraph Formatting** docker, to specify the spacing after the paragraph within the bounding frame of the paragraph text. For example, in our case, we have typed 150% as shown in Figure 10.15.
5. Type a percentage value in the **Line** spinner box in the **Paragraph and Line** category in the **Paragraph Formatting** docker, to specify the spacing between the lines of the paragraph within the bounding frame of the paragraph text. For example, in our case, we have typed typed 125% as shown in Figure 8.15.
6. Click the **Close** button in the **Paragraph Formatting** docker to close the docker, as shown in Figure 10.15.
7. The selected text is aligned according to the values given in the Paragraph Formatting docker.

After learning how to modify the spacing between the paragraph and lines of the paragraph text frame in the CorelDRAW document. Let us discuss the various effects available in CorelDRAW and how to apply them in the CorelDRAW document.

Applying Effects to Text

You can apply various effects, such as Drop Cap and Bulleted List. When you apply the Drop Cap effect to paragraph text, the initial letter of the paragraph is enlarged. You can also apply bulleted lists to format text. It also customize bullets by changing their size, position, and distance from text.

Applying a Drop Cap

You can customize a Drop Cap by changing its settings by specifying the distance between the Drop Cap and the body of text, or specify the number of lines of text that you want to appear next to the Drop Cap.

To apply a Drop Cap to the paragraph text, do this:

1. Select the text in the paragraph frame in which you want to apply the Drop Cap effect as shown in Figure 10.16.

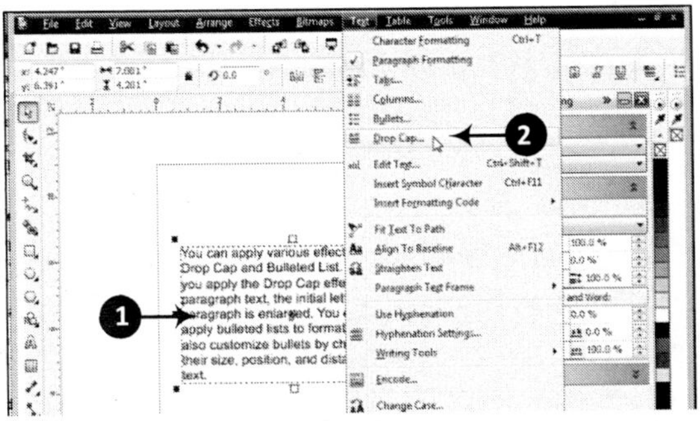

Figure 10.16

2. Select **Text** menu and choose **Drop Cap...** from the **Menu** bar as shown in Figure 10.16.

   The **Drop Cap** dialog box appears as shown in Figure 10.17.

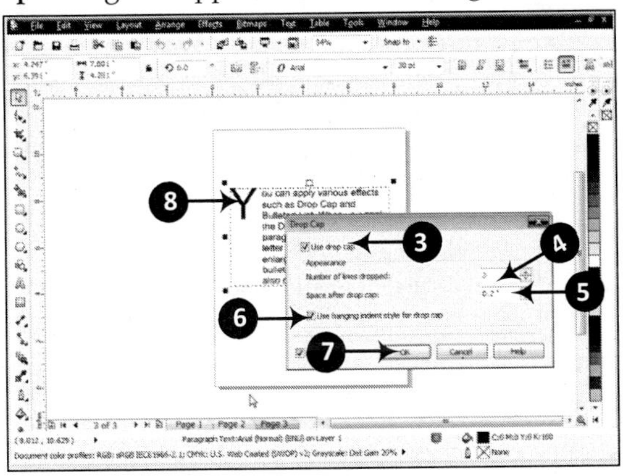

Figure 10.17 Drop Cap dialog box

3. Select the **Use drop cap** check box as shown in Figure 10.17.
4. Type a value in the **Number of lines dropped:** spinner box to specify the number of lines next to drop cap in the Appearance section. In our case, we have typed 3 (See Figure 10.17).
5. Type a value in the **Space after drop cap:** spinner box to specify the distance between the drop cap and the body of text. In our case, we have typed 0.2 (See Figure 10.17).
6. Select the **Use hanging indent style for drop cap** check box, to offset the drop cap from the body of text.
7. Click the **OK** button in the **Drop Cap** dialog box, as shown in Figure 10.17.

8. The selected paragraph text with the Drop Cap effect is applied as shown in Figure 10.17.

Next, we will discuss how to apply the Bullets list to the text.

Applying the Bullets Effect

You can also apply bullets to your text to emphasize text. You can also customize the appearance of the bullets by modifying elements, such as fonts and symbols you use.

To apply the bullets to text, do this:

1. Click the **Text** Tool in the **Toolbox**.
2. Select the paragraph text frame in which you want to apply bullet effect.
3. Select the **Text** menu and choose **Bullets...** from the **Menu** bar as shown in Figure 10.18.

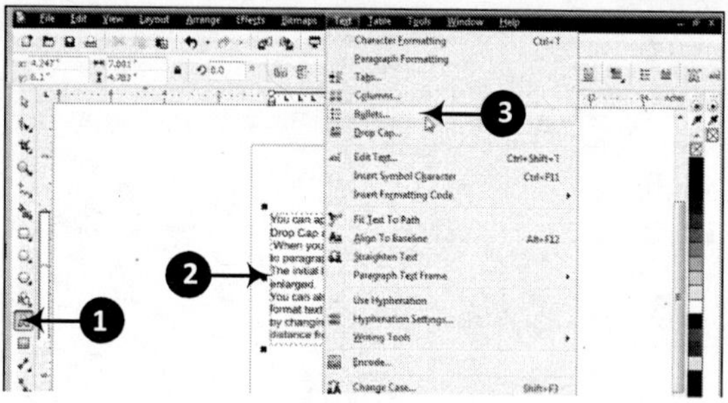

Figure 10.18 Selecting Bullets option

The **Bullets** dialog box appears as shown in Figure 8.18.

4. Click the check box to apply bullets list to the selected text as shown in Figure 10.18.
5. In the **Appearance** section, click the down arrow button in the **Font:** drop-down list. A drop-down list of various fonts is displayed as shown in Figure 10.19.

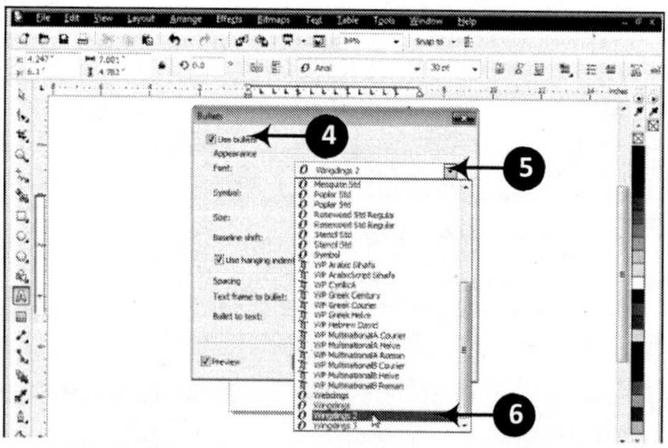

Figure 10.19 Selecting Font option

6. Select the desired font you want to use in the bullet list. In our case, we have selected the font names **Wingdings** as shown in Figure 10.19.
7. Click the **Symbol:** drop-down arrow button. It shows the list of various bullets items.
8. Select the symbol used to represent the bullet list. In our case, we have selected the **Diamond** symbol as shown in Figure 10.20.

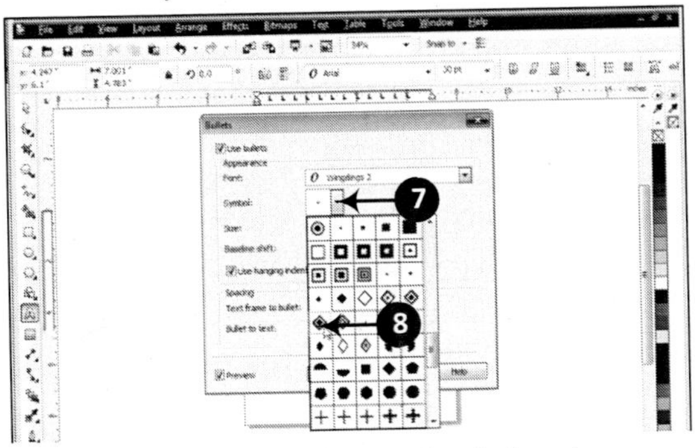

Figure 10.20 Selecting Symbol option

9. Type a value in the **Size:** spinner box for specifying the size of bullets. In our case, we have typed 22.2 pt (See Figure 10.21).
10. Type a value in the **Baseline shift:** spinner box to specify the distance between the bullets and base line. In our case, we have typed 1.0 pt (See Figure 10.21).
11. Select the **Use hanging indent style for bulleted lists** check box to apply a hanging indent to the bullet list as shown in Figure 10.21.

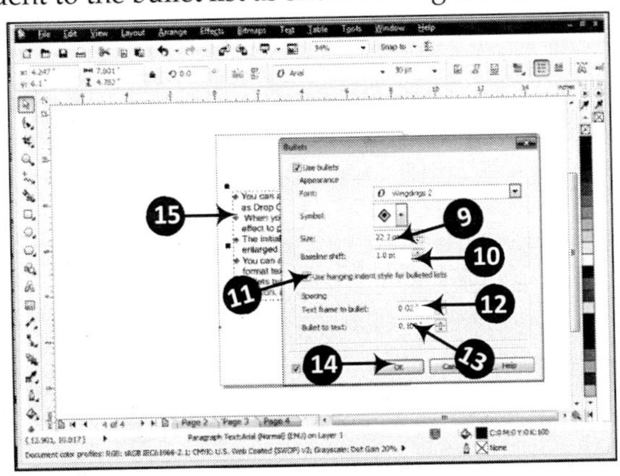

Figure 10.21 Bullet dialog box

12. Type a value in the **Text frame to bullet:** spinner box to specify the spacing you want to apply between the text frame and the bullets. In our case, we have typed 0.02.

13. Type a value in the **Bullet to Text:** spinner box to specify the spacing between the bullet character and the text for the bulleted item. In our case, we have typed 0.109.
14. Click the **OK** button in the **Bullets** dialog box as shown in Figure 10.21.
15. The text with Bullets appears as shown in Figure 10.21.

Wrapping Paragraph Text around an Object

You can change the shape of text by wrapping paragraph text around an object, artistic text, or a paragraph text frame. You can wrap text by using contour or square wrapping styles. You can also adjust the amount of space between paragraph text and the object or text, or you also remove any wrapping style.

To wrap paragraph text around an object, do this:

1. Select the Text Tool and create the Paragraph text as shown in Figure 10.22.
2. Draw a Complex star and keep it selected, as shown in Figure 10.22.
3. Click the **Wrap Paragraph Text** button on the **Property bar**. A drop-down list appears.

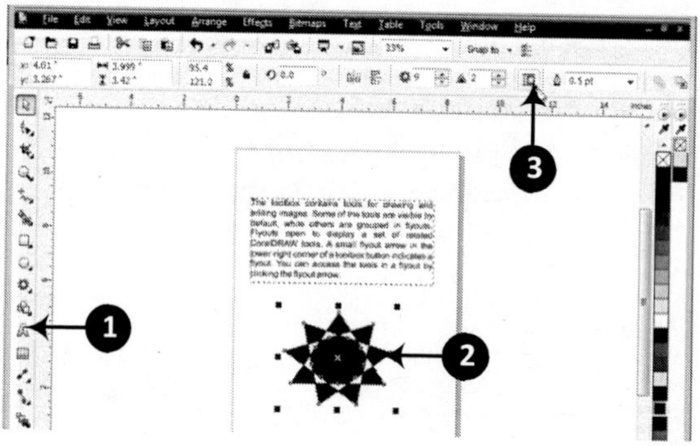

Figure 10.22 Selecting Wrap text option from the property bar

4. Select the **Text Flows Left** option in the **Square** section in the drop-down list, to specify how you want the text to be positioned when it is wrapped as shown in Figure 10.23.

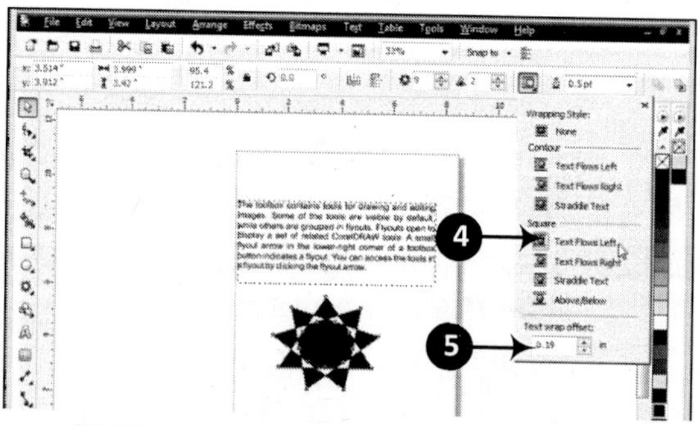

Figure 10.23 Selecting Wrap text flow left option

5. Click up or down arrow in the spinner box below the **Text wrap offset:** option to increase or decrease the space between wrapping text and object.

   Press the Enter key on the keyboard to apply the values you typed in the Wrap text drop-down list.

6. Drag the selected object to the right of the Paragraph text, as shown in Figure 10.24.

   As soon as you drag the object and place it in the right of the Paragraph text, the text will be moved to left of the object, as shown in Figure 10.24.

7. Click anywhere on the Drawing page to remove the control handles on the drawing as shown in Figure 10.25.

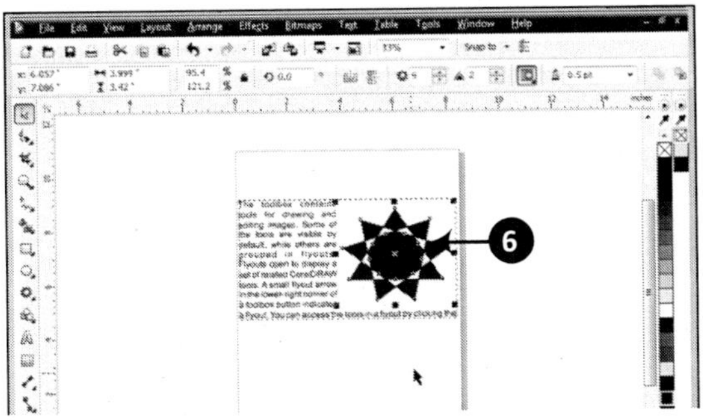

Figure 10.24 Drag the object between the text

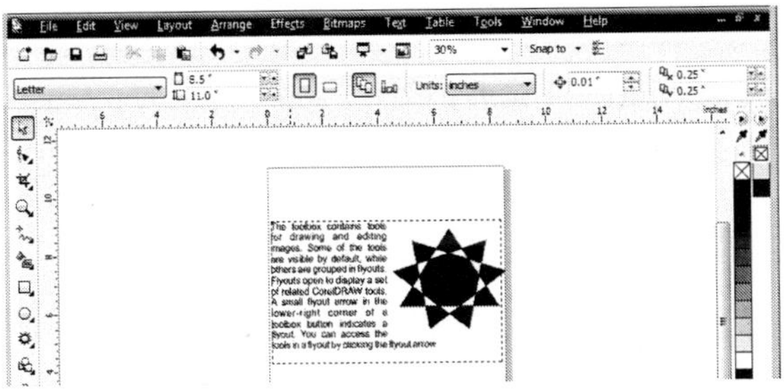

Figure 10.25 The object placed in the selected option

Fitting Text to an Object's Path

You can position artistic text along the path of an open object (for example, a line) or a closed object (for example, a square). For example, you can place the text horizontally, vertically or both. You can adjust the distance between the text and the path.

To add text along the path, do this:

1. Draw a **Circle** and keep it selected as shown in Figure 10.26.
2. Click **Text** menu and choose **Fit Text to path** as shown in Figure 10.26.
3. Click the down arrow button in the **Text Orientation** drop-down list.

4. Select the text orientation style from the drop-down list on the Property bar as shown in Figure 10.27.

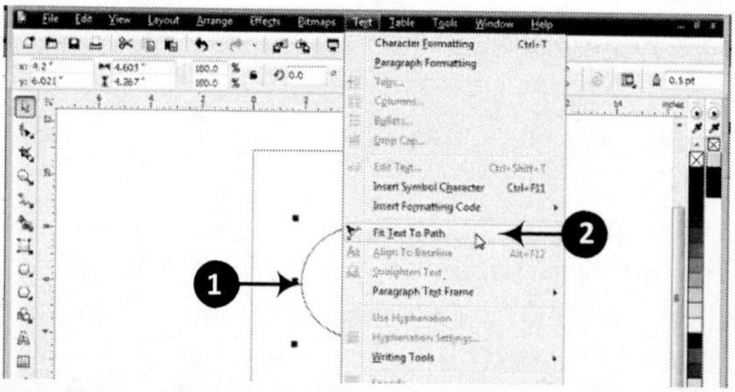

Figure 10.26 Selecting Fit Text to path from the Text menu

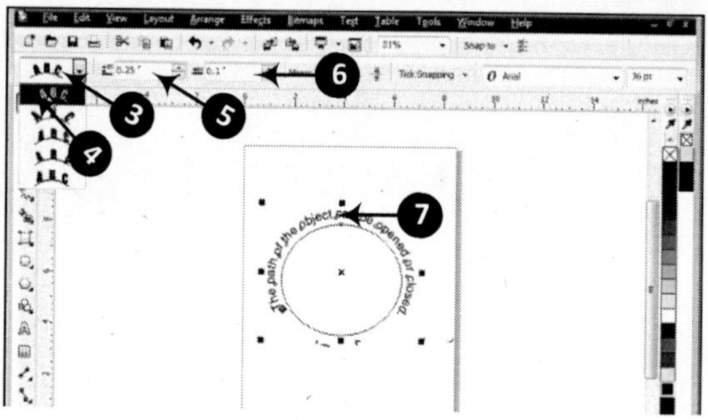

Figure 10.27 Type a text over an object

5. Select the **Distance from Path** in the Property bar by using the up or down arrow in the spin box as shown in Figure 10.27. This option to set the distance between the text and object's path.
6. Click the up or down arrow button in the **Horizontal Offset** spin box on the Property bar to set the horizontal position of the text along the path.
7. Type the text along the path from the point where a blinking cursor appears on the outer boundary of the circle as shown in Figure 10.27.
8. Click anywhere in the Drawing window, to deselect the text that we have typed on the path as shown in Figure 10.27.

After, you have learned to fit text to an objects path by setting various options. Now, let us learn how to convert text to curve object.

Converting Text to an Object using Curve Command

You have to know how to convert the Paragraph text to Artistic text and vice-versa. In the similar method, you can also convert the Artistic curve and Paragraph text to curve by using the Convert To Curve Command. Converting text into a curve object allows you to easily customize the shape of the object. When the text is converted to curve object, you can edit the shape of the individual characters of the text.

To convert text to a curve object, do this:

1. Create an Artistic text.
2. Select the **Artistic text** by using the **Pick** Tool on the **Drawing page** as shown in Figure 10.28.
3. Select the **Arrange** menu and choose **Convert To Curves** as shown in Figure 10.28.
4. The selected Artistic text is converted to a curve object.

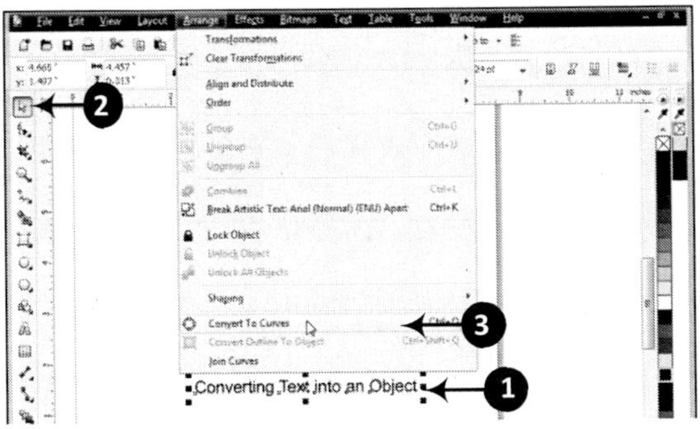

Figure 10.28 Selecting Convert To Curves option

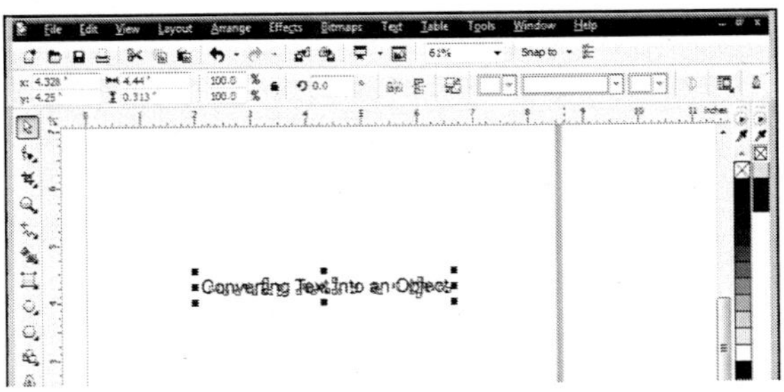

Figure 10.29 The selected text is converted to a curve object

Now, let us learn about breaking apart text.

Breaking Apart Text

When you convert text to curve object, you can provide the desired shape to the whole object. However, you want to edit a particular character, then you have to break the text apart. Breaking text apart means each character of the text behaves like a separate object. After breaking apart the text, you can edit the characters individually.

To break apart artistic text on the Drawing page, do this:

1. Select the text using the Pick Tool on the Drawing page as shown in Figure 10.30.
2. Click **Arrange** menu and choose **Break Curve Apart**.

The selected text breaks apart by enabling selection of each character of the text individually.

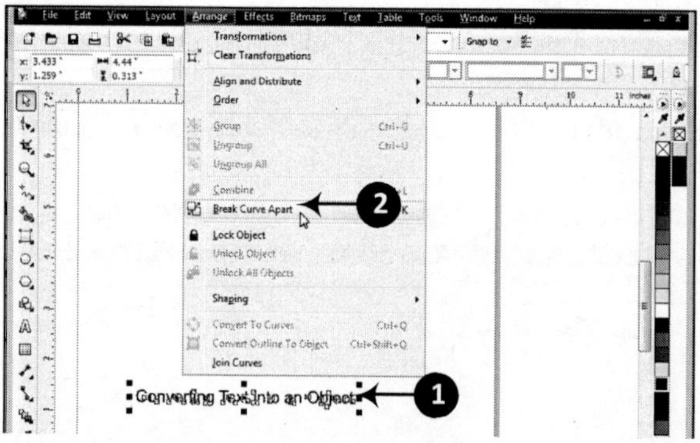

Figure 10.30 Selecting Break Curve Apart

3. Select a character which you want to edit and drag the control handles to resize it as shown in Figure 10.31.
4. Now, you can select individual character(s) and change their shapes. In addition, you can use the **Shape** Tool from the Toolbox to change the shape of the characters by dragging the editable nodes enabled after selecting **Shape Tool** as shown in Figure 10.32.

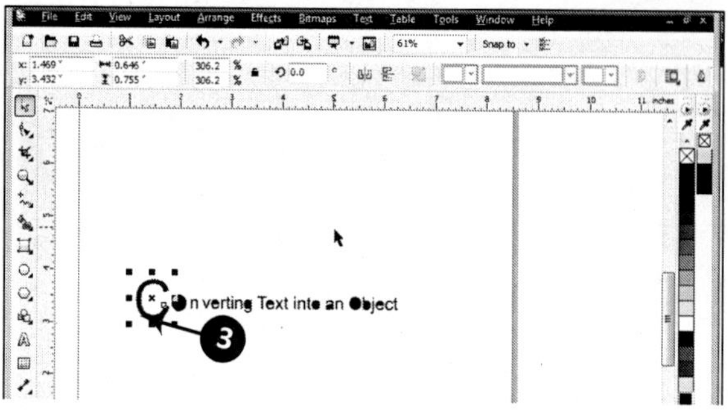

Figure 10.31 Drag the control handle to resize its shape

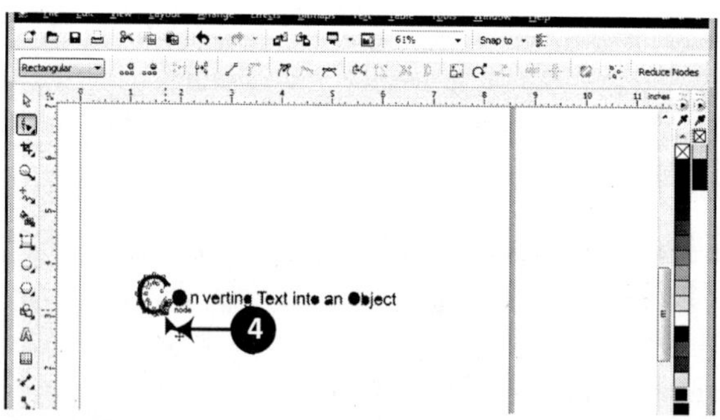

Figure 10.32 Drag the nodes to change its character shape

CHAPTER 11

Working with Bitmaps

Introduction

You can create vector graphics in CorelDRAW. As we know that all the images saved in CorelDRAW are of .cdr format and this format belongs to the vector images. You can import bitmaps (such as jpg and tiff files) in CorelDRAW and integrate them into your drawings. (Joint Photographic Experts Group), is a file extension for graphics file whereas TIFF (Tagged Image File Format) is a computer file format for raster graphics images.

In this chapter, you first understand the image types, such as bitmap and vector images. You will learn how to work with bitmap and vector images by converting vector images into bitmap images. You also learn to import a bitmap image into CorelDRAW document. You will also learn to modify a bitmap image by cropping, resampling and resizing it.

Changing Vector Images into Bitmap Images

Converting a vector graphic or object(s) to a bitmap, you can apply special effects in the CorelDRAW. The process of converting a vector graphic to a bitmap is also known as "rasterizing." When you convert the vector graphic, you can select the Color mode of the bitmap. The size of your file may increase or decrease depending on the Color mode you select. For example, a simple bitmap file created in MS Paint might have smaller file size with RGB Color mode; on the other hand, a Bitmap file created in Photoshop with CMYK Color mode might have larger file size.

To convert vector image into bitmap, do this:

1. Open a document containing a vector image, as shown in Figure 11.1.
2. Select an image by using the **Pick** Tool.
3. Select **Bitmaps** menu and choose **Convert to Bitmap...** from the Menu bar as shown in Figure 11.1.

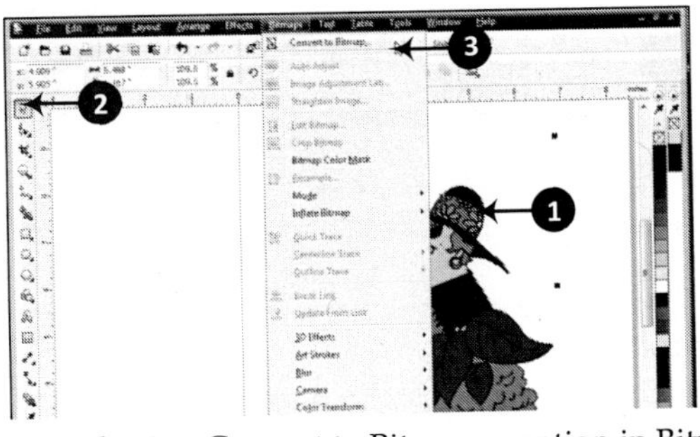

Figure 11.1 Selecting Convert to Bitmap... option in Bitmaps menu

A **Convert to Bitmap** dialog box appears as shown in Figure 11.2.

4. Click the down arrow button beside the **Resolution:** option. A drop-down list having various resolution options as shown in Figure 11.2.
5. Select the desired option from the drop-down list. In our case, we have selected **300** (dots per inch).

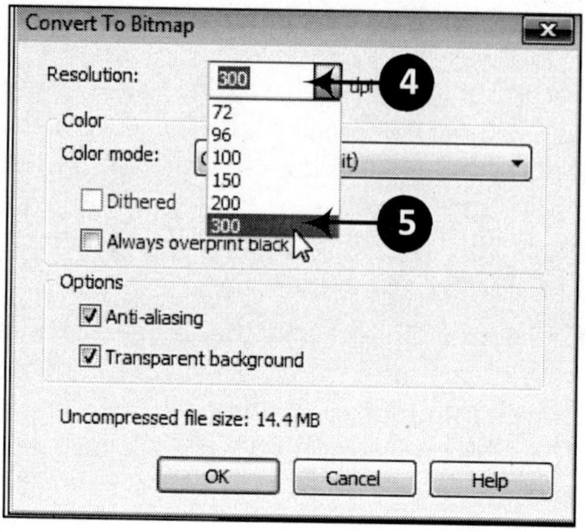

Figure 11.2 Convert To Bitmap dialog box

6. Click the down arrow button in the list box beside the **Color mode:** option under the **Color section**. A drop-down list appears as shown in Figure 11.3.
7. Select a Color mode on the drop-down list. In our case, we have selected as **CMYK Color (32-bit)**, as shown in Figure 11.3.
8. Click the **Anti-aliasing** check box in the **Options** section to smooth the edges of the bitmap as shown in Figure 11.3.

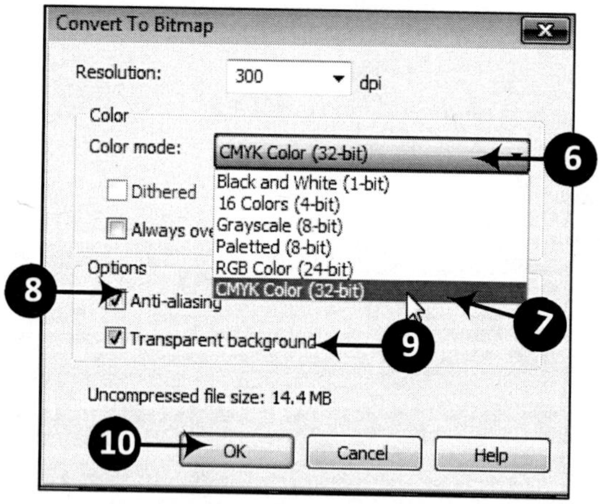

Figure 11.3 Selecting Color mode: options in the Convert To Bitmap dialog box

9. Click the **Transparent background** check box in the **Options** section to make the background of bitmap transparent.
10. Click **OK** button.

The vector image is converted into bitmap image as shown in Figure 19.4.

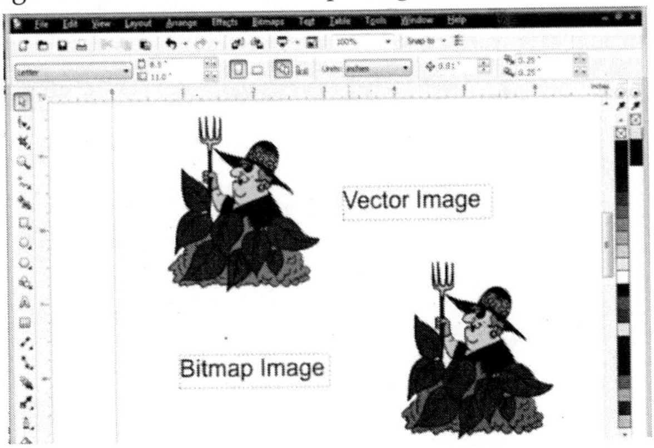

Figure 11.4 The vector image below is converted to bitmap

Converting Vector Images into a Bitmap when Exporting

Converting an image into a bitmap image while exporting helps you to work in an existing drawing without affecting the destination or the file type in which you have saved the current drawing.

To convert a vector image to a bitmap image while exporting, do this:

1. Select the image containing vector image as shown in Figure 11.5.
2. Select **File** menu and choose **Export...** from the **Menu** bar as shown in Figure 11.5.

   The **Export** dialog box appears as shown in Figure 11.6.

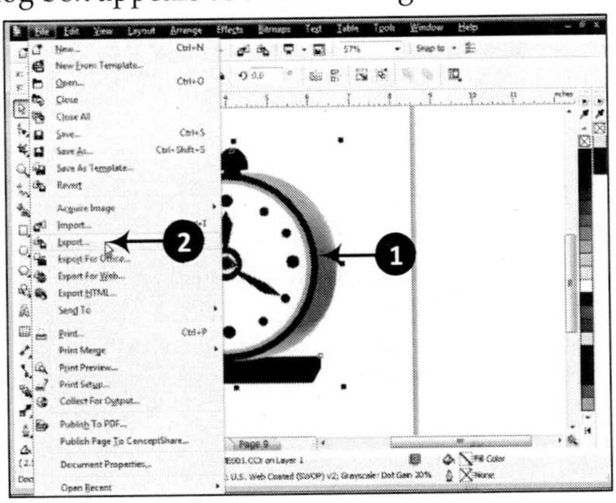

Figure 11.5 Selecting Export... option from the File menu bar

3. Navigate a location from the **Navigation** group located at the left side of the Export dialog box, to specify where you want to save your exported file.
4. Type the name for the image in the **File name:** drop-down list. In our case, we have typed the name **Export-bitmap** as shown in Figure 11.6.
5. Click the down arrow button of the **Save as type** drop-down list. A drop-down list appears.
6. Select a file extension for the exported image from the drop-down list. In our case, we have selected **BMP Window Bitmap**.
7. Click the **Export** button as shown in Figure 11.6.

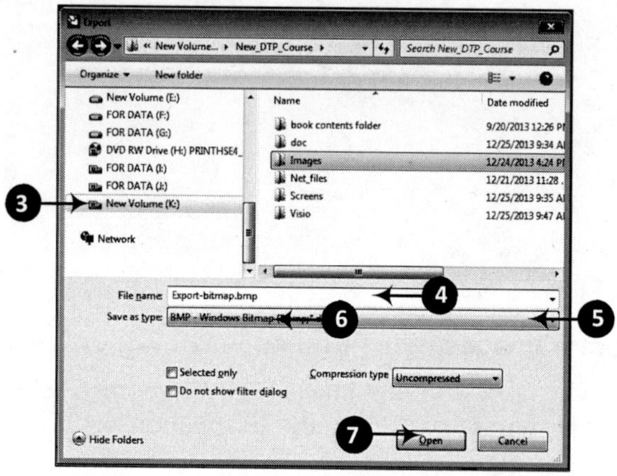

Figure 11.6 Export dialog box

As you click the **Export** button, the **Convert to Bitmap** dialog box appears as shown in Figure 11.7.

8. Type a value to specify the **Height:** and **Width:** of the exported image in the height and width spinner box of the **Image** Size section. In our case, we have typed **7.5 × 8.42** as shown in Figure 11.7.

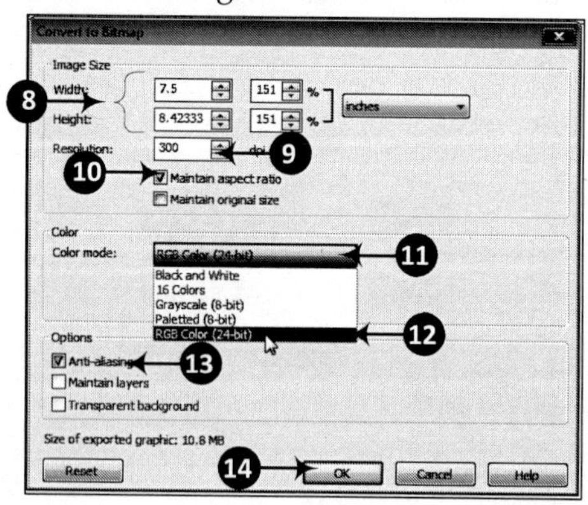

Figure 11.7 Convert to Bitmap dialog box

9. Type a value to specify the resolution for the image in the **Resolution:** spinner box of the Image Size section. In our case, we have typed **300 dip**.
10. Click the **Maintain aspect ratio** check box, to maintain the width and height of the image would not be changed if the image size is changed.
11. Click the down arrow of the **Color mode:** drop-down in **Color** section of the **Convert to Bitmap** dialog box (See Figure 11.7)
12. Select a Color mode from the drop-down list. In our case, we have selected **RGB Color (24-bit)**.
13. Click the **Anti-aliasing** check box in the **Options** section to smooth edges of the image (See Figure 11.7).
14. Click the OK button in the Convert to Bitmap dialog box as shown in Figure 11.7.

    The vector image will be converted to the bitmap and store to the location where you have exported it as shown in Figure 11.8.

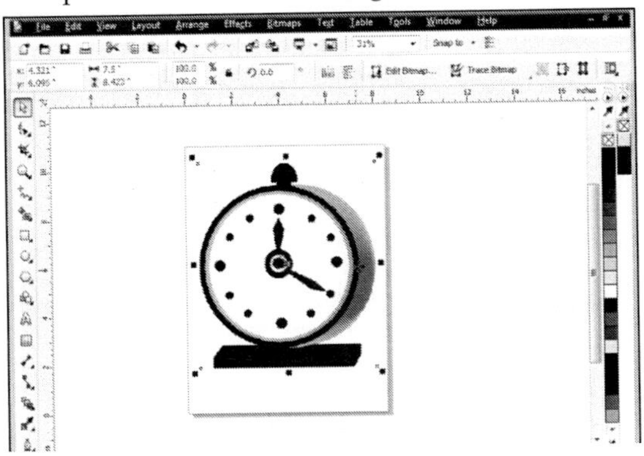

Figure 11.8 Export image converted to bitmap

After learning to export a vector image by converting it to a bitmap image, you can also import a bitmap image from other applications and use it in your CorelDRAW document as discussed in the next Section.

Importing a Bitmap

You can import a bitmap into a drawing either directly or by linking it to an external file. When you link to an external file, edits to the original file are automatically updated in the imported file. After you import a bitmap, the status bar provides information about its Color mode, size and resolution. You can import files created in other applications, such as Photoshop or Adobe Illustrator (AI) file.

To import a bitmap, do this:

1. Select the **File** menu and choose **Import** from the **Menu** bar as shown in Figure 11.9.

   The **Import** dialog box appears as shown in Figure 11.10.

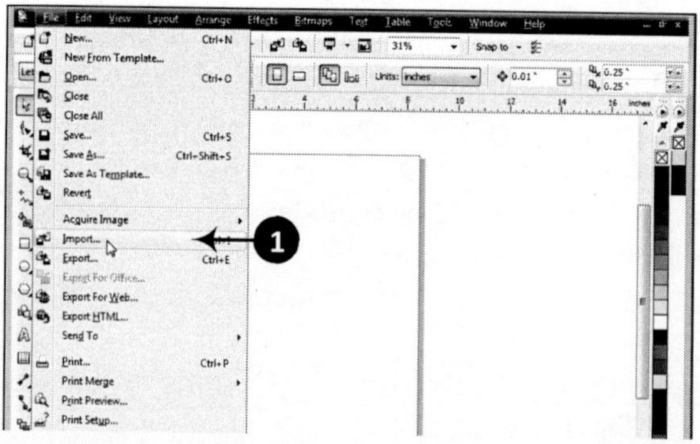

Figure 11.9 Selecting Import option from File menu

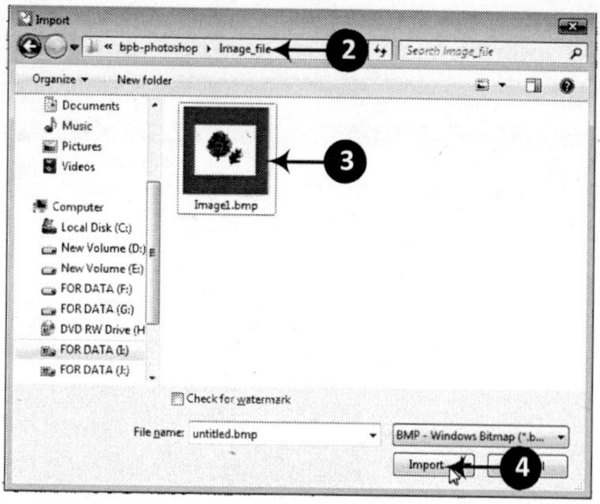

Figure 11.10 Import dialog box

2. Navigate the location where the bitmap file is stored. In our case, the navigate path is **Image_file** folder in the **I** drive.
3. Select the bitmap image you want to import on the **Drawing** page. In our case, we have selected the image **Image1.bmp** as shown in Figure 11.10.
4. Click the **Import** button in the Import dialog box.

   The shape of the mouse pointer changes and displays information, such as name and dimensions, of the image you want to import.
5. Place the mouse-pointer in the Drawing page where you want to place the imported graphic and click in the Drawing page, as shown in Figure 11.11.
6. The imported bitmap graphic appears, as shown in Figure 11.12.

After importing a bitmap image, you will learn how to crop, resample and resizing the image.

Modifying a Bitmap

After you add a bitmap to a drawing, you can crop, resample, and resize the bitmap. Cropping removes unwanted areas of a bitmap. When you resample a

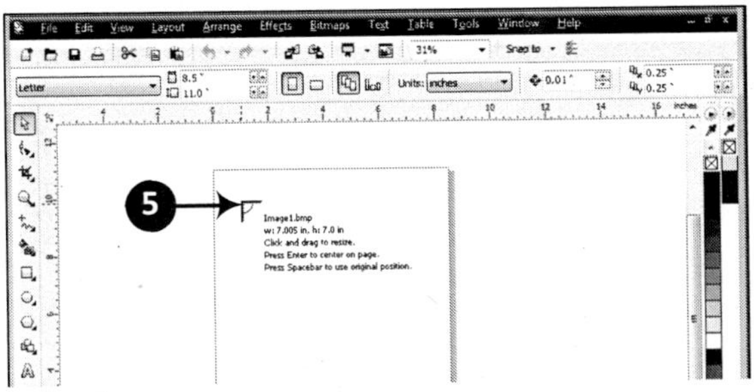

Figure 11.11 Place the mouse pointer on the drawing page

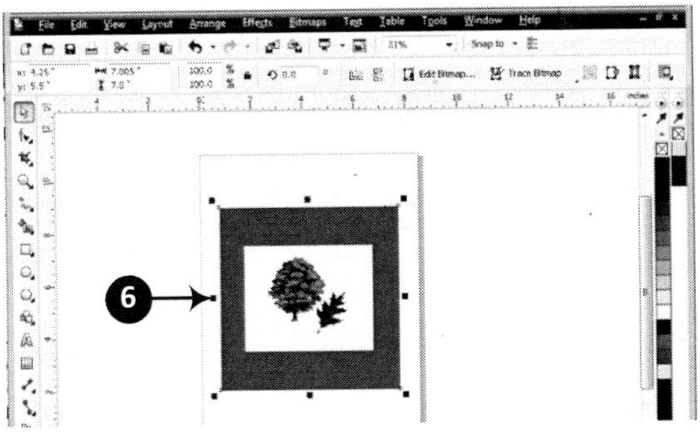

Figure 11.12 Imported graphic image

bitmap, you can change the image size, the resolution, or both by adding or removing pixels. For example, if you make an image larger without resampling, you can lose details because the image's pixels are spread over a greater area. By resampling, you can add pixels to preserve more detail from the original image. Resizing an image maintains the same number of pixels in a smaller or larger area. For example, you can lose details when you make an image large without resampling because the image's pixels are spread over a large area. Upsampling adds pixels to maintain some of the original's details.

Cropping a Bitmap

To crop a bitmap into a rectangular shape, you can use the Crop Tool. To crop a bitmap into an irregular shape, you can use the Shape Tool and the Crop bitmap command.

To crop a bitmap image, do this:

1. Open a document in CorelDRAW containing a bitmap image.
2. Select the image by using the **Pick** Tool as shown in Figure 11.13.
3. Click the **Bitmaps** menu and choose **Crop Bitmap** from the menu bar as shown in Figure 11.13.

   Nodes appear around the boundary of the image, which you can move to crop the image as required.

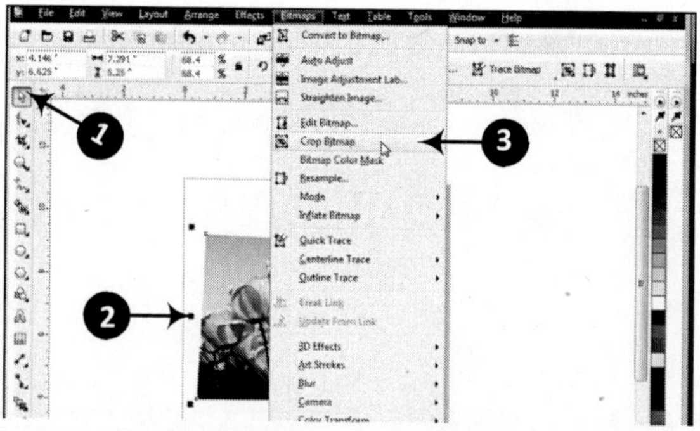

Figure 11.13 Selecting Crop Bitmap option

4. Select the nodes by using the **Shape** Tool option from the **Toolbox**.
5. Select and move the nodes to crop the image as required. The image, after performing the cropping operation is shown in Figure 11.14.

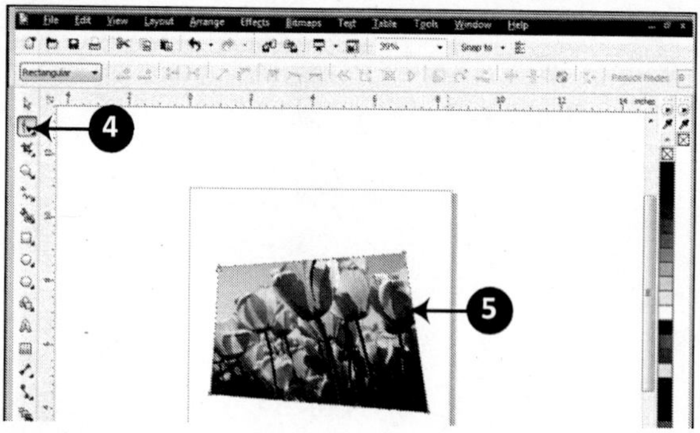

Figure 11.14 Drag the node to crop the image

Resampling a Bitmap

You can resample a bitmap image to improve its quality. This can be performed by the addition or removal of the pixels. When you resample a bitmap, you can change the image or the resolution, or both by adding or removing pixels. If you make an image larger without changing the resolution, the image may lose detail because the pixels are spread over a greater area.

To resample a bitmap image, do this:

1. Select a bitmap image as shown in Figure 11.15.
2. Click the **Bitmaps** menu and choose **Resample...** from the Menu bar as shown in Figure 11.15.
3. A Resample dialog box appears as shown in Figure 11.16.
4. Type a value in the **Resolution:** group in the **Horizontal:** and **Vertical:** spinner boxes.
5. Click the **Anti-alias** check box, as shown in Figure 11.16.

6. Select the **Maintain aspect ratio** check box to maintain the proportion of the bitmap image.
7. Select the **Maintain original size** check box to maintain the file size.
8. Click the **OK** button as shown in Figure 11.16.

   The image, after entering the values is shown in Figure 11.17.

   After resampling, let us learn how to resize a bitmap.

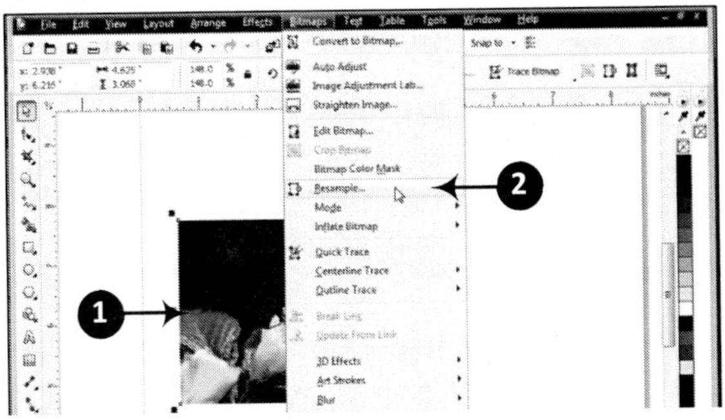

Figure 11.15 Selecting Resample option

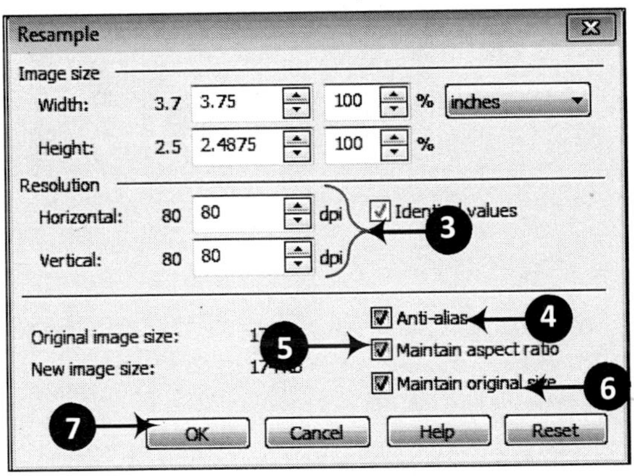

Figure 11.16 Resample dialog box

Figure 11.17 Resampling an image

Resizing a Bitmap

CorelDRAW allows you to resize a bitmap image. Resizing an image allows you to change the dimensions of the image maintaining the number of pixels.

To resize a bitmap image, do this:

1. Open a document containing an image.
2. Select the image by using the **Pick Tool**.
3. Click the **Bitmaps** menu and choose **Resample** from the Menu bar as shown in Figure 11.15.

   A **Resample** dialog box appears as shown in Figure 11.16.
4. Type a value in the **Image Size** group in the **Width:** and **Height:** spinner boxes as shown in Figure 11.18.

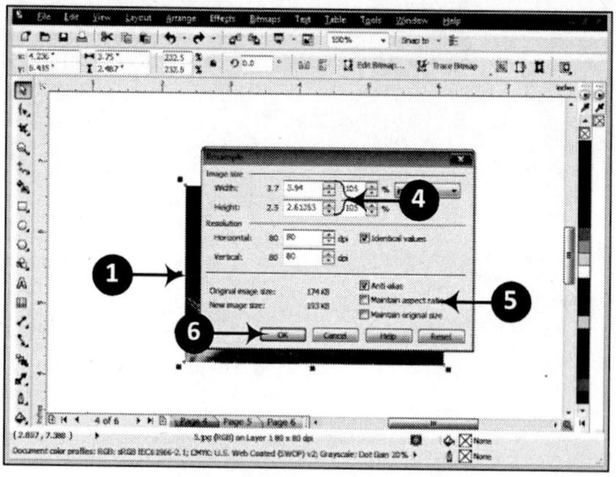

Figure 11.18 Setting options in Resample dialog box

5. Clear the **Maintain aspect ratio** check box so that the image is resized by the specified width and height as shown in Figure 11.18.
6. Click **OK** button.
7. The image is resized according to the values specified in the **Resample** dialog box as shown in Figure 11.19.

After resizing a bitmap, let us now learn how to use special effects to bitmap in the following Section.

Using Special Effects on Bitmap Images

You can apply various special effects to change the properties of bitmap images. Special effects change the properties of the image, such as Orientation and Color. There are number of effects to apply to a bitmap image:

3D effects: It lets you create the illusion of three-dimensional depth. These effects include 3-D Rotate, Cylinder and page curl.

Art strokes: It lets you apply hand-painted techniques. The art stroke media and styles include crayon, palette knife, Water Color, and pen and ink.

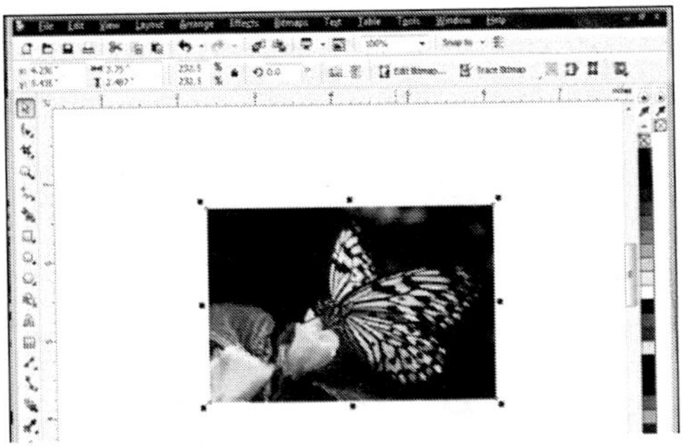

Figure 11.19 Resized image

Blur: It creates an image dim, dully, hazy and indistinct. Different Blur effects are Directional smooth, Low pass, and soften.

Camera: It lets you simulate the effect produced by diffusion filters of a diffusion lens.

Colour transform: It lets you create photographic illusions by using Colour reduction and replacements. These effects include Bit Plane, halftones, psychedelic, and solarizing.

Contour: It lets you highlight and enhance the edges of an image. The contour effects include Edge Detect and Find Edges.

Creative: It lets you apply various textures and shapes to an image. The creative effects include Frames, Particles, Scatter, Smoked Glass and Weather.

Distort: It lets you distort image surfaces. These effects include Block, Displace, Offset, Ripple and Tile.

Noise: It lets you modify the graininess of an image. The noise effects include Add Noise, Maximum, Median, Minimum, and Remove Noise.

Sharpen: It lets you create enhance edges of an image. The sharpen effects include Adaptive Unsharp, Directional Sharpen, High Pass, Sharpen and Unsharp Mask.

Plug-ins: It lets you apply effects from a third-party filter to bitmaps in CorelDRAW.

Applying 3D Effects to a Bitmap

CorelDRAW provide you these feature to create the illusion of three-dimensional (3D) depth in objects by adding contour, perspective, extrusion, bevel, or drop shadow effects.

To apply 3D Effects to a bitmap image, do this:

1. Select a bitmap image.
2. Select the **Bitmap** menu. Highlight **3D Effects**. A sub menu appears. Select **3D Rotate...** from the **Menu** bar as shown in Figure 11.20.

   A **3D Rotate** dialog box appears as shown in Figure 11.21.

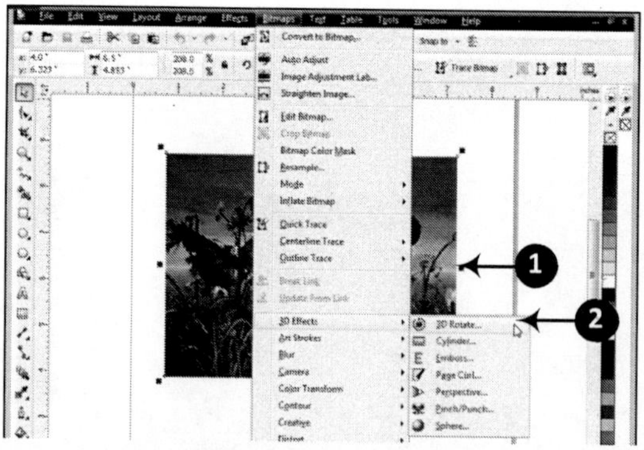

Figure 11.20 Selecting 3D Rotate... option from the Bitmap menu bar

3. Type values in the **Vertical:** and **Horizontal:** spinner boxes to rotate and position the object as shown in Figure 11.21.
4. Select the **Best fit** check box to ensure that the bitmaps stay within the boundary of the drawing page.
5. Click the **Preview** button to see the preview of the image.
6. Click the **OK** button to apply the effect.
7. Image after applying 3D Rotate effect is shown in Figure 11.22.

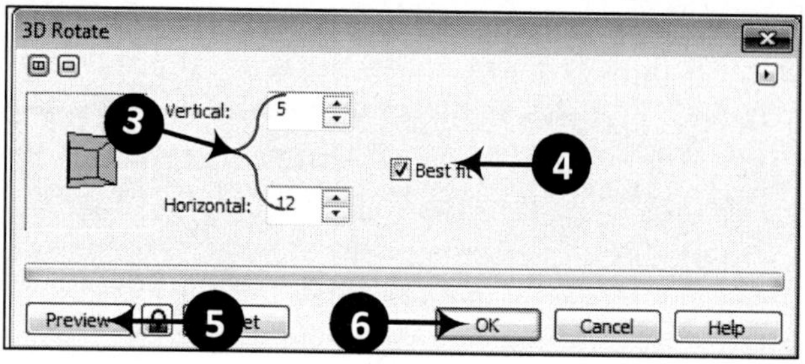

Figure 11.21 3D Rotate dialog box

Figure 11.22 Image after 3D Rotate effect

Applying Color Transform Effects to a Bitmap

CorelDRAW allows you to apply various Color Transform effects, such as Bit Plane, Halftone, Psychedelic and Solarize. These effects create pictorial illusions using the Color reduction and replacements.

To apply Color Transform effects to a bitmap image, do this:

1. Select a bitmap image.
2. Select the **Bitmaps** menu. Highlight **Color Transform**. A sub menu appears. Select **Bit Planes...** from the Menu bar as shown in Figure 11.23.

   A **Bit Planes** dialog box appears as shown in Figure 11.24.
3. Type a value in any one of the three options: **Red**, **Green**, and **Blue**. When you select the value of one option, the value of the other two options automatically changes. Or you can drag the slider to change the value.

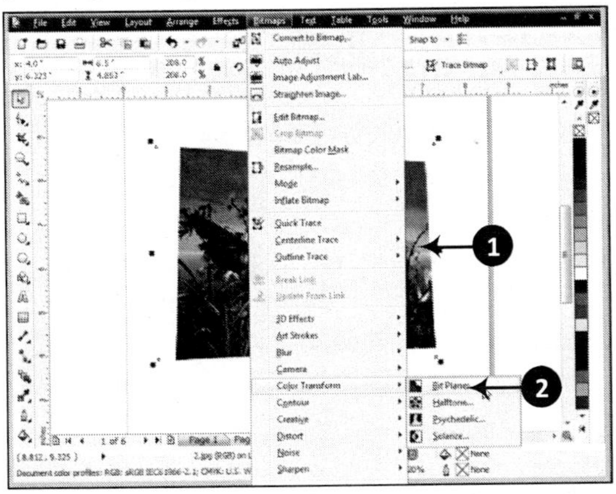

Figure 11.23 Selecting Color Transform option

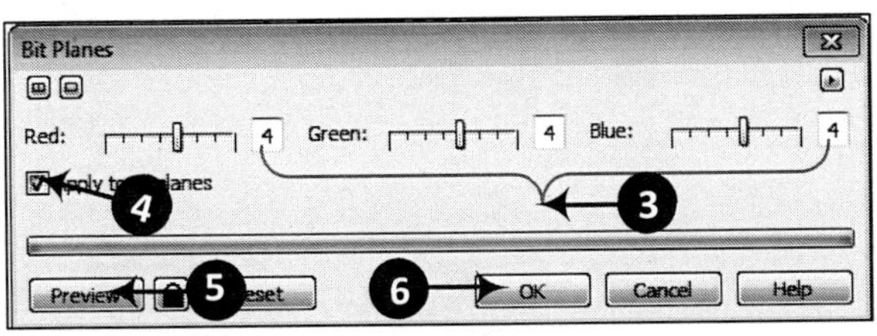

Figure 11.24 Bit Planes dialog box

4. Select the **Apply to all planes** check box.
5. Click the **Preview** button to see the preview of the image.
6. Click the **OK** button to apply the effect, as shown in Figure 11.24.
7. The **Color Transform** effect is applied to the selected image, as shown in Figure 11.25.

After applying Color transition effect, let us learn how to apply sharpen effect.

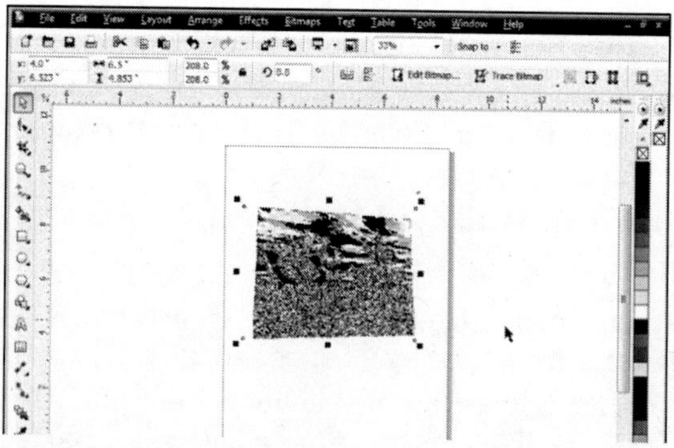

Figure 11.25 Color Transform effect is applied in the image

Applying Sharpen Effects to a Bitmap

You can apply a sharpen effect to focus and enhance the edges of a bitmap image. The Sharpen effects make the edges of an image more prominent. This helps in hiding the minor focusing errors. It includes Adaptive Unsharp, Directional Sharpen, High Pass, Sharpen and Unsharp Mask.

To apply Sharpen effect to a bitmap, do this:

1. Select a bitmap image.
2. Select **Bitmaps** menu. Highlight **Sharpen** and then choose **Adaptive Unsharp...** from the Menu bar as shown in Figure 11.26.
3. An **Adaptive Unsharp** dialog box appears as shown in Figure 11.27.

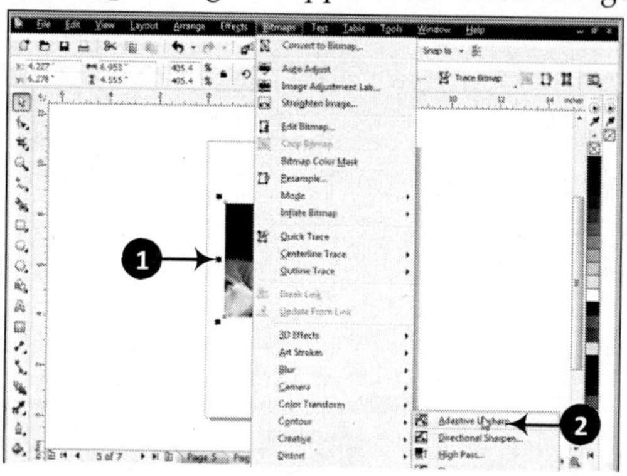

Figure 11.26 Selecting Adaptive Unsharp option

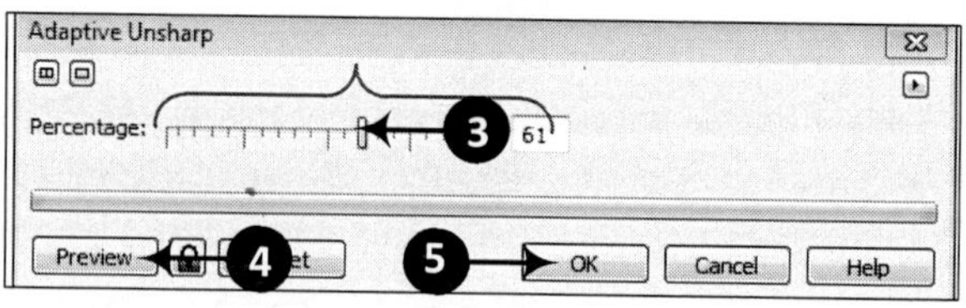

Figure 11.27 Adaptive Unsharp dialog box

4. Move the slider beside **Percentage:** option to change the value. You can also type a value for the percentage in the text box.
5. Click the **Preview** button to see the preview of the image.
6. Click the **OK** button to apply the effect.
7. You can see the image after applying **Adaptive Unsharp**, as shown in Figure 11.28.

After applying sharpen effect to a bitmap, let us how to trace a bitmap image in the next Section.

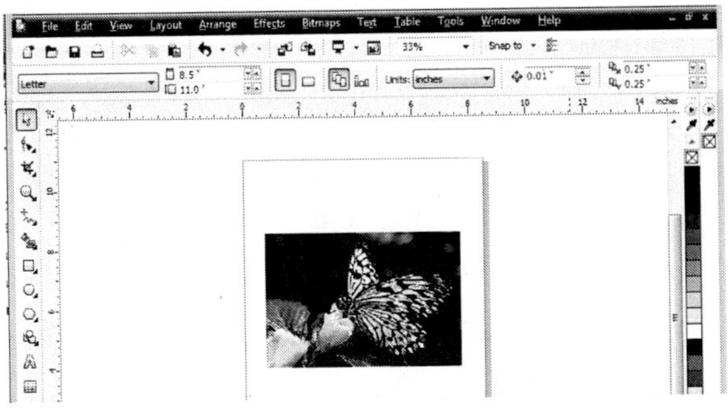

Figure 11.28 Image after applying Adaptive Unsharp feature

Tracing Bitmaps

CorelDRAW lets you trace bitmaps to convert them to fully editable and scalable vector graphics. You can trace artwork, photos, scanned sketches, or logos and then easily integrate them into your designs.

The Quick Trace Command in CorelDRAW

You can trace a bitmap by using the Quick Trace command.

To trace a bitmap by using Quick Trace, do this:

1. Select a bitmap image.
2. Select the **Bitmaps** menu and choose **Quick Trace** from the Menu bar.

   Now, traced image is shown in Figure 11.29.

Figure 11.29 Traced image

CHAPTER 12

Working with PageMaker 7

Introduction

PageMaker software is designed for business professionals, small-office users, and educators who want to create professional-quality documents for print and electronic distribution and also who want to create high-quality Publications, such as brochures and newsletters. It is a Publication development Tool used for creating print or electronic reading material. PageMaker's features enable you to create Publications using either formatted templates or original designs.

The user makes it possible to integrate with other software products, such as spreadsheets and graphic design programs. Data from spreadsheets can be imported into PageMaker, merged, and used to create mailing labels. PageMaker incorporates industry printing standards for output to high- and low-end printers.

This Chapter gives you a detail overview about PageMaker and takes you through the basics of effectively working in this package.

In this Chapter, you will learn how to start PageMaker 7 and window elements. Next, you will learn how to create a new document and setting Page Size in PageMaker. And then you will also learn how to create text using the Text Tool and text blocks. Finally, you will learn how to change paragraph spacing and to set indents and tabs.

Starting Pagemaker 7

To start PageMaker, do this:

1. Click the **Start** menu highlight **Programs**, highlight **Adobe** and then highlight **PageMaker** and choose **PageMaker 7** as shown in Figure 12.1.
2. PageMaker opens the opening window as shown in Figure 12.2 appears.

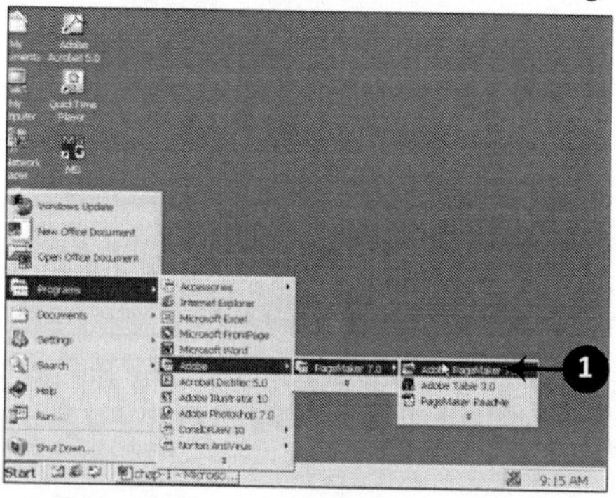

Figure 12.1 Starting PageMaker

PageMaker Window Elements

The PageMaker window is the working space for creating and producing documents. The PageMaker window elements are marked as shown in Figure 12.2 and explained here under.

- **Title bar**–The Title bar appears at the top of the PageMaker window. When the size of the window is less than the maximum size, you can move the entire window by clicking on the Title bar and dragging the mouse to a new position.

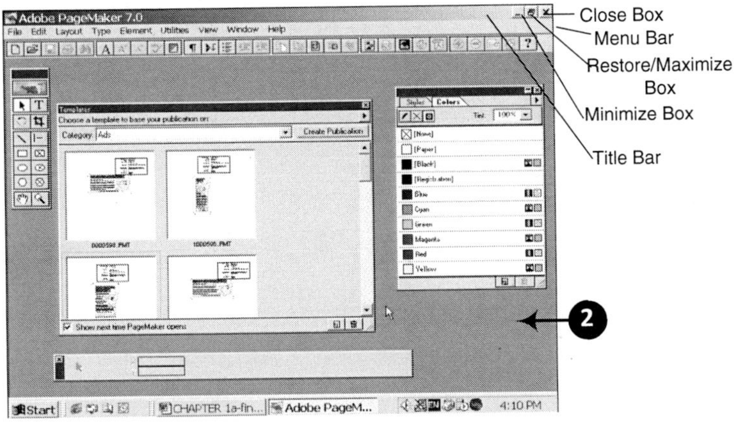

Figure 12.2 Opening screen of PageMaker

- **Close box**–The Close box is located at the right corner of the PageMaker window. Click the Close box once to close the active window.
- **Restore box / Maximize box**–On the left of the Close Box is the Restore box. This appears only when the PageMaker window is maximized. Once you click the Restore box it is replaced by the Maximize Box.
- **Minimize box**–On the left of the Restore/Maximize box, is the Minimize box. Clicking the Minimize box reduces the PageMaker window to a button on the Taskbar.
- **Menu bar**–The Menu bar is located below the Title bar and contains the Pull-down menus.

The Work Area

When you create a Publication, PageMaker opens a Publication window that contains an empty page centered on the pasteboard (See Figure 12.3). The pasteboard is the entire work area, and the page is the area within the pasteboard, which is printed.

The elements of the work area are marked in Figure 12.3 and explained below.

- The Toolbox includes Tools for creating or editing objects.

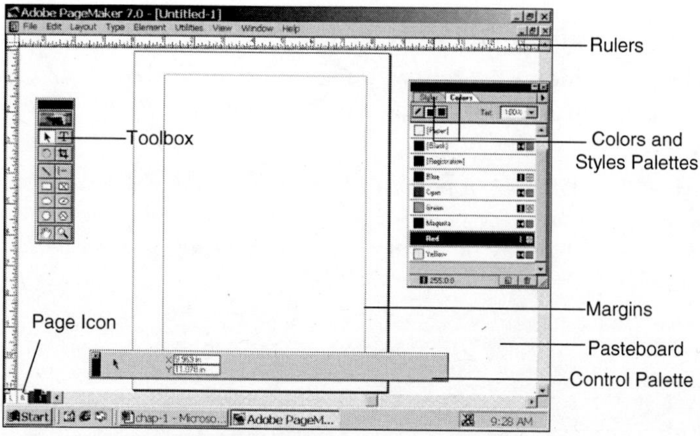

Figure 12.3 Work Area

- Margins appear as dotted lines.
- A Page icon shows the master pages (Left and Right) and the regular pages in the Publication.
- Rulers help you align objects on the page.
- The Colors and Styles palettes are used to add, delete, and edit colors and styles.
- The Pasteboard stores items for later use.
- The Control Palette provides commands for making precise changes to text and graphics.

Viewing the Page

PageMaker offers a number of views of your document pages. You can shrink the image to see the whole page, or see varying enlargements of the page up to 400% of actual size. When a new document is created, it is initially displayed in the Fit in Window view (See Figure 12.4). You see the whole page and the edges of the PageMaker pasteboard at each side of the page. This view is ideal for seeing the overall design of a page. You can change views of the page at any time. You can scroll within the window using the scroll bars or the Hand Tool.

To change the view size of your page, do this:

1. Click the **View** menu. The various view options are displayed (See Figure 12.4).
2. **Zoom In (Ctrl+)**-Displays the page at the next higher magnification.
   - **Zoom Out (Ctrl-)**-Displays the page at the next lower magnification.
   - **Entire Pasteboard (Shift+Ctrl+0)**—Shrinks the page to a postage-stamp size, and shows the entire width (and contents) of the pasteboard (See Figure 12.5).

- **Zoom To** – Displays the Zoom To submenu.
- **Actual size (Ctrl+1)** – Shows an exact one-to-one representation of the page, as shown in Figure 12.6. Use this view when adjusting lines, text or graphics, or when typing text on a page.
- **Fit in Window (Ctrl+0)** – Shows the full page in the window, no matter how large is the subject matter.

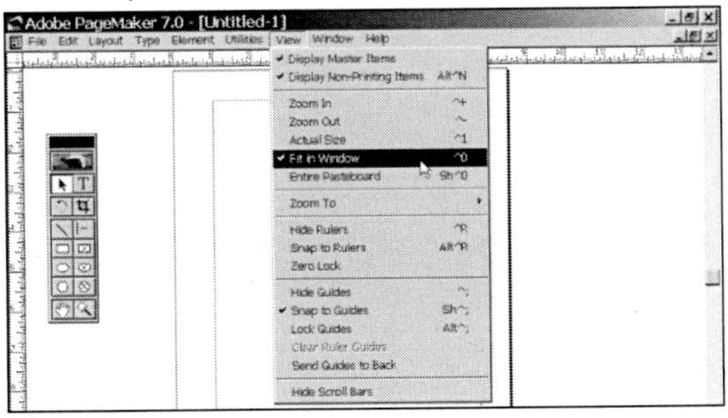

Figure 12.4 Selecting Fit in Window from the View menu

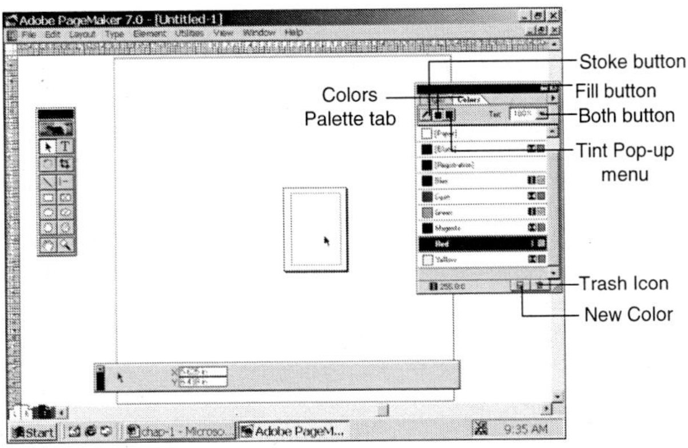

Figure 12.5 A pasteboard view size shows a thumbnail layout of the page

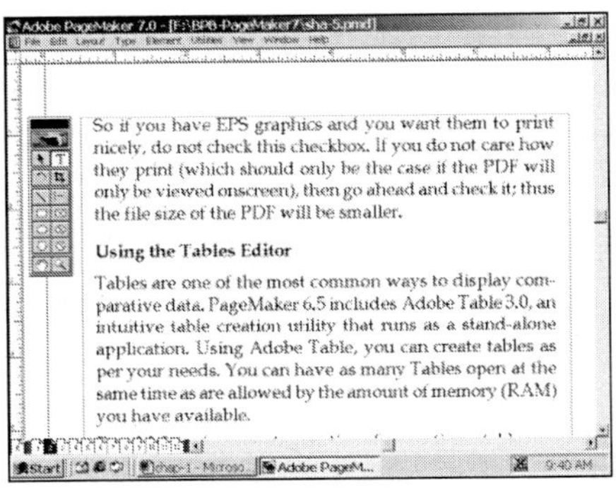

Figure 12.6 Actual view size of the same page

Toolbox

The Toolbox is displayed by default (See Figure 12.7). The Toolbox contains all the Tools you require to compose your page. When you click the mouse pointer on a Tool, the mouse changes to that Tool when you move the pointer outside the boundaries of the Toolbox. The Tools in the Toolbox are shown in Figure 12.7 Let us discuss each of them in brief.

Pointer Tool: Use the pointer to select any kind of object on the page, including blocks of text, lines, boxes, circles, and imported graphics. When selected, the objects display sizing handles (See Figure 12.8).

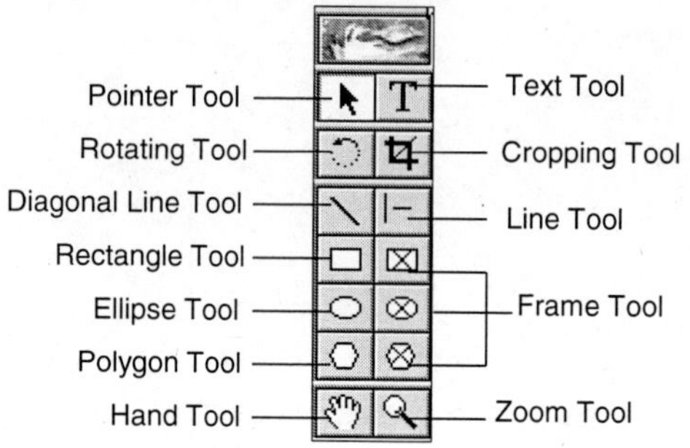

Figure 12.7 PageMaker Toolbox

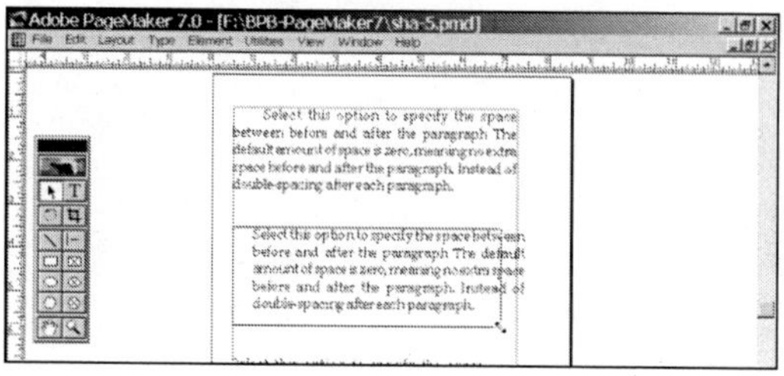

Figure 12.8 Selected objects are sized by their handles

- **Rotating Tool:** This Tool allows you to rotate a selected item to any of 360° of rotation in 0.01° increments. To use the Tool, first click the item you want to rotate with Pointer Tool. Then click the Rotating Tool. Move the crosshairs to the center of rotation for the item, press and hold down the mouse button, and draw a line with the crosshairs in the direction you want to rotate. When you have established the degree of rotation you want, release the mouse button. You can force the rotation to 45° increments by holding down the **Shift** key while draging the rotating lever.
- **Diagonal Line Tool:** Use this Tool to draw diagonal lines. You can select a diagonal line with the Pointer Tool and click on either handle to resize the line or change its angle.
- **Rectangle Tool:** This Tool draws square-cornered boxes. Click the mouse button to position the upper-left corner of the box and drag the Box Tool

icon to the right and down to create the box. Holding down the **Shift** key while drawing creates a square.

- **Ellipse Tool:** Use this Tool to draw circles and ovals. You can draw ovals much like boxes. Start in the upper-left side and drag toward the lower right. Holding down the Shift key while drawing creates a circle.
- **Polygon Tool:** Use this Tool to draw regular-sided (i.e., all the sides have the same length) polygons.
- **Hand Tool:** Use this Tool to move the entire image around on the screen.
- **Text Tool:** Clicking the Text Tool changes the pointer to an insertion point for typing, editing, highlighting text and formatting the text.
- **Cropping Tool:** Use this Tool to crop (reduce the image area of) graphics and scanned photos.
- **Line Tool:** This Tool draws vertical and horizontal lines. You can shorten or lengthen the lines with the Pointer Tool by clicking on either handle.
- **Box frame Tool:** Use this Tool to create rectangular frames into which you may place text or pictures.
- **Ellipse frame Tool:** This Tool creates oval and circular frames for text or images.
- **Polygon frame Tool:** This Tool creates multisided frames for text and pictures.
- **Zoom Tool:** This Tool is used to change the magnification of your page view.

Floating Palettes

PageMaker provides you with the option of having different palettes on the screen, which help you in efficiently working with your Publication. The different palettes are:

- Control palette
- Colors
- Styles
- Layers
- Master pages
- Hyperlinks

To control the display of palettes, do this:

1. Click the **Window** menu and choose the **Palette** or press **Ctrl + '** you want to display.
2. When the Palette is displayed, the option changes to **Hide Control Palette** option (See Figure 12.9).

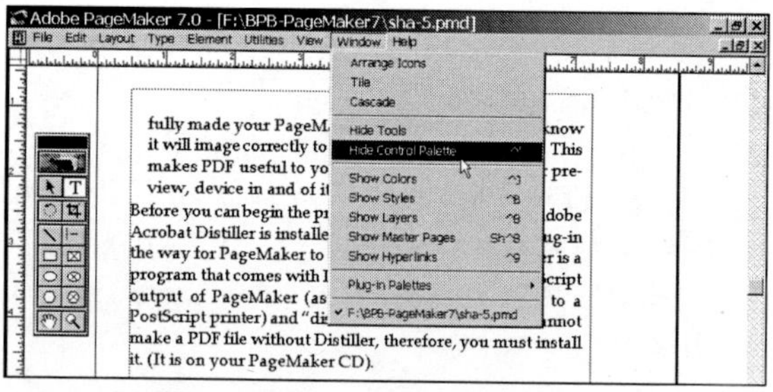

Figure 12.9 Window menu

Colors and Styles Palettes

The Color and Styles palettes appear in the same group (See Figure 12.10).

The Colors palette is used to apply colors or view the name or kind of color applied to the selected text or object. The other functions of the Colors palette are shown in the palette menu. To display the colors palette menu click the right arrow (See Figure 12.10).

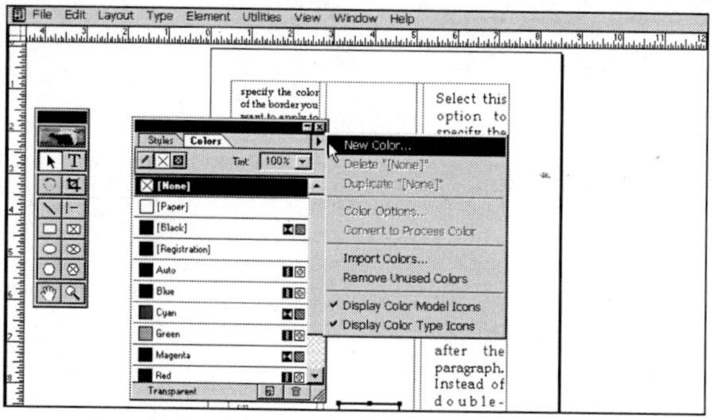

Figure 12.10 Colors Palette menu

The Styles palette is used to apply a style. Just click in a paragraph with the Text Tool and then click a style name in the palette. The other functions of the Styles palette are displayed in the palette menu (See Figure 12.11).

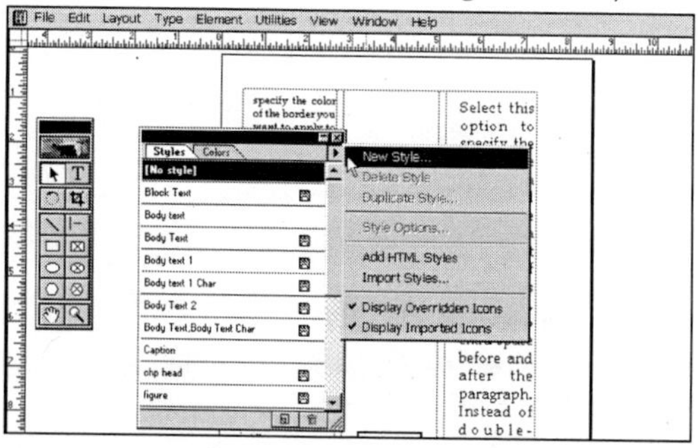

Figure 12.11 Styles Palette menu

Layers and Master Palettes

The Layers and Master palettes appear in the same group.

The Layers palette is used to create, edit, lock, and delete layers from your Publication. The palette functions are located in the palette menu.

The Master palette is used to create and apply masters, and use the master page icons on the bottom of the window when you want to go to a master page for editing. The palette functions are located in the palette menu.

Master page icons and **page number icons:** The lower-left corner of the window is the Master Page icons and the page icon, displaying the page numbers.

Using the Zoom Tool

The Zoom Tool lets you magnify or reduce the display of any area in your Publication. You can also double-click the Tool to jump to Actual Size, or press **Alt** key as you double-click the Tool to go to Fit in Window view.

To magnify or reduce with the Zoom Tool, do this:

1. Select the Zoom Tool.

   The pointer becomes a magnifying glass with a plus sign in its center, as shown in Figure 12.12 indicating that the Zoom Tool will magnify your view of the image. The magnifying glass shows a minus sign in its center in reduction mode.

   To toggle between magnification and reduction, press the ***Ctrl*** *key.*

2. Position the magnifying glass at the center of the area you want to magnify or reduce, and then click, to zoom in or zoom out.

   Continue clicking until the Publication is at the magnification level you want. When the Publication has reached its maximum magnification or reduction level, the center of the magnifying glass appears blank.

To magnify part of a page by dragging, do this:

1. Select the Zoom Tool.
2. Drag to draw a marquee around the area you want to magnify as shown in Figure 12.13.

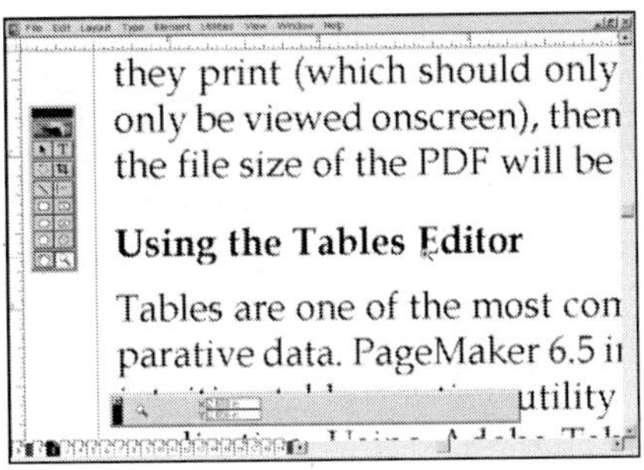

Figure 12.12 Zoom Tool icon

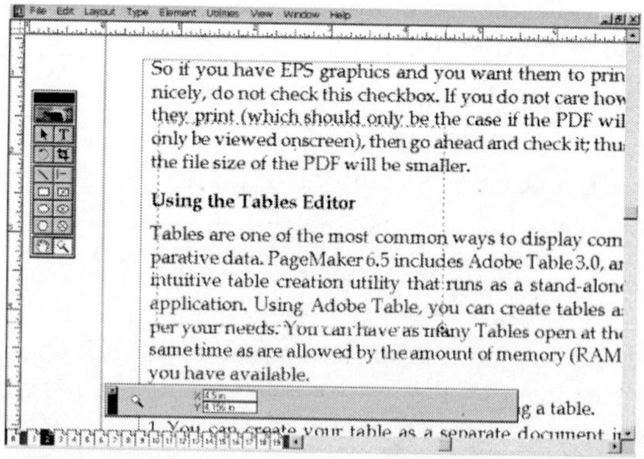

Figure 12.13 Magnifying a part of the page

To zoom in or out while using another Tool, do this:

1. Press **Ctrl+Spacebar** keys together to zoom in. Press **Ctrl+Alt+Spacebar** keys together to zoom out.
2. Click to zoom in or out, or drag to select an area you want to zoom in or out.

Using the Rulers

The rulers give you accuracy in laying out a page. As you move the mouse pointer or Tool icon across the page, reference marks also move on the horizontal and vertical rulers, indicating the current position of the mouse, as shown in Figure 12.14.

Displaying the Rulers (Ctrl+R)

If rulers are not displayed in the document window, you can activate them by pressing **Ctrl+R** keys together. The default measurement system for the rulers is in inches, but you can change to any of the several measurement systems, such as cms (Centimeters), etc., at any time.

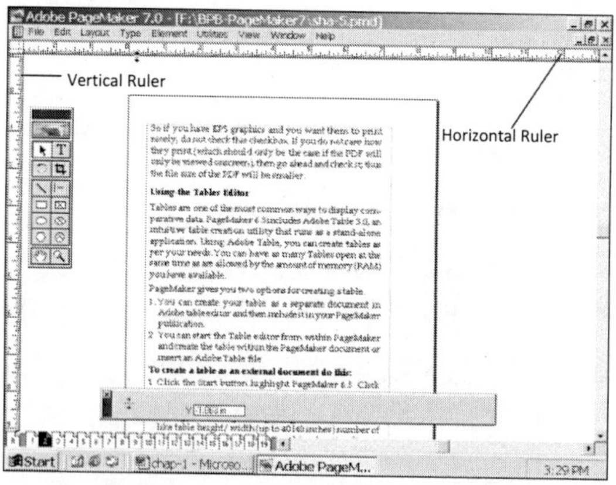

Figure 12.14 Vertical and Horizontal Rulers

Creating Publication

While using PageMaker 7, you work with a Publication. In other words, a document prepared in PageMaker is referred to as a Publication and the file is saved with the extension .PMD (PageMaker Document).

The Publication has the text objects and graphic objects. The text objects are also called stories. The graphics objects may contain drawings prepared with PageMaker or scanned images imported from another application software. While opening a Publication you can open an existing Publication or a new Publication, or a Publication prepared in an earlier version of PageMaker.

To open an existing Publication designed in PageMaker 7, do this:

1. Click **File** menu and choose **Open...** . The **Open Publication** dialog box appears as shown in Figure 12.12.
2. Select the Publication you want to open.
3. PageMaker keeps a record of the last eight Publications you have worked with.
4. To open any one from the last eight Publications, click the **File** menu and choose **Recent Publications** as in Figure 12.16.
5. Select **Original** or **Copy**.
6. Click **OK**.

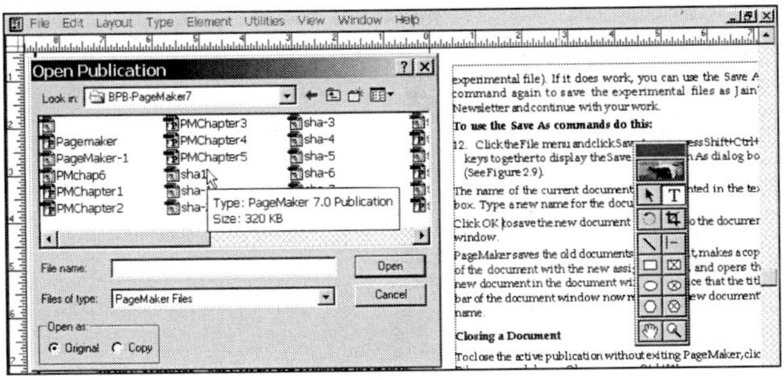

Figure 12.15 Open Publication dialog box

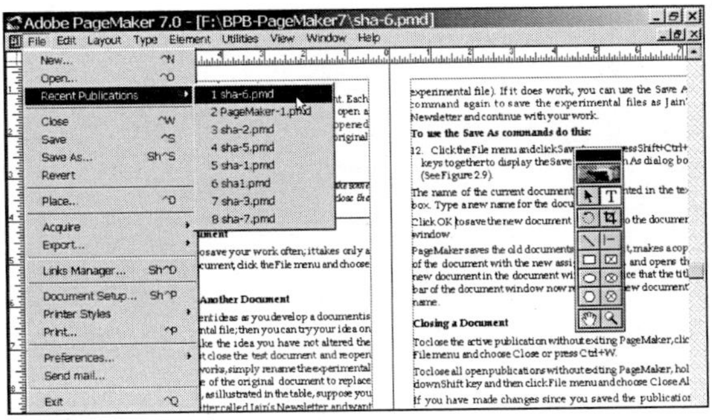

Figure 12.16 Select option available in Recent Publications in the File menu

Creating a New Document

To create new document, do this:

1. Click the **File** menu and choose **New...** or press **Ctrl+N** keys together. PageMaker displays the **Document Setup** dialog box as shown in Figure 12.17.

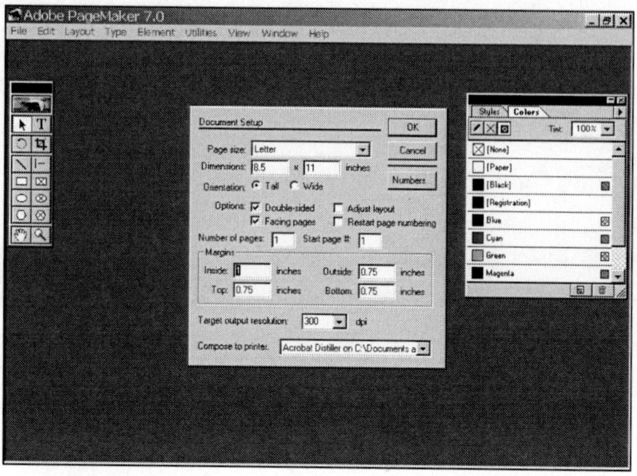

Figure 12.17 Document Setup Dialog Box

2. The **Options** in the **Document Setup** dialog box are:

   Page size–Indicates the size of paper. For this document, based on the printer you have selected.

   Dimensions– Indicates the overall width and height (in inches) of the paper specified in the Page List box. You can enter your own dimensions here to define a custom page size.

   Orientation–The default orientation is Tall (also called Portrait). Wide orientation turns the page 90° (also called Landscape). Depending on the page dimensions you enter above, PageMaker selects the Tall or Wide radio button orientation automatically.

3. In **Options:** area there are two types:

   Double sided–Click this option if you will be printing on both sides of the paper. Selecting this option lets you set the inside and outside margin.

   Facing pages–Click this option if you want left and right pages to be displayed together.

   Number of pages–In this text box, type the number of pages you initially plan for the Publication. You can always add or delete pages later, if necessary.

   Start page #–This check box indicates which number to start numbering the pages with (for example, if you want your first page number to be 7 and your second page to be 8, and so on, enter 7 in the text box).

Margins–The default margins for a new document are displayed in Figure 12.17. However, you can change the margins if you wish.

Setting the Margins

You can change the margin size and the page size to suit your need. Remember, the page size is the overall size of the printed page. Margins are the inner boundaries of that page, which define where the printer prints text and graphics. The margins that you specify are applied to the document master as well as to all pages in the document.

Margins appear on the pages as pink (horizontal) and blue (vertical) non-printing lines.

To change the margin settings, do this:

1. In the Document Setup dialog box, position the mouse pointer in the Margins Measurement text box you want to change, and click the mouse button to highlight the current entry (See Figure 12.17).
2. Type the new margin value. If the default margins are in inches and you want to enter a pica value, simply type P after the value. When you click **OK** or press **Enter key** to leave the dialog box, PageMaker converts the inch measurement to equivalent pica (for example, 1 inch is converted to 6 picas).
3. Press **Tab** to move to the next margin text box you want to change. *Alternatively*, click the margin text box you want to change.
4. When you have finished, click **OK** or press **Enter** key to display the new document window.

Setting the Page Size

PageMaker comes configured with standard paper sizes like A3, A4, etc., based on the capability of your laser printer. You cannot print a larger page size than your printer can physically handle, but you can always specify a smaller size.

To change the page size, do this:

1. Position the mouse pointer over the first dimension text box and click the mouse button to highlight the current dimensions.
2. Type the new dimension. If the default dimensions are in inches and you want to enter a pica value, simply type P after the value. When you click **OK** or press **Enter key** to leave the dialog box, PageMaker converts the inch measurement to equivalent Picas (for example, 8.5×14 inch is converted to 51×84 picas).
3. Press **Tab** to move to the second dimension text box or click the second dimension box. Enter its value.
4. When you are finished, click **OK** or press **Enter** key to move to the new document window.

Setting the Page Orientation

If you find after setting a different page size, that the page width is actually the height because you entered the page dimension values in the wrong order, you can easily change the orientation without re-entering the page dimensions.

To change the page orientation, do this:

1. In the **Document Setup** dialog box, to change a Tall document to a Wide document, click the **Wide** radio button. To change Wide to Tall orientation, click the **Tall** radio button.
2. Click **OK** or press **Enter** key to return to the document window.

The Page Icons

You can easily move from one page to another when you are working on a Publication with multiple pages. You can go directly to a specific page or thumb through pages in sequential or random order. You can also view master pages.

To move between Publication pages, do this:

1. Click a page icon along the bottom of the layout window. (Click the left or right arrows to view lower-or higher-numbered page icons.)
2. Click **Layout** menu and choose **Go to page...** . Or press **Alt+Ctrl+G** keys together and type the page number you want.
3. To go to the previous page, press the **Page Up** key; to go to the next page, press the **Page Down** key.
4. To move sequentially through the Publication, press **Shift** key and click **Layout** menu and choose **Go to page...** . To stop the slide show, click the mouse, or press any key on the keyboard.

Inserting and Removing Pages

PageMaker gives you complete freedom to add or remove pages. You specify where you want to add a page, or where you want to delete page. Then select the command from the Page pull-down menu. The pages you add have the page setup parameters you specified for your existing pages.

Inserting a Page

To insert a page, do this:

1. Click the **Layout** menu and choose **Insert Pages...** . The **Insert Pages** dialog box appears as shown in Figure 12.18.

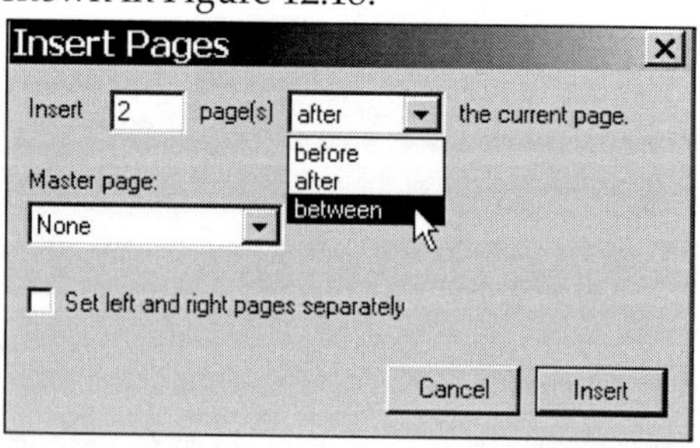

Figure 12.18 Insert Pages dialog box

2. Select the page before or after the page you want to add. Say, you want to add a page after page 10, go to either page 10, or to the current page by using **Go To** command or press **Alt+Ctrl+G** keys together.
3. The insertion point is positioned in the **Insert Page(s)** text box, which shows a default value of 2. Enter the number of pages to insert, or accept the default value.
4. Click one out of the three options before, after, between from the drop-down lists:

   page(s) before the current page–Clicking this button inserts a new page before the page you are on. Your current page number increases by the number of inserted pages.

   page(s) after the current page–Clicking this button adds a new page after the page you are on.

   page(s) between the current page–If you have selected Double sided pages in the Page Setup dialog box for this document, your pages are displayed as two-page spreads. Clicking this button allows you to add pages between the two pages currently displayed. Using this option changes the front and back orientation of the remaining two-page pairs in your document.
5. You can also choose which Master Page to base the inserted pages on—either the current Document Master or another Master Page you have designed (using the drop-down menu available from the Window: Master page palette). Click the **Master page:** drop-down list and select the Master Page you want.
6. **Set left and right pages separately**–Click this (check box) option if you want to set left and right pages separately.
7. Click **Insert** to return your document.

Removing a page

It would be a good idea to move to the page you want to remove before actually removing it. This way you can confirm that it is indeed the page you want to be deleted.

To remove the page, do this:

1. Click the **Layout** menu and choose **Remove Pages...** . The **Remove Pages** dialog box displaying a message appears as shown in Figure 12.19.

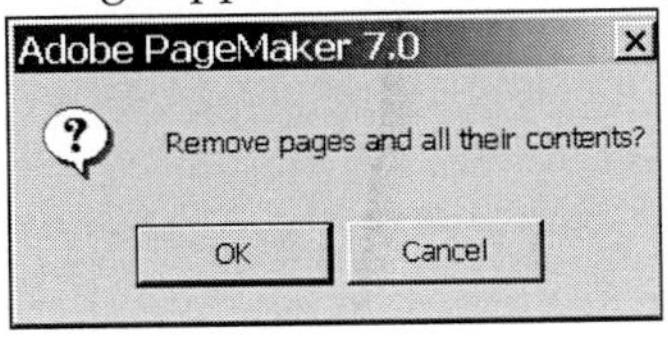

Figure 12.19 PageMaker displays a warning message

2. The insertion point is positioned in the **Remove page(s)** text box. The

Remove page(s) and **through:** text boxes display the page number you are on.

3. If you are removing only one page, enter the same page number in both text boxes (for example, if you want to remove page 27, type 27 in both text boxes). If you want to remove more than one page, type the beginning and ending page numbers, inclusive, in the two text boxes (for example, if you want to remove pages 27 through 34, type those numbers in the two text boxes)
4. Click **OK**. PageMaker displays a dialog box warning you that the contents of the pages will be deleted (See Figure 12.19). Click **OK** to confirm the removal and return to your document. Click **Cancel** to cancel the deletion.

Setting Page Numbers

When you create a new document, PageMaker sets the number of pages to 1 and highlights the text box. You can enter any number of pages up to 999.

To change the number of pages, do this:

1. Type the number of pages in the **Number of Pages:** text box of the **Document Setup** dialog box.
2. If you want the page number to start with a number other than 1, place the insertion point in the **Start page #:** text box, and click the mouse button.
3. Type the new beginning page number. Press **Tab** to move to the # of Pages text box.
4. Click **OK** or press **Enter** to move the new document window. For multipage documents, you need not be concerned with setting the correct number of pages—you can add more pages or delete excess pages at any time.
5. You cannot change the page size, orientation, or margin values for a single page within a multipage document. Any changes to the dialog box are global, and therefore, affect all pages of the document.

Saving a New Document

To save a new document, do this:

1. Click **File** menu, and choose **Save** to display the **Save Publication:** dialog box (See Figure 12.20). Or press **Ctrl+S** keys together.
2. The insertion point is positioned in the **File name:** text box. In this box type a file name for this document.
3. The default folder for the dialog box is Adobe PageMaker 7, where PageMaker's programs are located. To change the folder, click the drive or folder you would like using standard **Save** dialog box.
4. Select Publication in the **Save as type:** drop-down list.
5. Click **Save** to return to your document.

You assign a file name only once to a new document. Each subsequent time you open the document, you in fact open a copy of the document. Any changes made to the opened document are made to the copy until it is saved, then the original is updated with the changes.

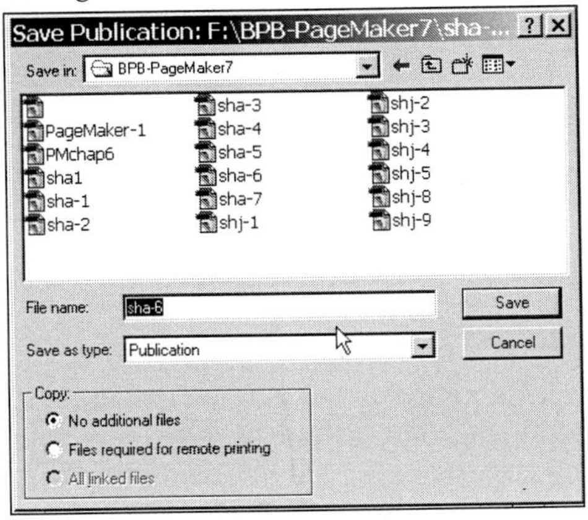

Figure 12.20 Save Publication: dialog box

Closing a Document

To close the active Publication, do this:

1. Click **File** menu and choose **Close** or press **Ctrl+W** keys together.
2. The document is closed without exiting PageMaker.

To close all open Publications, do this:

1. Hold down **Shift** key and then click **File** menu and choose **Close All.**

   All open documents are closed without exiting PageMaker.

   If you have made changes since you saved the Publication, PageMaker asks if you want to save those changes. (If you are closing more than one Publication, PageMaker prompts you to save any Publication containing Unsaved changes (See Figure 12.21). You can save changes, ignore them, or cancel using Close command.

2. If you want to save changes but have not yet named the Publication, PageMaker prompts you to save changes, by providing a dialog box. Type the file name and save the document, if you press Yes button.

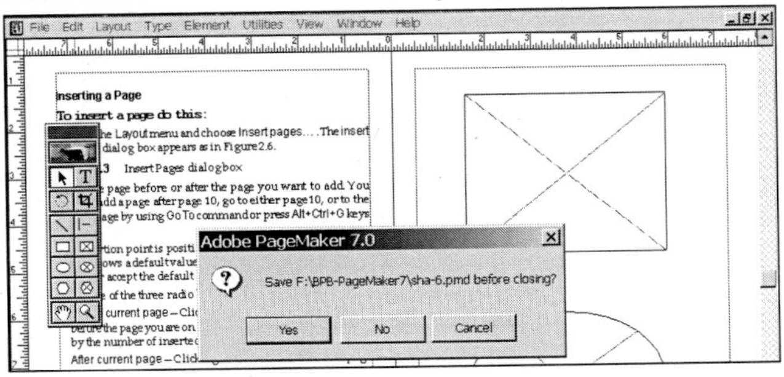

Figure 12.21 PageMaker prompts for saving a document

Working with Text

PageMaker 7 lets you create two types of text objects. One type of object is text blocks and another is text frames. PageMaker includes a special kind of object called a frame. A frame behaves in many ways like any other PageMaker graphic object. The way of working with text blocks and frames is more or less the same. While inserting text in your document, you directly enter the text in the PageMaker document or you can prepare your text in a word processor like Microsoft Word, etc., and then import the text in a PageMaker Publication. It is always advisable to type your text in Microsoft Word and then import it in PageMaker.

Using the Text Tool

While working with text in PageMaker, you have to use the Text Tool. The Text Tool is located in the upper-right corner of the Toolbox, and the icon appears with a letter T. If you click the icon, you get the I-beam text pointer (See Figure 12.22). You can toggle between the Text Tool and the Pointer Tool by pressing **Ctrl+Spacebar** keys together.

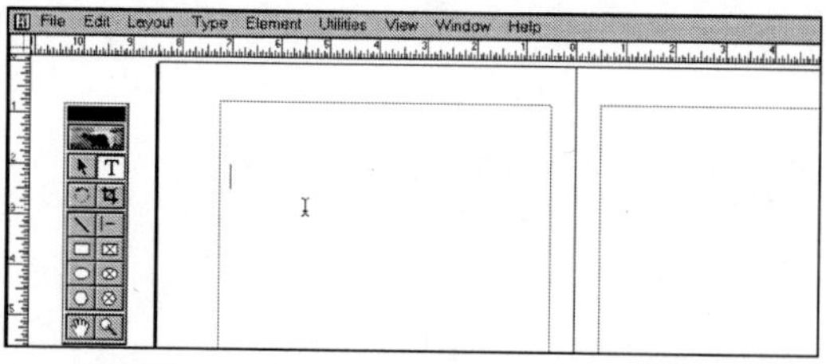

Figure 12.22 Text Tool and I beam text Pointer

To create text using Drag and Drop, do this:

1. Open both PageMaker and your Word Processing program so that both are visible onscreen.
2. Drag and drop selected pieces of text from one document to the other (See Figure 12.23). It shows a piece of text being dragged from Word into PageMaker.
3. You can drag and drop text or graphics from other programs like Photoshop, Illustrator, and WordPro, etc.

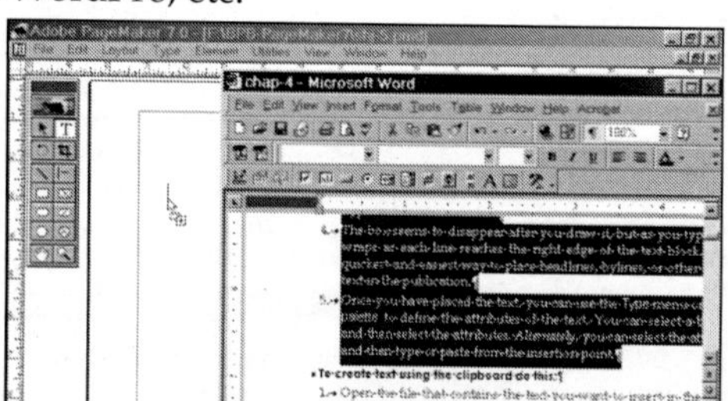

Figure 12.23 Drag Text from Word to PageMaker

To create text using the place command, do this:

1. First, prepare the page(s) on which you will place the text. Decide how many columns per page and how many pages you need to fill.
2. Click the **File** menu and choose **Place...** . The **Place** dialog box appears as shown in Figure 12.24.
3. In the **Look in:** box specifies the location of the file from the files list. Select the file you want to place and click Open button.
4. The file you select is ready to be placed.

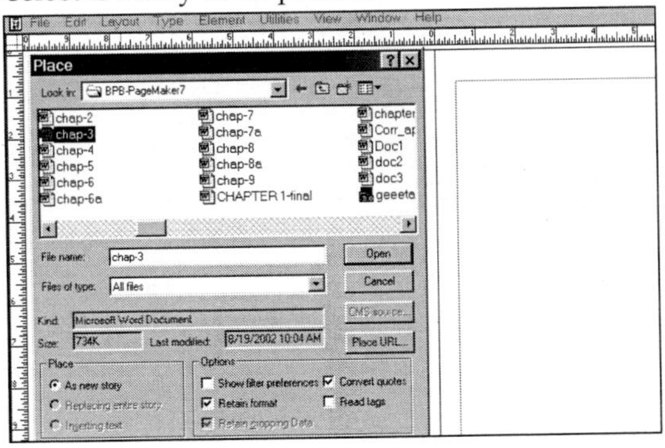

Figure 12.24 Place dialog box

PageMaker has two layout methods.

- Manual
- Automatic

The two methods are discussed in the following sections:

The Manual Text Icon

Manual text flow is the slowest method. The icon looks like a tiny page of text. It places only that much text as the column can hold; then it stops. A red arrow at the bottom of the text block indicates that there is more text to place.

To place more text, you must position the icon in the next column or text block to fill, and click again.

If you click anywhere between two column guides without dragging out a text block, the Manual icon fills a column from the click point to the lower margin or another text block.

To use Manual text flow, do this:

1. Click the **Layout** menu and turn off **Autoflow**. Press the **Ctrl** key to temporarily covert the **Autoflow** icon to a **Manual** icon.
2. Using the Manual icon, text stops flowing when it reaches the bottom of a column or if it hits another text block lower in the column. The bottom windowshade displays a down-arrow tab, indicating that you must reload your Manual text icon by single-clicking the tab to place the next text block in the thread (See Figure 12.25).

The Autoflow Text Icon

Automatic text flow, or Autoflow, is the fastest way to place text on a page. The curvy line of the Autoflow text placement icon suggests the way text blocks thread together on a page to create a story (See Figure 12.26).

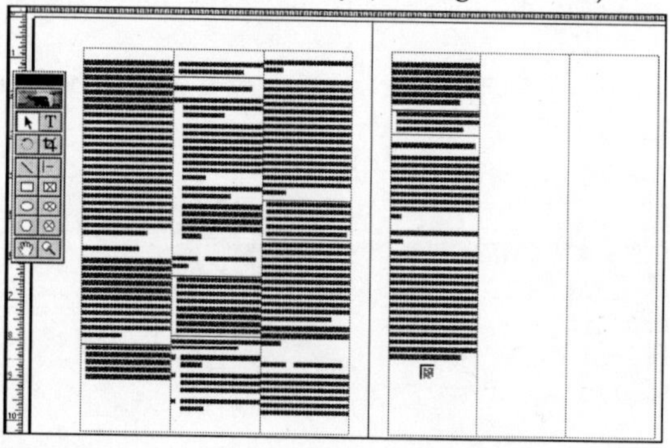

Figure 12.25 By clicking the down arrow tab, the tab changes into Manual icon

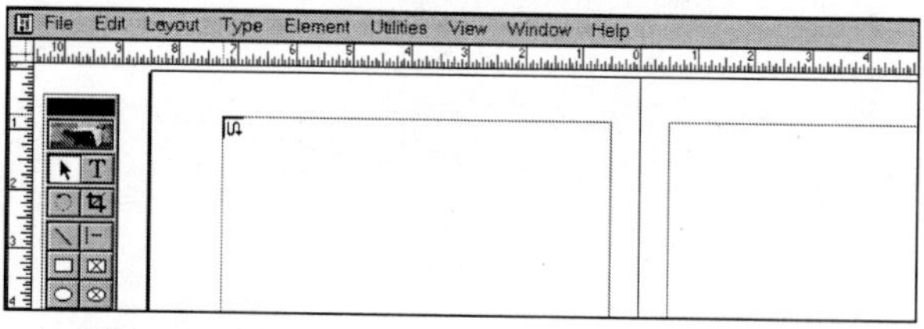

Figure 12.26 Automatic text flow icon

Autoflow functions – By placing an entire story at a time, automatically jumping from column to column and from page to page, placing text between empty column guides as it goes. If the Autoflow text icon reaches the last page of your Publication and needs more room to finish placing a story, it adds pages to finish the job.

To use the Autoflow text, do this:

1. Click the **Layout** menu and choose **Autoflow**.
2. You can use Autoflow on a temporary basis by pressing the **Ctrl** key when the Manual icon is showing.
3. Autoflow works best for the initial placement of a large story that takes many pages, such as all the pages of a book chapter or a technical report.

You can slow down the autoflow process so that you can see each page as it fills with text. If you decide to stop text placement for a while, but you still have some unplaced text, you have the following two options:

- If you already have at least one block on the page, click on any Tool in the Toolbox to switch off the text placement icon.

- The last text block you placed displays a down arrow, as shown in Figure 12.27. To resume text placement, click the down arrow to reload your text placement icon with the rest of the story.

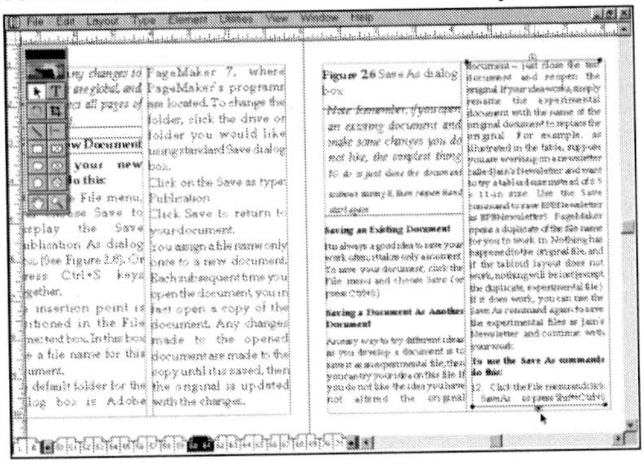

Figure 12.27 Text placement icon

Text Blocks

PageMaker considers a block of text as an object instead of a string of words. Although text blocks contain text, you can move and size them as you would move and size graphic objects. The text blocks act as a container for the text.

When text block objects are combined, they make up a complete PageMaker story. They are threaded together from top to bottom, and from beginning to end. As blocks are expanded or reduced, the text thread flows freely between them, fillng each block with text.

A story can have one text block, or it can have hundreds. The thread of text blocks in a book is simply a story running from page one to the final page in serial order. However, the thread in a newsletter, newspaper, or a magazine will be more complicated. For example, a story on page 1 in a newsletter might continue on page 5, with a dozen other stories located on the intervening pages. Even though the story is separated by many pages, the page 1 story's text blocks are threaded together and text flows among them. Together, the text blocks constitute a thread that makes up a complete story. Unless you break the threads, they always stay linked automatically.

Figure 12.28 shows text blocks. The horizontal lines across the top and bottom of each text block are called windowshades. Pull the tabs attached to each windnowshade up or down so that they roll and unroll portions of the story's text like a roller-type windowshade. As the text block expands and contracts in this manner, the text inside the block is squeezed in and out of the other blocks in the thread.

Some windowshade tabs contain a symbol which indicates the following:

1. A plain, empty windowshade tab at the top or bottom of a text block ensuring that no text is left to be rolled out as shown in Figure 12.29.

A plus sign tab in the top or bottom windowshade shows that there is more text, but it is located in an adjacent text block in the thread—either before or after the selected one.

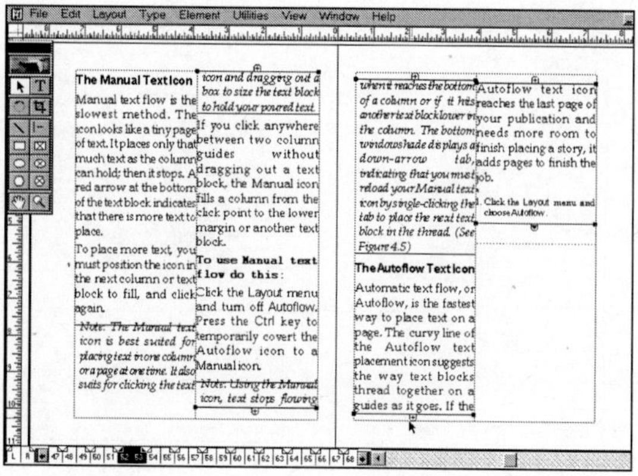

Figure 12.28 PageMaker story with a text block

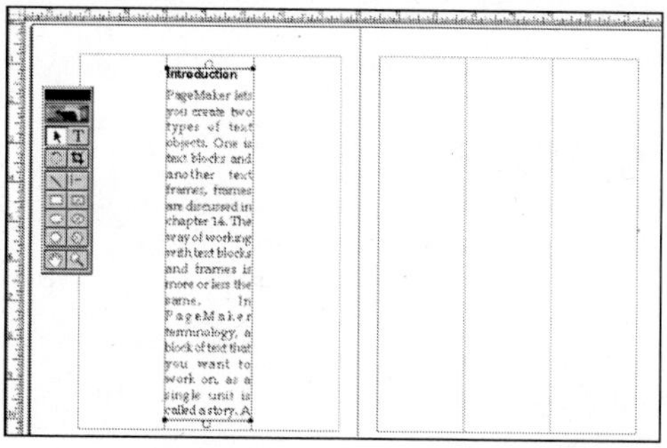

Figure 12.29 A text block with empty windowshade

2. A down arrow in red color indicates that there is more text, but it has not been placed.

In Figure 12.30, notice what happens when the bottom windowshade of the second text block is moved upward. The move leaves less room in that text block for the text (less room in the container). As a result, the excess text in that block spills down the story thread into the next text block in the thread.

Text Wrap

The Text Wrap command controls the way text flows around an independent graphic element.

To specify text wrap options, do this:

1. Select the graphic with the Pointer Tool.
2. Click **Element** menu and choose **Text Wrap...** command to display the **Text Wrap** dialog box as shown in Figure 12.31.

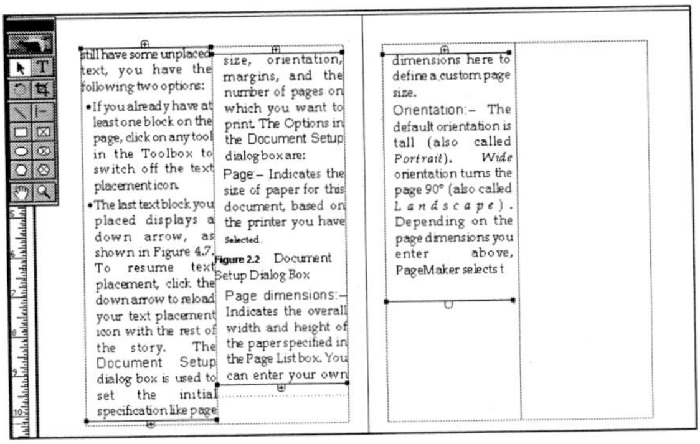

Figure 12.30 Bottom windowshade of the second text block is moved upward

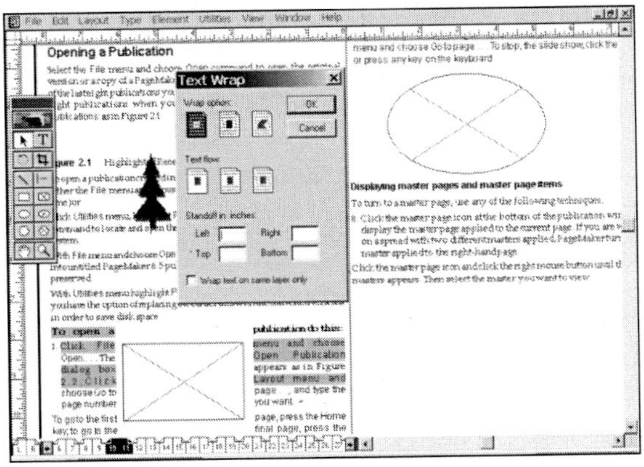

Figure 12.31 Text Wrap dialog box

3. Pick the **Wrap option:** you want by clicking the icon.
   - The first icon represents text flowing over the graphic.
   - The second icon flows text around the graphic's boundary.
   - If you have modified the boundary to mask the shape of the graphic, then the third icon will be selected.

To change the area and shape of the boundary, click the graphic to select its boundary. Notice the diamond-shaped handles. Drag a handle to change the shape of the boundary. You can create more sizing handles by clicking along the boundary where you want them to be appeared.

4. **Text flow** options are:
   - The first icon is called the *column break* icon. Click it and text stops flowing when it encounters a graphic and begins again on the next column.
   - The second icon is called the *jump-over* icon. Click it and text stops when it encounters a graphic but starts again immediately following the graphic (it jumps over the graphic).

- The third icon is called the *wrap-all-sides* icon; click it and text flows around all sides of a graphic (See Figure 12.32).

5. Click **Wrap text on same layer only** check box if the text on the same layer as the graphic is to be wrapped.
6. Finally, enter the amount of standoff around the graphic. The standoff is the margin between the graphic and the wrapped text.
7. Click **OK** to return to your document.

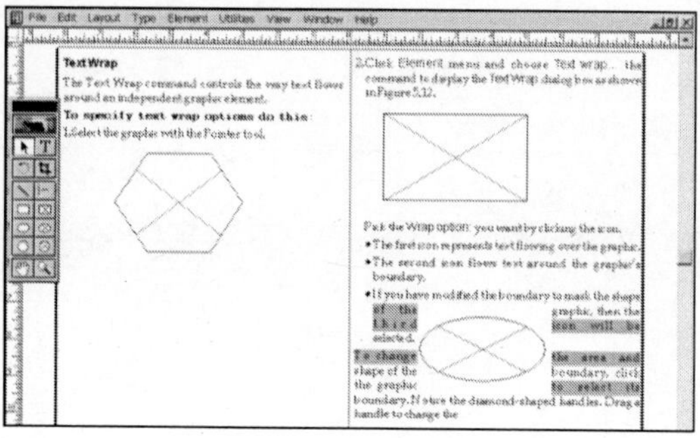

Figure 12.32 Text flow in three different ways

Character Formatting

Character formatting includes various aspects of text attributes, such as font, size, position, leading, case, etc.

To change Character formatting, do this:

1. Select the text to be changed.
2. Click the **Type** menu and choose **Character...** . The **Character Specifications** dialog box appears as shown in Figure 12.33. *Alternatively,* double-click the Text Tool to bring up the same dialog box. Or press **Ctrl+T** keys together.

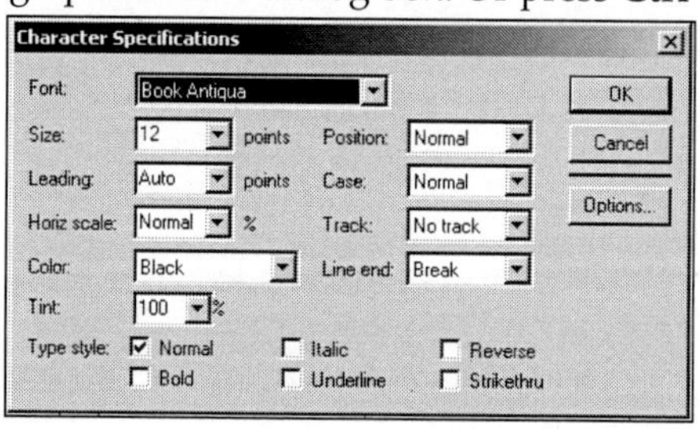

Figure 12.33 Character Specifications dialog box

The Character Specifications dialog box options are discussed below.

Font:–From the drop-down list, choose the font you want to use for the text.

Leading:–Leading is the vertical space between two lines of text. Too little leading causes descenders of the upper line (the tails of the lowercase g and p) to overlap the ascenders of the lower line, as shown in Figure 12.34. If there is too much space between the two lines, it is difficult for the eye to track down the page. As the font size is changed, so must the leading measurement should change. The correct leading for a given size is normally about 120% of the type size (so that if the type size is 10 points, the leading is usually 12 points).

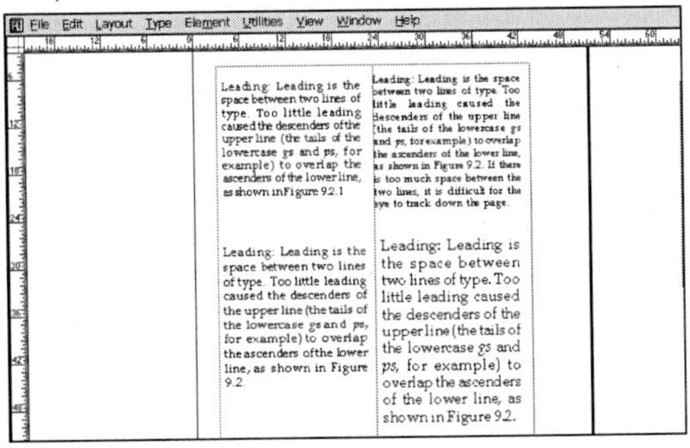

Figure 12.34 Different type of Leading

3. If you select Auto feature, PageMaker automatically calculates the leading. Otherwise you can specify the leading in points.

   Horiz scale:-To adjust the Width of Character (like leading) is something you generally do not think about with PageMaker. However, for special effects, very bold headlines, or designing a unique logo, changing the character width can help you achieve a special look. The default width of all characters is normal, or 100% of the width. You can change the percentage of the width value from 5% to 250% of normal in as small as 0.1% increments. This changes the width of individual characters proportionately from 70 to 130% of normal value.

   Color:-Assigns the selected text a color, based on the colors you have defined for this document.

   Position-Used mostly in typesetting equations, this feature allows you to set type as subscript characters (dropped below the baseline) or superscript characters (raised above the baseline).

   Case-Allows you to set type in all capital letters, all small capital letters, or leave it as typed.

   Track:-Tracking is similar to kerning in that it adjusts the spacing between letters, but kerning only adjusts the space between certain pairs of letters and does not affect the spacing between words. On the other hand, tracking adjusts the spaces between all letters and words in equal proportion. If you select a headline to squeeze, everything in the headline shifts toward the margin to which the text is aligned. Figure 12.35 shows an example of the effects of tracking.

   Type style:-The options are Normal, Bold, Italic, Underline, Reverse,

Strikethrough. Choosing the type style has the same effect as clicking the **Type** menu and choosing **Type Style** sub menu (See Figure 12.35).

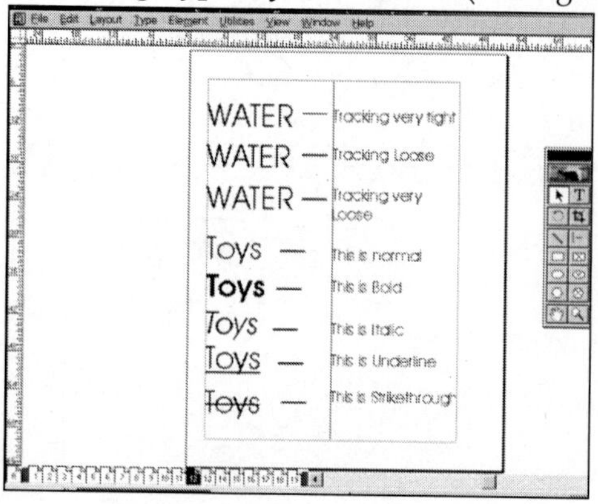

Figure 12.35 Different types of tracking (the word WATER) and applying typeface (the word Toys)

To Change type options, do this:

1. In the **Character Specifications** dialog box click **Options...** button. The **Character Options** dialog box appears as shown in Figure 12.36. You find options for altering the look of small caps, superscript and subscript characters. Their default values are fine for most of the documents.

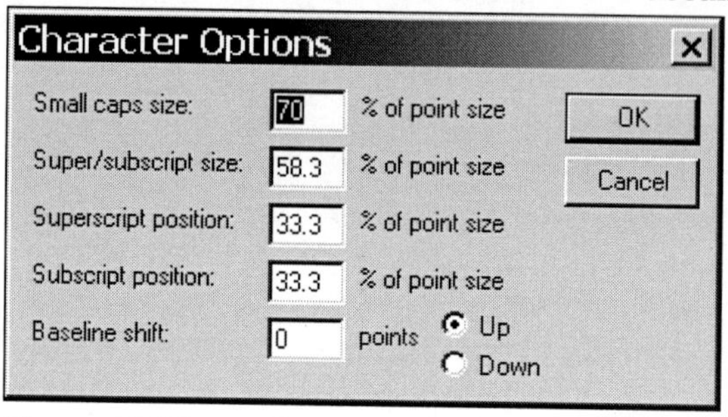

Figure 12.36 Character Options dialog box

2. The options in the Character Options are:

   Small caps size:–To change the size of the small caps, enter a different percentage in the text box. The percentage you enter is proportional to the type size. For example, if you enter 50%, and the typeface was set at 24 Points, then the *small cap* size would be about 12 points.

   Super/subscript size position:– Superscript characters are positioned above the normal baseline of the type (like a footnote in-text reference). Subscript characters drop below the baseline. To change the size of these characters, enter a different percentage value in the text box, that is, above or below the baseline, relative to the surrounding type. In other words, the default value of 33.3% means that a superscript character is 33.3% of the character's em size above the baseline of the surrounding type. (The em size is the width of the letter m in the size and typeface you have selected). You can also specify separately the positions for superscript and subscript.

Baseline shift:–The baseline is an invisible line on which all texts rest. If you were to specify points for the vertical ruler to align the tick marks on the ruler to the leading value of your text, the invisible baselines would actually be aligned to the ruler. To shift the baseline is to move the baseline for selected text up or down. Enter the amount of Shift you want in Points with steps as small as 0.1 point values. Then click either the Up or Down radio button to tell PageMaker in which direction you want to shift the baseline. When you have finished, click OK to return to your document.

Paragraph Formatting

Paragraph formatting includes the setting of indent values in paragraphs, specifying the space before and after a paragraph, setting the text alignment orientation and controlling how paragraphs split among columns and between pages.

To change paragraph formatting, do this:

1. Select the paragraph for which you want to change the specification.
2. Click the **Type** menu and choose **Paragraph...** or press **Ctrl+M** keys together to display the **Paragraph Specifications** dialog box as shown in Figure 12.37.

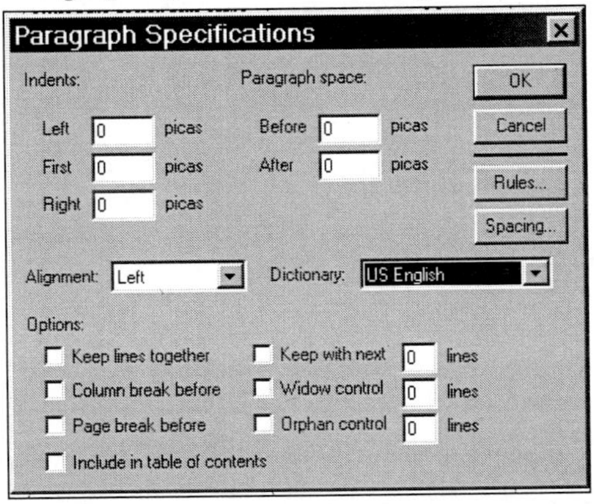

Figure 12.37 Paragraph Specifications dialog box

Changing Indents

Paragraph indents are specified in the **Indents:** section of the Paragraph Specifications dialog box.

3. Change the left indent value by clicking in the **Left** text box and entering a new value. The left margin of the paragraph is indented by the amount of the value entered (See Figure 12.38).

4. Change the first line indent value by clicking in the First text box and entering a value. If a value has been entered in the Left text box above, entering a negative value here outdents the first line by the amount of the negative value entered, while the remaining lines of the paragraph are indented the amount entered in the Left text box (See Figure 12.38).
5. Change the right indent value by clicking in the **Right** text box and entering value. The right edge of the paragraph is indented by the amount of the Right value entered (See Figure 12.38).

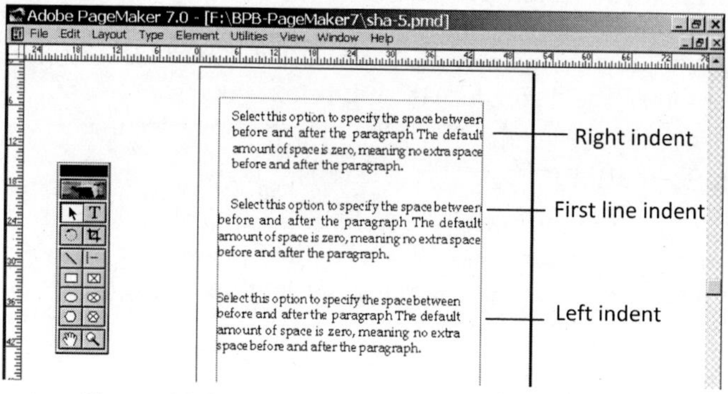

Figure 12.38 Different paragraph indents

Paragraph Spaces

The space above and below a paragraph is specified in the **Paragraph Space:** section of the **Paragraph Specifications** dialog box. You control the vertical space between paragraphs by specifying the amount of space to insert before or after selected paragraphs or all paragraphs of a certain style. The default amount of space is zero, meaning no extra space before and after the paragraph.

6. To specify the space before the paragraph, enter a value in **Before** text box (See Figure 12.37). To specify the space after the paragraph enter a value in **After** text box (See Figure 12.37).

Alignment

You can change the alignment of text in a paragraph in the **Alignment:** box of the **Paragraph Specifications** dialog box. This is equivalent to using the **Alignment...** command on the **Type** pull down menu.

7. Click the **Alignment:** pop-up list as shown in Figure 12.37 to make your choice or Left, Right, Center, Justify, or Force Justify (See Figure 12.39).

Setting Indents and Tabs

Indents and tabs are powerful Tools for positioning text. Indents move text inward from the right and left edges of a text object, and tabs position text at specific locations in a text object. You can create left- and right-aligned tabs; center tabs, which center text around the tab; and decimal tabs, which align characters at a decimal point. You can also apply a leader of any style to any tab.

A leader is a repeated pattern, such as a series of dots or dashes, between the tab and the preceding text.

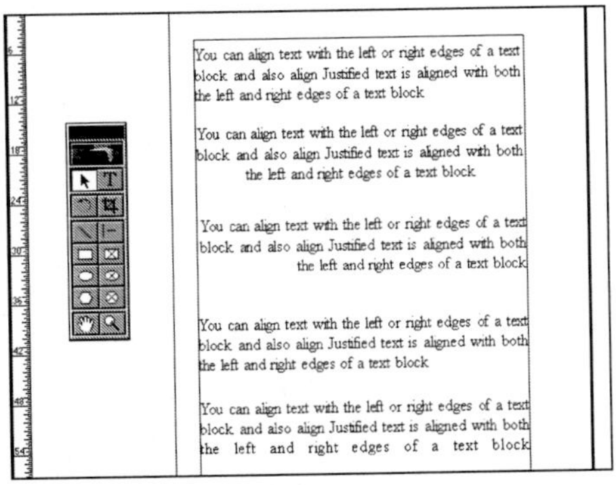

Figure 12.39 Different alignment option

To set tabs with the Indents/Tabs ruler, do this:

1. In the **Layout** view, click the insertion point in a paragraph, or select a group of paragraphs.
2. Click the **Type** menu and choose **Indents/Tabs**. The **Indents/Tabs** dialog box appears as shown in Figure 12.40.

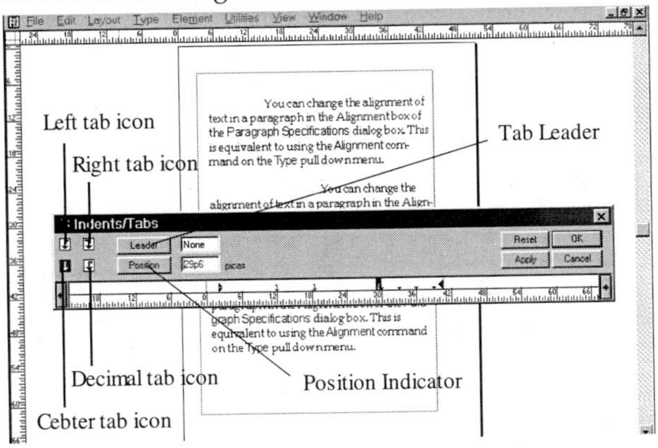

Figure 12.40 Indents/Tabs dialog box

3. Click one of the tab-alignment icon (left, right, center, or decimal) you want to set (See Figure 12.41). You can see example of all four alignments.

   Left tab: Text typed at these tabs aligns the left edge of the stop.

   Right tab: Text typed at these tabs aligns the right edge.

   Center tab: A center tab stop, centers your text around the tab stop.

   Decimal tab: Decimal tab stops, align columns of numbers on the decimal point.
4. Click a tab location on the ruler to position the new tab, or move an existing tab by dragging its marker along the ruler.

5. If you want the tab **leadered**, select the tab and choose an option from the **Leader** text box.
6. Click **Apply** to preview the changes to your text, and then click **OK** to accept the changes.

To move, delete or repeat a tab, do this:

1. In the **Layout** view, click the insertion point in a paragraph, or select a group of paragraphs.
2. Click the **Type** menu and choose **Indents/Tabs**. The **Indents/Tabs** dialog box appears as shown in Figure 12.41.
3. To move the tab, drag it or type the new location in the **Position** box, and then choose **Move** Tab from the Position submenu.
4. To delete the tab, drag it off the ruler or choose **Delete Tab** from the **Position** submenu.
5. To create a series of tabs the same distance the selected tab is from the preceding tab (or from the tab ruler's zero point), choose **Repeat Tab** from the **Position** submenu.
6. Click **Reset** button to clear all tabs in the selected text and restore the default tabs for the document.

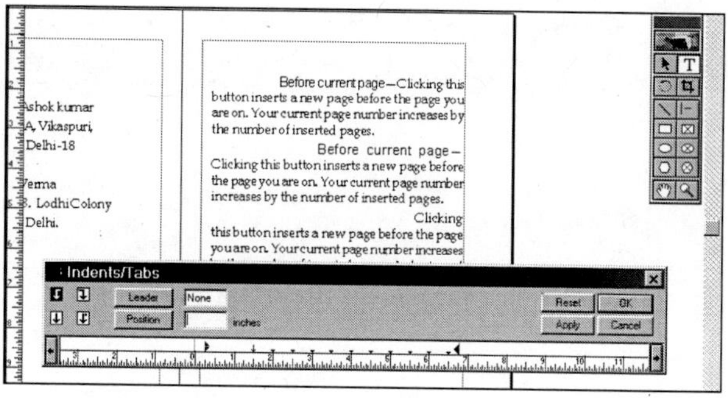

Figure 12.41 Different alignment tabs

Appendix

Answer the Following Questions

CorelDRAW X5

1. Describe the process of opening and closing of CorelDRAW files.
2. What are the save options?
3. What are the advanced saving options?
4. How would you import and export CorelDRAW files?
5. How would you use the Backup options?
6. Describe the various options of Polygon tool.
7. Describe the process of filling and outlining the shapes.
8. How would you group and ungroup the objects?
9. How would you lock and unclock the objects?
10. How would you rotate the various shapes?
11. How would you duplicate an object?
12. Describe the process of aligning the various objects.
13. Describe the process of combining various objects.
14. How would you find and replace objects?
15. How many freehand tools are there in CorelDRAW?
16. Describe the working of each one of them.
17. Describe the process of creating and moving of the text blocks.
18. How would you rotate the text?
19. Describe the process of creating a Drop Cap in text.
20. Describe how would you fit text to a path?
21. How would you find and replace the text?
22. How would you draw a straight line?

Photoshop CS6

1. Describe the ways of starting Photoshop.
2. Describe the new commands of Photoshop CS6.
3. Describe the various commands of File menu.
4. Describe the commands available under Edit menu.
5. What is available under Layer menu? Describe.
6. Describe the various commands of View menu.
7. Describe the various tools available under the toolbar.
8. Describe the various tools available for painting under toolbox.
9. Describe the working of Art History Brush.

10. Describe the various options of type tool.

PageMaker 7.0

1. Describe the various new features of PageMaker.
2. Describe briefly the activities of PageMaker.
3. Which are the various popular paper and page sizes?
4. Describe how two pages are made on one page.
5. Describe the various tools on the toolbar.
6. Describe the various options available under Preference.
7. Which are the extra preference commands in PageMaker?
8. Describe the various methods of starting PageMaker.
9. Describe how you would setup the dimensions of a new page.
10. How would you check the size of a page? Explain.
11. Explain the steps taken in placing the text in the publication.
12. What all you can change from the character dialog box? Explain.
13. Describe the various options of the Paragraph dialog box.
14. How would you set up paragraph rules? Explain.
15. Describe the process of setting Indents/Tab.
16. Describe the usefulness of setting Styles.
17. How do the hyphenation command works? Explain.
18. What are master pages?
19. How would you set the page numbers in a publication?
20. How would you open a PageMaker publication? Describe.
21. Describe how would you Find a word in Story Editor and Change it to other?
22. Describe briefly the process of Spell Checking in PageMaker.
23. Explain the difference between Cut and Copy commands.
24. Describe the use of Multiple Paste.
25. Describe the process of setting up of 2 pages on a single sheet of paper using the columns commands.
26. How would you use the command Control Palette? Explain.
27. What are the uses of Book command? Explain.
28. Explain the process of creating Table of Contents.
29. Describe the completer process of creating Index in PageMaker.
30. What are the various options under the Print command? Explain.